FOLKLORE: AN ANNOTATED BIBLIOGRAPHY

AND

INDEX TO SINGLE EDITIONS

FOLKLORE: AN ANNOTATED BIBLIOGRAPHY AND INDEX TO SINGLE EDITIONS

By

Elsie B. Ziegler

The F. W. Faxon Company
Westwood, Mass.
1973

International Standard Book Number 0-87305-100-9

Library of Congress Card Number 73-77289

Printed in the United States of America

To my husband, Carlos, and my three daughters—Jane, Ann, and Judy—for sharing their "family time."

ACKNOWLEDGMENTS

The author is grateful to The Free Library of Philadelphia, Central Children's Department, The Chester County District Library Staff, and the West Chester State College Francis Harvey Green Library Staff for facilitating the use of their collections.

It is with special gratitude the author acknowledges the help of the West Chester State College Computer Service Center in the preparation of this book.

And finally, the author wishes to express appreciation to Joyce Hendrickson, Bruce Hartshorne, and Marion Wilson for their assistance in compiling this book.

Contents

Purpose. The purpose of this book is to aid librarians, teachers and researchers of folklore in locating appropriate folklore for story hours, reading units, social studies units, voluntary reading and analysis.

Arrangement. This book is divided into the following six sections: Part I, Annotated Title Bibliography; Part II, Subject Index; Part III, Motif Index; Part IV, Country Index; Part V, Type of Folklore Index; and Part VI, Illustrator Index.

Part I—Annotated Title Bibliography. This section presents a comprehensive description for each type of folklore. It is arranged alphabetically by title. Cross references are given for the different versions.

Example: 0001 Three Sillies, The
by Joseph Jacobs
Illus. Margot Zemach
New York, Holt, Rinehart, and Winston, 1963 unp.

While drawing beer, the poor couple's daughter predicts that if she has a son he might be killed by an ax on the ceiling when he goes to draw beer. Her suitor says he will not marry her until he finds three people as silly as she. He finds them.

Subjects   —   cow
moon
trousers
Jacobs, Joseph

Motifs   —   Humor
Fools and Simpletons

Country   —   United Kingdom

Type of
Folklore   —   Folk tales

See Also   —   0002 Jack and The Three Sillies

Upon looking up the cross reference 0002 Jack and the Three Sillies, the following information could be found:

0002   Jack and the Three Sillies
Reteller, Richard Chase
Illus. Joshua Tolford
Boston, Houghton Mifflin Co., 1950, 39p.

Jack starts out to sell a cow but through a series of exchanges he ends up with a stone. His irritated wife leaves home and vows not to return until she finds three people more foolish than Jack. This is easily done.

Subject   —   shirt
Jack Tales
tall tales
moon
cow

Motifs   —   Humor
Fools and Simpletons

Country   —   U.S.—Variants of the European Stories

Type of
Folklore   —   Folk Tales

See Also   —   0001 Three Sillies, The

Part II—Subject Index. Subjects were gleaned from each type of folklore the author read. The subjects are arranged alphabetically with titles listed in which that subject has been mentioned. For example, both The Three Sillies and Jack and the Three Sillies could be located by looking under the subject "moon." These two stories would be listed as well as others in which the moon was mentioned to some degree.

Example: Moon

0174 Angry Moon, The
0279 Buried Moon
0383 Dancing Stars, The
0167 Good Llama, The
0073 Humpy
0002 Jack and the Three Sillies
0094 Kap and the Wicked Monkey
0351 Painting the Moon
0001 Three Sillies, The
0353 Why the Sun and the Moon live in the Sky

After finding the needed titles, complete information could be found in the annotated title bibliography.

Part III. Motif Index. Certain themes are prevalent in folklore. These characteristics are termed motifs. In the two folk tales mentioned above, the motifs are humor and fools and simpletons. The humor in both folk tales is based on the incredible way some of the characters think. Fools and simpleton characters can be found in both stories. In The Three Sillies there are characters who display an inconceivable type of logic: the fiance and her parents cry about something that might happen in the future; one woman endeavors to lodge her cow on the roof to graze instead of bringing the grass to the cow; a man tries to jump into his trousers and can't think of another way to get into them; and last, men try to get the moon's reflection out of the water.

In Jack and the Three Sillies there are four characters that are fools and simpletons: Jack, the husband, trades a healthy cow for a stone; the farmer tries to rake the moon's reflection out of the pond; a farmer's wife hitches her husband to the plow instead of using their mule in this capacity; and the fourth, another farmer's wife, tries to beat her husband's head through the shirt in order to make a neck hole.

Similarly, in both stories the main character is capable of thinking normally and is capable of resolving the different predicaments. It is through viewing contrasts of the characters' normal and absurd actions in the different episodes that one finds it easy to classify them as humor and fools and simpletons motifs.

The following sixteen motifs of Huck and Kuhn are used:[1]

humor	trickery
magic objects	realistic events
magic transformation	talking animals
enchanted people	pourquoi
tasks and trials	local legendary heroes
wit prevails	supernatural creatures
fools and simpletons	friendly animals
wishes	legendary heroes

In addition to the above, nature calamaties and religion motifs are used.

Part IV. Country Index. This section is divided into ten areas of the world. The areas are arranged alphabetically in the following order:

Africa	North America
Central America	Oceania
Europe	South America
Far East	South Asia
Middle East	Southeast Asia

These areas are in turn subdivided into countries within the areas. For example, The Three Sillies would be located under the area, Europe and then the subdivision, United Kingdom. Jack and the Three Sillies would be found under the area, North America and then the subdivision, U.S.—Variants of the European Stories.

Part V. Type of Folklore Index. This section presents the many facets of folklore in the ensuing order:

Epics	Legends
Fables	Myths
Folk Songs, Ballads	Nursery Rymes
Folk Tales	

Part VI. Illustrator Index. This section alphabetically categorizes the folklore under the individual illustrator.

---

[1] Charlotte S. Huck and Doris Young Kuhn, *Children's Literature in the Elementary School* (New York: Holt, Rinehart and Winston, Inc.), pp.169-180.

0542 ALADDIN

0404 Aladdin, The Story of

Reteller, Naomi Lewis
Illus. Barry Wilkinson
New York, Henry Z. Walck, Inc., 1971. 48p.

Aladdin finds himself buried alive in an underground vault with an old lamp. As he raises his arms for prayer, he touches a magic ring an evil sorcerer had lent him and a magic genie appears who does his every wish.

SUBJECTS	–		COUNTRY	–	Iran
		Allah			
		Aladdin and the Lamp			
		Geni and the Lamp			
		Lamp, Magic			
		Ring (Magic)			
		Sultan			
		Magician			

MOTIFS	–	Magic Objects	TYPE OF FOLKLORE	–	Folk Tales
		Trickery			
		Wit Prevails			
		Magic Transformation			
		Religion			

0402 ALADDIN AND THE WONDERFUL LAMP

Reteller, Jean Hersholt
Illus. Fritz Kredel
New York, George Macy Companies, Inc., 1949. 39p.

Similar to title no. 0404 Aladdin, The Story of.

SUBJECTS	–		COUNTRY	–	Iran
		Allah			
		Aladdin and the Lamp			
		China			
		Geni and the Lamp			
		Lamp, Magic			
		Ring (Magic)			
		Sultan			
		Magician			

MOTIFS	–	Magic Objects	TYPE OF FOLKLORE	–	Folk Tales
		Trickery			
		Wit Prevails			
		Magic Transformation			
		Religion			

0402 ALADDIN AND THE WONDERFUL LAMP

See – 0542 Aladdin

0404 ALADDIN, THE STORY OF

See – 0542 Aladdin

0107 ALI-BABA AND THE FORTY-THIEVES

Arabian Nights
Illus. Not Given
New York, Thomas Nelson and Sons, 1928. 40p.

> Ali Baba discovers a gang's hidden treasure. His greedy brother investigates for himself and the thieves capture and murder him. The thieves then search for Ali Baba's home, but his slave girl's wit foils them.

SUBJECTS – Greediness   COUNTRY – Iran
         Loyalty
         Robber(s)   TYPE OF
         Arabian Nights   FOLKLORE – Folk Tales

MOTIFS   – Wit Prevails
         Trickery
         Magic Objects

0141 ALL IN THE MORNING EARLY

Reteller, Sorche Nic Leodhas
Illus. Evaline Ness
New York, Holt, Rinehart and Winston, 1963. unp.

> In this counting chain tale Sandy is joined by first one huntsman, two ewes, three gypsies, four farmers, five wee lads, all the way to 10 bonnie lassies.

SUBJECTS – Cumulative Tale   COUNTRY – United
         Counting   Kingdom
         Chain Tale
         Formula Tale   TYPE OF
                              FOLKLORE – Folk Tales
MOTIFS   – Humor
         Talking Animals
         Friendly Animals

0370 ALWAYS ROOM FOR ONE MORE

Reteller, Sorche Nic Leodhas
Illus. Nonny Hogrogian
New York, Holt, Rinehart and Winston, 1965. unp.

> The good-natured Lachie invites in every traveler during a storm. The walls of his house reach the breaking point. His guests repay his generosity by building a house double in size. Music is included.

SUBJECTS – Scotland, Folksong   COUNTRY – United
         Sharing of House   Kingdom
           with Travelers
                              TYPE OF
MOTIFS   – Humor   FOLKLORE – Folk Songs,
                                       Ballads

0301 ANDY JACKSON'S WATER WELL

Reteller, William O. Steele
Illus. Michael Ramus
New York, Harcourt, Brace and Company, 1959, 80p.

> With the help of his Indian friend Chief Tickle Pticher, Andy Jackson finds and brings back a well to the people of Nashville during a drought. Some say he later became President.

SUBJECTS	–	Drought	COUNTRY	–	U.S.–Native
		Andrew Jackson			Tall Tales of
		Nashville, Tennessee			the Paul Bun-
		Tennessee			yan Variety
MOTIFS	–	Humor	TYPE OF		
		Local Legendary	FOLKLORE	–	Folk Tales
		Heroes			
		Nature Calamities			

0174 ANGRY MOON, THE

Reteller, William Sleator
Illus. Blair Lent
Boston, Little, Brown and Company, 1970. 48p.

> Lapowinsa, an Indian girl, laughs at the moon and becomes its prisoner. With the aid of an old grandmother's magic, Lupan finds Lapowinsa and resuces her.

SUBJECTS	–	Tlingit Indians	COUNTRY	–	U.S.–Tales
		(Alaskan)			From the
		Moon			North Ameri-
		Sky Country			can Indians
		Stone Transf. Into			
		Mountain			
		Arrows Make Sky			
		Rope			
		Fish Eye			
		Rose Transf. Into			
		Rose Thicket			
MOTIFS	–	Magic Objects	TYPE OF		
		Magic Transforma-	FOLKLORE	–	Folk Tales
		tion			
		Wit Prevails			
		Trickery			
		Supernatural			
		Creatures			

0531 ANT AND THE GRASSHOPPER

0205 John J. Plenty and Fiddler Dan

Reteller, John Ciardi
Illus. Madeleine Gekiere
New York, J. B. Lippincott Company, 1963. unp.

> The industrious ant works all summer storing food for winter while the grasshopper fiddles his time away, but both survive the winter.

SUBJECTS	–	Grasshopper	COUNTRY	–	Greece
		Ant			
		Industrious Ant versus			
		Lazy Grasshopper			
		Aesop			
MOTIFS	–	Talking Animals	TYPE OF		
			FOLKLORE	–	Fables

0532 ARAB AND HIS CAMEL

0406 Camel In the Tent

Reteller, Katherine Evans
Illus. Katherine Evans
Chicago, Ill., Albert Whitman & Company, 1961. unp.

> Similar to an Aesop fable a merchant loses the fine clothes he made for the Sultan's daughters when he lets his camel inside his tent.

SUBJECTS	– Camel Tricks Merchant	COUNTRY	– Greece
	Sultan		
MOTIFS	– Humor	TYPE OF	
	Talking Animals	FOLKLORE	– Fables
	Fools and Simpletons		

0533 ARGONAUTS

0045 Clashing Rocks: The Story of Jason, The

Reteller, Ian Serraillier
Illus. William Stobbs
New York, Henry Z. Walck, Inc., 1964. 96p.

> Jason must prove his fitness by bringing back the golden fleece that will restore prosperity to his kingdom. Jason sets out on his task with the argonauts, a brave crew of fifty men.

SUBJECTS	– Clashing Rocks	COUNTRY	– Greece
	Courage		
	Giant(s)		
	Gods		
	Serpent's Teeth		
	Fate		
MOTIFS	– Magic Objects	TYPE OF	
	Tasks and Trials	FOLKLORE	– Myths
	Supernatural Creatures		
	Wit Prevails		
	Religion		

0173 AUTUN AND THE BEAR

Reteller, Anita Feagles
Illus. Gertrude Barrer-Russell
New York, Young Scott Books, 1967. unp.

> Autun, a man of conviction, travels on a viking ship to Denmark, Norway, and Rome before returning to his homeland.

SUBJECTS	– Bear(s)	COUNTRY	– Iceland
	Vikings		
	Pilgrimage		
	Royalty		
	Friendship		
	Denmark		
	Norway		
MOTIFS	– Religion	TYPE OF	
	Legendary Heroes	FOLKLORE	– Legends
	Realistic Events		

0076 BABA YAGA

Reteller, Ernest Small
Illus. Blair Lent
Boston, Houghton Mifflin Company, 1966. 48p.

Marusia and the hedgehog nearly become stew while matching wits
with the witch Baba Yaga. The black sunflower is the key to their
freedom. The black horse and rider and white horse and rider represent
night and day.

SUBJECTS	–	Witch(es) Flower, Black Sunflower Hedgehog Turnip(s) Baba Yaga	COUNTRY	–	U.S.S.R.
MOTIFS	–	Supernatural Creatures Magic Transforma- tion Magic Objects	TYPE OF FOLKLORE	–	Folk Tales

0312 BABOUSHKA AND THE THREE KINGS

Reteller, Ruth Robbins
Illus. Nicolas Sidjakov
Berkeley, California, Parnassus Press, 1960. unp.

The old woman Baboushka declines three strangers' offer to join them
as they follow a star to where the babe is born. Baboushka changes
her mind, but cannot find the trail to the babe.

SUBJECTS	–	Baboushka Christmas Music	COUNTRY	–	U.S.S.R.
MOTIFS	–	Religion	TYPE OF FOLKLORE	–	Folk Tales

0248 BADGER, THE MISCHIEF MAKER

Reteller, Kay Hill
Illus. John Hamberger
New York, Dodd, Mead & Company, 1965. 95p.

Badger delights in playing tricks on everyone he meets. Glooscap,
a wise and friendly god of the Wabanaki Indians, keeps an eye
on him and he finally learns what kindness and love can mean.

SUBJECTS	–	Gooscap (God of the Wabanaki Indians) Algonquin Nation Boodin (Wizards) Hairstring (Magic)	COUNTRY	–	Canada
MOTIFS	–	Humor Supernatural Creatures Trickery Religion Local Legendary Heroes	TYPE OF FOLKLORE	–	Legends

0268 BAKER AND THE BASILISK, THE

Reteller, Georgess McHargue
Illus. Robert Quackenbush
New York, The Bobbs-Merrill Company, Inc., 1971. 32p.

Hans, an apprentice, is fired by the ill-tempered Garhibl, Vienna's best baker, when Garhibl finds Hans is in love with his daughter. Garhibl says when his rooster lays an egg Hans may marry his daughter. The rooster hatches a basilisk, and Hans wins the hand of Garhibl's daughter.

SUBJECTS	–	Basilisk (Monster)	COUNTRY	–	Austria
		Baker			
		Apprentice			
		Judge(s)			
		Justice			
		Rooster			
		Vienna			

MOTIFS	–	Wit Prevails	TYPE OF	
		Humor	FOLKLORE	– Folk Tales
		Supernatural Creatures		
		Tasks and Trials		

0020 BEAUTY AND THE BEAST

French Version by LePrince de Beaumont, Trans. by P. H. Muir
Illus. Erica Ducornet
New York, Alfred A. Knopf, 1968. 51p.

A lovely girl is given to the beast to punish her father who picked a rose from the beast's garden. When she promises to marry the creature he turns into a handsome prince.

SUBJECTS	–	Kindness	COUNTRY	–	France
		Beast			
		Fairy			
		Mirror			

MOTIFS	–	Magic Objects	TYPE OF	
		Magic Transformation	FOLKLORE	– Folk Tales
		Supernatural Creatures		

0191 BEESWAX CATCHES A THIEF

Reteller, Ann Kirn
Illus. Ann Kirn
New York, W. W. Norton & Company, Inc., 1968. unp.

The animals of the jungle rule that only those who work on the water hole project may drink from it. By placing beeswax on his shell, Tortoise captures Jackal who has not worked. Jackal escapes by pleading against one punishment.

SUBJECTS	–	Beeswax, Capture by B.	COUNTRY	–	Congo (Brazzaville)
		Animals, Jungle			
		Drought			

Jackal
Theft
Cooperation
Punishment, Chooses
  Type of

MOTIFS	– Trickery	TYPE OF
	Talking Animals	FOLKLORE – Folk Tales
	Wit Prevails	
	Humor	

See also 0193   **Clever Turtle, The**
         0304   **Punia and the King of the Sharks**

0502 BEOWULF

0227 By His Own Might: The Battles of Beowulf

By Dorothy Hosford
Illus. Laszlo Matulay
New York, Henry Holt and Company, 1947. 69p.

Strength, courage, and loyalty are exemplified as Beowulf kills the monster Grendel and Grendel's mother. He then returns to his land to rule for fifty years. He dies a hero from wounds in his victory over the dragon.

SUBJECTS	– Anglo-Saxons	COUNTRY	– United
	Fate		Kingdom
	Dragon Kills Beowulf		
	God		
	Beowulf		
	Courage		

MOTIFS	– Religion	TYPE OF
	Legendary Heroes	FOLKLORE – Epics
	Supernatural	
	Creatures	

0374 Beowulf

Reteller, Rosemary Sutcliff
Illus. Charles Keeping
New York, E. P. Dutton and Company, Inc., 1962. 93p.

Similar to title no. 0227 By His Own Might: The Battles of Beowulf. There are descriptive sentences on the all father, Wyrd, the weaver of the fates of men. p. 48, 68, 80, 88, and 90.

SUBJECTS	– Anglo-Saxons	COUNTRY	– United
	Dragon Kills Beowulf		Kingdom
	Fate		
	God		
	Courage		
	Beowulf		

MOTIFS	– Supernatural	TYPE OF
	Creatures	FOLKLORE – Epics
	Legendary Heroes	
	Religion	

0373 Beowulf the Warrior

Reteller, Ian Serraillier
Illus. Severin
New York, Henry Z. Walck Incorporated, 1961. 48p.

Similar to title no. 0227 By His Own Might: The Battles of Beowulf.

SUBJECTS	– Anglo-Saxons	COUNTRY	– United
	Dragon Kills Beowulf		Kingdom
	Fate		
	God		
	Courage		
	Beowulf		

MOTIFS	– Supernatural	TYPE OF	
	Creatures	FOLKLORE	– Epics
	Legendary Heroes		
	Religion		

0375 Beowulf, Story of

Reteller, Scrafford Riggs
Illus. Henry A. Pitz
New York, D. Appleton-Century Company, Inc., 1933. 84p.

Similar to title no. 0227 By His Own Might: The Battles of Beowulf.

SUBJECTS	– Anglo-Saxons	COUNTRY	– United
	Dragon Kills Beowulf		Kingdom
	Fate		
	God		
	Courage		
	Beowulf		

MOTIFS	– Supernatural	TYPE OF	
	Creatures	FOLKLORE	– Epics
	Legendary Heroes		
	Religion		

0374 BEOWULF

See – 0502 Beowulf

0373 BEOWULF THE WARRIOR

See – 0502 Beowulf

0375 BEOWULF, STORY OF

See – 0502 Beowulf

0250 BIG FRAID LITTLE FRAID

Reteller, Ellis Credle
Illus. Ellis Credle
New York, Thomas Nelson & Sons, 1964, unp.

Examples of practical jokes and the dread of the supernatural in early America are presented in this story.

SUBJECTS	– Ghosts	COUNTRY	– U.S.–Native
	Monkey		Folk Tales
	North Carolina		
	Frontier and Pioneer		
	Life		

MOTIFS	— Supernatural Creatures Humor	TYPE OF FOLKLORE — Folk Tales

0300 BIG MOSE

Reteller, Katherine B. Shippen
Illus. Margaret Bloy Graham
New York, Harper & Brothers, 1953. 90p.

Big Mose, who lived in New York City 100 years ago, is such a big man he could step over a horse and buggy. He is a kind man who spends his life helping others.

SUBJECTS	— Mose Humphrey New York Tall Tales	COUNTRY	— U.S.–Native Tall Tales of of the Paul Bunyan Variety

MOTIFS	— Humor Local Legendary Heroes	TYPE OF FOLKLORE — Folk Tales

0327 BILLY BOY

Reteller, Richard Chase
Illus. Glen Rounds
San Carlos, California, Golden Gate Junior Books, 1966. unp.

"Tell me where have you been Billy Boy, Billy Boy . . . I have been down the lane for to court Miss Mary Jane. She's a young thing and cannot leave her mother." Seventeen verses with the melody are provided for this Appalachian folk song.

SUBJECTS	— Appalachian Mountain Song Billy Boy Folksong	COUNTRY	— U.S.– Folksongs

MOTIFS	— Humor	TYPE OF FOLKLORE — Folksongs, Ballads

0386 BISHOP AND THE DEVIL

Reteller, Ian Serraillier
Illus. Simon Stern
New York, Frederick Warne & Co., Inc., 1971. unp.

The Bishop sells his soul to the devil in order to get his new church bell over the Alps, but he is saved when the barnyard fowl crow making the sun rise earlier than the devil expected.

SUBJECTS	— Bishop Tricks Devil Christianity	COUNTRY	— United Kingdom

MOTIFS	— Religion Humor Supernatural Creatures	TYPE OF FOLKLORE — Legends

0105 BLACK HEART OF INDRI, THE

Adapted by Dorothy Hoge
Illus. Janina Domanska
New York, Charles Scribner's Sons, 1966. unp.

> Although Indri is an ugly fellow with webbed feet and hands and the face of a toad, he has much power because he controls the stream of the water of life. Told his ugliness will disappear if he will live with virtue for nine days and nights, he learns that his ugliness only disappears when he tries to make others happy.

SUBJECTS	–	Water Spirit (Sprite) Forest Sprites Greediness Love, Selfless Mandarin Toad	COUNTRY	–	China (Mainland)
MOTIFS	–	Supernatural Creatures Magic Transformation Trickery Talking Animals	TYPE OF FOLKLORE	–	Folk Tales

0558 BLIND MEN AND THE ELEPHANT

0121 Blind Men and the Elephant, The

Reteller, Lillian Quigley
Illus. Janice Holland
New York, Charles Scribner's Sons, 1959. unp.

> Six blind men feel an elephant's side, tusk, trunk, knee, ear, and tail, respectively, but they cannot agree on what they have felt.

SUBJECTS	–	Blind Men Dispute Over Description of Elephant Elephant Rajah	COUNTRY	–	India
MOTIFS	–	Humor Realistic Events	TYPE OF FOLKLORE	–	Fables

0120 Blind Men and the Elephant, The

Reteller, John Godfrey Saxe
Illus. Paul Galdone
New York, Whittlesey House, McGraw-Hill Book Company, Inc., 1963. unp.

> This version differs from title no. 0120 Blind Men and the Elephant, The in that it is written in rhyme.

SUBJECTS	–	Blind Men Dispute Over Description of Elephant Elephant	COUNTRY	–	India
MOTIFS	–	Humor Realistic Events	TYPE OF FOLKLORE	–	Fables

0121 BLIND MEN AND THE ELEPHANT, THE

See – 0558 Blind Men and the Elephant

0120 BLIND MEN AND THE ELEPHANT, THE

See – 0558 Blind Men and the Elephant

0314 BLUE JACKAL, THE

Reteller, Mehlli Gobhai
Illus. Mehlli Gobhai
Englewood Cliffs, N. J., Prentice-Hall, Inc., 1968. unp.

Long howl, the jackal, is timid, but when he falls into a barrel of indigo blue, the animals in the forest do not recognize him and he becomes powerful until he makes the mistake of howling with the other jackals.

SUBJECTS	–	Jackal	COUNTRY	–	India
		Deceptive Appearances			
		Panchatantra Tale			
		Timidity			

MOTIFS	–	Religion	TYPE OF FOLKLORE	–	Fables

0388 BLUE MOUNTAIN, THE

Reteller, Beth Lewis
Illus. Adrienne Adams
New York, Alfred A. Knopf, 1956. 59p.

All the princesses want to marry the prince. A mountain climb is set to determine who will marry him. With the help of leprechauns and the fairy queen, his beloved princess wins.

SUBJECTS	–	Fairy Queen	COUNTRY	–	United Kingdom
		Royalty			
		Leprechaun Helps			
		Princess Climb Mt.			

MOTIFS	–	Humor	TYPE OF FOLKLORE	–	Folk Tales
		Supernatural Creatures			
		Tasks and Trials			

0556 BOJABI TREE

0124 Bojabi Tree, The

Reteller, Edith Rickert
Illus. Gleb Botkin
Garden City, New York, Doubleday, Doran & Company, Inc., 1928. 47p.

When a great famine comes, the jungle sends the rat, pig, and goat to ask Leo the Lion the name of the fruit from a strange tree and if it is edible. They forget so the tortoise is sent and he remembers by making up a song about the tree.

SUBJECTS	–	Tortoise	COUNTRY	–	Africa
		Famine			

Formula Tale
Rat
Pig(s)
Goat(s)
Forgetting (Forget-
    fulness)
Chain Tale

MOTIFS	– Wit Prevails	TYPE OF
	Talking Animals	FOLKLORE – Folk Tales
	Friendly Animals	

0192 BOJABI TREE, THE

Reteller, Edith Rickert
Illus. Anna Braune
Garden City, N.Y., Doubleday and Company, Inc., 1958. 47p.

Similar to Title No. 0124 Bojabi Tree, The. Different Illus.

SUBJECTS	– Famine	COUNTRY – Africa
	Tortoise	
	Formula Tale	
	Rat	
	Pig(s)	
	Goat(s)	
	Forgetting (Forget-	
	fulness)	
	Chain Tale	

MOTIFS	– Wit Prevails	TYPE OF
	Talking Animals	FOLKLORE – Folk Tales
	Friendly Animals	

0192 BOJABI TREE, THE

See – 0556 Bojabi Tree

0124 BOJABI TREE, THE

See – 0556 Bojabi Tree

0541 BRAHMIN

0119 Tiger, The Brahman, and the Jackal, The

From the Tales of the Punjab by Flora Annie Steel
Illus. Mamoru Funai
New York, Holt, Rinehart and Winston, Inc., 1963. unp.

The Brahman frees a tiger from his cage but the tiger attempts to repay the kindness by eating the Brahman. Only the wily jackal is clever
enough to save him.

SUBJECTS	– Arrogance	COUNTRY – India
	Brahman	
	Jackal	
	Tiger	
	Justice	
	Judge(s)	

| MOTIFS | – Religion | TYPE OF |
| | Trickery | FOLKLORE – Fables |

12

> Wit Prevails
> Talking Animals
> Humor

See also **0202**   **One Good Deed Deserves Another**

0522 BRAVE LITTLE TAILOR

0013 Valiant Tailor, The

By Grimm, The Brothers, Reteller, Kurt Werth
Illus. Kurt Werth
New York, The Viking Press, 1965. 32p.

The little tailor's first feat of killing seven flies with one blow cannot match his future accomplishments of outwitting giants, and completing tasks assigned by the king before he can marry his daughter.

SUBJECTS	–	Giant(s)	COUNTRY	–	Germany
		Boar			
		Tailor(s)			
		Royalty			
		Fly (Flies)			
		Unicorn			
		Grimm, The Brothers			

MOTIFS	–	Supernatural Creatures	TYPE OF FOLKLORE	–	Folk Tales
		Trickery			
		Tasks and Trials			

See also **0087**   **Sixty At a Blow**

0162 BRAVE SOLDIER JANOSH

Reteller, Victor G. Ambrus
Illus. Victor G. Ambrus
New York, Harcourt, Brace & World, Inc., First American ed., 1967, unp.

Janosh, a brave soldier, tells the villagers in one of his many tales how he singlehandedly defeats Napoleon and his army.

SUBJECTS	–	Soldier(s)	COUNTRY	–	Hungary
		Shirt			

MOTIFS	–	Humor	TYPE OF FOLKLORE	–	Folk Tales

0523 BREMEN TOWN MUSICIANS

0217 Bremen Town Musicians, The

By Grimm, The Brothers
Illus. Paul Galdone
New York, McGraw-Hill Book Company, 1968. 32p.

The ass, dog, cat, and rooster decide to make music together after they become of little use to their masters. Their music helps to frighten some robbers from a house. They decide to stay in the house.

SUBJECTS	–	Cat	COUNTRY	–	Germany
		Dog(s)			
		Donkey			
		Musician(s)			

Rooster
Robber(s)
Grimm, The Brothers

| MOTIFS | — Humor | TYPE OF | |
| | Talking Animals | FOLKLORE | — Folk Tales |

0038 Traveling Musicians, The

By Grimm, The Brothers
Illus. Hans Fischer
New York, Harcourt, Brace and Company, 1944. unp.

A donkey, dog, cat, and rooster are ill treated by their masters so they go to the city. On the way they rout robbers from their house, confiscate their stolen goods and live to a ripe old age.

SUBJECTS	— Cat	COUNTRY	— Germany
	Dog(s)		
	Donkey		
	Musician(s)		
	Rooster		
	Robber(s)		
	Grimm, The Brothers		

| MOTIFS | — Humor | TYPE OF | |
| | Talking Animals | FOLKLORE | — Folk Tales |

0217 BREMEN TOWN MUSICIANS, THE

See — 0523 Bremen Town Musicians

0407 BUNDLE OF STICKS, A

Reteller, Katherine Evans
Illus. Katherine Evans
Chicago, Ill., Albert Whitman & Company, 1962. unp.

Three brothers are taught a lesson in teamwork when after they take over their father's Persian rugmaking business, they each want the prize for the most handsome rug.

SUBJECTS	— Cooperation	COUNTRY	— Greece
	Rugmaker, Old R.		
	Teaches Sons a		
	Lesson		

| MOTIFS | — Wit Prevails | TYPE OF | |
| | Humor | FOLKLORE | — Fables |

0279 BURIED MOON, THE

By Joseph Jacobs
Illus. Susan Jeffers
Englewood Cliffs, New Jersey, Bradbury Press, 1969. unp.

Moon is rescued by brave townsfolk from the evil ones after she comes to earth to see the evil that lurks when she doesn't shine.

SUBJECTS	— Helpfulness	COUNTRY	— United
	Moon		Kingdom
	Wise Women		
	Witch(es)		
	Jacobs, Joseph		

STORIES BY TITLE

MOTIFS	– Supernatural Creatures Religion	TYPE OF FOLKLORE	– Folk Tales

0026 BURNING RICE FIELDS, THE

See – 0543 Wave

0227 BY HIS OWN MIGHT: THE BATTLES OF BEOWULF

See – 0502 Beowulf

0159 CALLOW PIT COFFER, THE

Reteller, Kevin Crossley-Holland
Illus. Margaret Gordon
New York, The Seabury Press, First American Edition, 1969. 48p.

Two men defy the powers of the supernatural to pull a coffer of gold
and silver from the callow pit when England's King Stephen reigns, but
they do not reckon with the giant hand that emerges from the water.

SUBJECTS	– Coffer Poverty	COUNTRY	– United Kingdom
MOTIFS	– Religion Supernatural Creatures	TYPE OF FOLKLORE	– Folk Tales

0406 CAMEL IN THE TENT

See – 0532 Arab and His Camel

0299 CAP'N DOW AND THE HOLE IN THE DOUGHNUT

By Le Grand
Illus. Le Grand
New York, Abingdon-Cokesbury Press, 1946. unp.

Capt. Dow needs both hands to steer his schooner through the storm
so he sticks his doughnut over one of the spokes of the wheel. Some
say this is the true story of how the doughnut got its hole.

SUBJECTS	– Captain Jason Dow Doughnuts Maine Tall Tales	COUNTRY	– U.S.–Native Tall Tales of the Paul Bunyan Variety
MOTIFS	– Humor Local Legendary Heroes Pourquoi Stories	TYPE OF FOLKLORE	– Folk Tales

0293 CAPTAIN ICHABOD PADDOCK, WHALER OF NANTUCKET

Reteller, Ann Malcolmson
Illus. Unada
New York, Walker and Company, 1970. unp.

In an effort to catch Crooked Jaw the whale, Capt. Paddock jumps
inside the whale where he meets the devil and a witch mermaid. Each
Thursday he visits the witch mermaid inside the whale until Mrs.
Paddock's silver harpoon enters the whale and kills the witch
mermaid.

STORIES BY TITLE

SUBJECTS	– Captain Ichabod Paddock Devil Mermaid Nantucket Whalers Tall Tales Whale Massachusetts	COUNTRY	– U.S.–Native Tall Tales of the Paul Bunyan Variety
MOTIFS	– Supernatural Creatures Humor Local Legendary Heroes	TYPE OF FOLKLORE	– Folk Tales

0117 CARPET OF SOLOMON

Reteller, Sulamith Ish-Kishor
Illus. Uri Shulevitz
New York, Pantheon Books, 1966. 57p.

King Solomon thinks a magic carpet from the king of demons makes him as powerful as the Lord God Almighty. He sees the error of his ways and prays for forgiveness.

SUBJECTS	– Carpet God Eagle Humility Invisibility Vision Solomon Pride	COUNTRY	– Israel
MOTIFS	– Magic Objects Religion Supernatural Creatures Talking Animals Legendary Heroes	TYPE OF FOLKLORE	– Legends

0295 CASEY JONES: THE STORY OF A BRAVE ENGINEER

Author Anonymous
Illus. Glen Rounds
San Carlos, California, Golden Gate Junior Books, 1968. unp.

Engineer Casey Jones dies in a wreck trying to get the mail through and is the symbol of those fearless engineers who pride themselves on being on time and sticking to their posts at all costs. Music is included.

SUBJECTS	– Casey Jones Music Railroads Tall Tales	COUNTRY	– U.S.–Native Tall Tales of the Paul Bunyan Variety
MOTIFS	– Humor Local Legendary Heroes	TYPE OF FOLKLORE	– Folk Songs, Ballads

0366 CHALLENGE OF THE GREEN KNIGHT, THE

See — 0513 Sir Gawain and the Green Knight

0321 CHANTICLEER AND THE FOX
See — 0504 Cock and the Fox

0503 CHICKEN LITTLE

0278 Henny Penny

Reteller, Paul Galdone
Illus. Paul Galdone
New York, The Seabury Press, 1968. unp.

> Henny Penny is struck by an acorn and thinks the sky is falling. On her way to tell the king, she and her friends are tricked by the fox who offers them a shortcut and they are never seen again.

SUBJECTS	– Cumulative Tale	COUNTRY	– United
	Chain Tale		Kingdom
	Animals With Strange		
	Names		
	Acorn (Hits		
	Chicken's Head)		
	Formula Tale		
MOTIFS	– Humor	TYPE OF	
	Talking Animals	FOLKLORE	– Folk Tales

0358 Henny Penny

Reteller, William Stobbs
Illus. William Stobbs
Chicago, Follett Publishing Company, 1970. 26p.

> This version differs from the title no. 0278 in its ending. Cocky-Locky warns Henny Penny of Foxy-Woxy's trickery and she escapes to her home.

SUBJECTS	– Animals With Strange	COUNTRY	– United
	Names		Kingdom
	Cumulative Tale		
	Chain Tale		
	Formula Tale		
MOTIFS	– Humor	TYPE OF	
	Talking Animals	FOLKLORE	– Folk Tales

0381 CHINESE STORY TELLER, THE

Reteller, Pearl S. Buck
Illus. Regina Shekerjian
New York, The John Day Company, 1971. unp.

> The farmer finds a magic ring but it is stolen after his wife brags of their good fortune. Their cat and dog find it, but when the cat takes all the credit, the dog becomes angry and hates cats to this day.

SUBJECTS	– Cat, Reason Dog	COUNTRY	– China
	Fights C.		(Mainland)
	Vanity		
	Ring Brings Good		
	Luck		
MOTIFS	– Trickery	TYPE OF	
	Wit Prevails	FOLKLORE	– Folk Tales

Talking Animals
Pourquoi Stories
Magic Objects

0518 CINDERELLA

0270 Cinderella

From the Opera by Gioacchino Rossini, Reteller, Beni Montresor
Illus. Beni Montresor
New York, Alfred A. Knopf, 1965. unp.

Angelina is sent to the kitchen to work when her mother dies. With
the aid of a friend she attends a ball and dances with the prince who is
disguised as a valet. Later she marries the prince and lives happily ever
after.

SUBJECTS	–	Beggar(s)(Super- natural Creature) Pumpkin Kindness Royalty Opera Music	COUNTRY	–	Italy
MOTIFS	–	Magic Transforma- tion Magic Objects Supernatural Creatures	TYPE OF FOLKLORE	–	Folk Tales

See also   0352   **Vasilisa the Beautiful**
          0063   **Cinderella or the Little Glass Slipper**

0063 Cinderella or The Little Glass Slipper

A Free Trans. From the French of Charles Perrault
Illus. Marcia Brown
New York, Charles Scribner's Sons, 1954. unp.

Cinderella is helped by her fairy godmother and goes to the prince's
ball despite her wicked stepmother and two stepsisters. The prince
falls in love with Cinderella and finds her by using the glass slipper as
a clue.

SUBJECTS	–	Royalty Rat Mouse (Mice) Pumpkin Lizards Fairy Kindness Perrault, Charles	COUNTRY	–	France
MOTIFS	–	Magic Transforma- tion Magic Objects Supernatural Creatures	TYPE OF FOLKLORE	–	Folk Tales

See also   0352   **Vasilisa the Beautiful**
          0270   **Cinderella**

0270 CINDERELLA

See – 0518 Cinderella

STORIES BY TITLE

0063 CINDERELLA OR THE LITTLE GLASS SLIPPER

See — 0518 Cinderella

0045 CLASHING ROCKS: THE STORY OF JASON, THE

See — 0533 Argonauts

0193 CLEVER TURTLE, THE

Reteller, A. K. Roche
Illus. A. K. Roche
Englewood Cliffs, N. J., Prentice-Hall, Inc., 1969. unp.

Turtle tricks the townsfolk after he is caught crushing all the corn in the cornfield. About to be punished, he asks them not to throw him in the river. They decide that is just what they will do, and he paddles away unharmed,

SUBJECTS	—	Turtle	COUNTRY	—	Portugal–
		Punishment, Chooses			Angola
		Type of			
MOTIFS	—	Humor	TYPE OF		
		Wit Prevails	FOLKLORE	—	Folk Tales
		Trickery			
		Talking Animals			

See also **0191   Beeswax Catches a Thief**
         0304   Punia and the King of the Sharks

0221 COBBLER'S DILEMMA, THE

Reteller, Kurt Werth
Illus. Kurt Werth
New York, McGraw-Hill Book Company, 1967. 32p.

When a poor cobbler receives three magic objects, he is told to say nothing about them but he cannot contain his knowledge. The wise man takes back the magic objects making the cobbler wiser for his experience.

SUBJECTS	—	Cobbler	COUNTRY	—	Italy
		Magic Basket, Cock			
		and Broomstick			
		Wise Man			
MOTIFS	—	Humor	TYPE OF		
		Magic Objects	FOLKLORE	—	Folk Tales
		Trickery			

0504 COCK AND THE FOX

  0321 Chanticleer and the Fox

By Geoffrey Chaucer, Reteller, Barbara Cooney
Illus. Barbara Cooney
New York, Thomas Y. Crowell Company, 1958. unp.

The wily fox catches the vain cock off guard but the cock outwits him.

SUBJECTS	—	Rooster Tricked	COUNTRY	—	United
		By Fox's Flattery			Kingdom
		Pride			

Canterbury
Tales

| MOTIFS | — Trickery
Humor
Wit Prevails
Talking Animals
Religion | TYPE OF
FOLKLORE | — Fables |

0505 COCK ROBIN

0235 Cock Robin and Jenny Wren

By Mother Goose
Illus. Barbara Cooney
New York, Charles Scribner's Sons, 1965. unp.

This is a chain tale in which Cock Robin's death by his friend Sparrow is mourned by his animal friends.

| SUBJECTS | — Cock Robin
Chain Tale
Mother Goose
Formula Tale
Cumulative Tale
Animal Weddings
  (Cock Robin and
  Jenny Wren) | COUNTRY | — United
Kingdom |
| MOTIFS | — Talking Animals | TYPE OF
FOLKLORE | — Nursery
Rhymes |

0235 COCK ROBIN AND JENNY WREN

See — 0505 Cock Robin

0506 COCK, THE MOUSE, AND THE LITTLE RED HEN

0325 Rooster, Mouse, and Little Red Hen, The

Reteller, Nova Nestrick
Illus. Bonnie & Bill Rutherford and Eulalie
New York, Platt & Munk, 1961. 28p.

Father Fox easily catches the mouse the rooster and Little Red Hen. However, Little Red Hen uses her wit to free all three and Father Fox returns home emptyhanded.

| SUBJECTS | — Cock, Mouse, Little
  Red Hen
Fox(es) | COUNTRY | — United
Kingdom |
| MOTIFS | — Talking Animals
Wit Prevails
Trickery | TYPE OF
FOLKLORE | — Folk Tales |

0324 Rooster, The Mouse, and the Little Red Hen, The

Reteller, Felicite Lefevre
Illus. Tony Sarg
Philadelphia, Pa., MacRae Smith Company, n. d. 103p.

This differs from title no. 0325 in its ending. Father Fox loses his balance and tumbles into the stream where fish imprison him in the fairy caves.

SUBJECTS	–	Cock, Mouse, Little Red Hen Fox(es)	COUNTRY	–	United Kingdom
MOTIFS	–	Talking Animals Wit Prevails Trickery	TYPE OF FOLKLORE	–	Folk Tales

0125 COCONUT THIEVES, THE

Reteller, Catharine Fournier
Illus. Janina Domanska
New York, Charles Scribner's Sons, 1964. unp.

When Turtle and Dog go to steal Leopard's coconuts, Turtle must save himself by trickery when Dog fails to help. Turtle forgives Dog and the next time they go to steal the coconuts, Dog tricks Leopard by making a fearful noise.

SUBJECTS	–	Coconut(s) Dog(s) Friendship Snake Selfishness Turtle Theft	COUNTRY	–	Africa
MOTIFS	–	Friendly Animals Talking Animals Trickery Wit Prevails	TYPE OF FOLKLORE	–	Folk Tales

0218 COUNT CARROT

Reteller, Frank Jupo
Illus. Frank Jupo
New York, Holiday House, 1966. unp.

The giant Count Carrot befriends the poor and rewards the honest. After a thousand year sleep he awakes to find an inhabited wilderness. He learns from experience what the inhabitants are like.

SUBJECTS	–	Experiences With Human Beings– Giants Giant(s) Sleep Extended Over Many Years	COUNTRY	–	Germany
MOTIFS	–	Magic Transformation Wit Prevails Trickery Supernatural Creatures Enchanted People	TYPE OF FOLKLORE	–	Folk Tales

0092 CRANE MAIDEN, THE

By Miyoko Matsutani, English Version By Alvin Tresselt

Illus. Chihiro Iwasaki
New York, Parents' Magazine, 1968. unp.

A crane becomes a maiden to repay a kindness to an old couple. She weaves beautiful cloth for them but says they must not watch her at work. The old woman's curiosity gets the best of her and she steals a glance.

SUBJECTS	–	Crane	COUNTRY	–	Japan
		Love, Selfless			
		Kindness			
		Childless (Couple			
MOTIFS	–	Magic Objects	TYPE OF		
		Magic Transforma-tion	FOLKLORE	–	Folk Tales

0236 CRANE WITH ONE LEG, THE

Reteller, Paul Schaaf
Illus. Jozef Wilkon
New York, Frederick Warne & Co. Inc., English Translation, 1964. unp.

A nobleman in Italy finds it is selfish not to share after he kills a crane and his cook gives some of the delicacy to a friend.

SUBJECTS	–	Crane	COUNTRY	–	Italy
		Sharing			
		Nobleman			
MOTIFS	–	Realistic Events	TYPE OF		
			FOLKLORE	–	Folk Tales

0194 CROCODILE AND HEN

Reteller, Joan M. Lexau
Illus. Joan Sandin
New York, Harper & Row, 1969. unp.

The Lizard explains that Hen and Crocodile are brothers even though their outward appearances differ: they both lay eggs.

SUBJECTS	–	Brothers, Why Hen and Crocodile Are	COUNTRY	–	Bakongo
		Crocodile			
		Hen			
MOTIFS	–	Humor	TYPE OF		
		Talking Animals	FOLKLORE	–	Folk Tales
		Pourquoi Stories			

0534 DAEDALUS AND ICARUS

0319 Fall From the Sky: The Story of Daedalus

By Ian Serraillier
Illus. William Stobbs
New York, Henry Z. Walck, Incorporated, 1966. 61p.

Daedalus, a master craftsman, kills his nephew Talos who surpassed him in creativeness. A series of disasters befalls Daedalus. His son Icarus is killed when he flies too near the sun and his wings melt.

STORIES BY TITLE

SUBJECTS	– Daedalus Flies On Artificial Wings Invention Icarus' Wings Melt Jealousy Wings, Flight On Artificial W.	COUNTRY	– Greece
MOTIFS	– Legendary Heroes Trickery Wit Prevails	TYPE OF FOLKLORE	– Myths

0237 DAME WIGGINS OF LEE AND HER SEVEN WONDERFUL CATS

By A Lady of Ninety. ed. With Additional Verses By John Ruskin
Illus. Robert Broomfield
New York, McGraw-Hill Book Company, Inc., 1963. unp.

Everytime Dame Wiggins goes to market in search of something, she
returns to find her cats doing something else. The pattern relates
similarly to that of Old Mother Hubbard.

SUBJECTS	– Cat Dame Wiggins	COUNTRY	– United Kingdom
MOTIFS	– Humor	TYPE OF FOLKLORE	– Nursery Rhymes

0383 DANCING STARS, THE

Reteller, Anne Rockwell
Illus. Anne Rockwell
New York, Thomas Y. Crowell Company, 1972. unp.

This is the mythical story of the creation of a constellation. The moon
tricks six little Indian brothers who like to run and dance together
into dancing forever in the sky.

SUBJECTS	– Constellation, Origin of Brothers Tricked By Moon Moon	COUNTRY	– U.S.–Tales From the North American Indians
MOTIFS	– Pourquoi Stories Supernatural Creatures	TYPE OF FOLKLORE	– Folk Tales

0342 DERBY RAM, THE

Reteller, Anonymous
Illus. Rick Schreiter
Garden City, New York, Doubleday & Company, Inc., 1970. unp.

This rollicking nursery rhyme ballad depicts some adventures in life of
a vagabond street singer.

SUBJECTS	– Vagabond Ram	COUNTRY	– United Kingdom
MOTIFS	– Humor	TYPE OF FOLKLORE	– Nursery Rhymes

0357 DICK WHITTINGTON
See — 0507 Dick Whittington and His Cat

0507 DICK WHITTINGTON AND HIS CAT

0365 Dick Whittington and His Cat

Reteller, Marcia Brown
Illus. Marcia Brown
New York, Charles Scribner's Sons, 1950. unp.

> Poor Dick Whittington is befriended by Mr. Fitzwarren. Mr. Fitz-warren's ship sails and Dick gives him a cat to trade. When the cat rids the king's palace of rats and mice, Dick is handsomely rewarded. In time, he becomes Lord Mayor of London Town.

SUBJECTS	– Cat Dick Whittington	COUNTRY	– United Kingdom
MOTIFS	– Realistic Events	TYPE OF FOLKLORE	– Folk Tales

0357 Dick Whittington

Reteller, Kathleen Lines
Illus. Edward Ardizzone
New York, Henry Z. Walck, Inc., 1970. 48p.

> This version differs from title no. 0365 Dick Whittington and His Cat in its emphasis on Dick Whittington's accomplishments for the betterment of London. Background notes: p46-48.

SUBJECTS	– Cat Dick Whittington	COUNTRY	– United Kingdom
MOTIFS	– Realistic Events	TYPE OF FOLKLORE	– Folk Tales

0365 DICK WHITTINGTON AND HIS CAT
See — 0507 Dick Whittington and His Cat

0356 DIONYSOS AND THE PIRATES: HOMERIC HYMN NUMBER SEVEN

Reteller, Penelope Proddow
Illus. Barbara Cooney
New York, Doubleday & Company, Inc., 1970. unp.

> The pirate captain wants to keep Dionysos for ransom, but the god turns into a lion and transforms the captain's crew into dolphins when they jump overboard to escape. Dionysos befriends the helmsman who did not want to keep him for ransom.

SUBJECTS	– Dionysis Fate Gods Pirates Dionysos	COUNTRY	– Greece
MOTIFS	– Supernatural Creatures Religion Magic Transformation	TYPE OF FOLKLORE	– Myths

0280 DIVERTING ADVENTURES OF TOM THUMB, THE

See – 0517 Tom Thumb

0285 DON'T COUNT YOUR CHICKS

Retellers, Ingri & Edgar Parin D'Aulaire
Illus. Ingri & Edgar Parin D'Aulaire
Garden City, New York, Doubleday & Company, 1943. unp.

When the old woman has collected three dozen eggs, she sets off to sell them. While daydreaming about what she will do with her money from the eggs, she drops the eggs and breaks them.

SUBJECTS	– Dreaming, Day Woman and Hen	COUNTRY	– Scandinavia
MOTIFS	– Humor	TYPE OF FOLKLORE	– Folk Tales

See also   0315   Maid and Her Pail of Milk, The

0010 DONKEY RIDE, THE

See – 0520 Man, The Boy, and The Donkey, The

0185 DUMPLINGS AND THE DEMONS, THE

Reteller, Claus Stamm
Illus. Kazue Mizumura
New York, The Viking Press, 1964. unp.

Old Tarobei follows a dumpling to the statue of Jizo, god of children. He is welcomed and told how to play a trick on some demons who come to the cave of Jizo to gamble.

SUBJECTS	– Demons Dumpling (Could Talk and Roll) Jizo, god of the children	COUNTRY	– Japan
MOTIFS	– Humor Supernatural Creatures Religion	TYPE OF FOLKLORE	– Folk Tales

0371 DWARF LONG-NOSE

See – 0529 Longnose the Dwarf

0349 EAGLE MASK: A WEST COAST INDIAN TALE

Reteller, James Houston
Illus. James Houston
New York, Harcourt, Brace & World, Inc., 1966. 63p.

The story of Skemshan, young prince of the eagle clan, and the endurance trials, rituals, and celebrations that mark the coming of age of this future chieftain.

SUBJECTS	– Eagle Indians, North- western America Initiation Rituals	COUNTRY	– North America– Indians of North America

MOTIFS	—	Supernatural Creatures Realistic Events Tasks and Trials Pourquoi Stories	TYPE OF FOLKLORE — Folk Tales

0156 EGGS, THE

Reteller, Aliki
Illus. Aliki
New York, Pantheon Book, 1969. unp.

A sea captain fails to pay his restaurant bill when he rushes to save his ship from a storm. Many years later he offers to pay the innkeeper who multiplies the bill many times over. A skillful lawyer helps the captain win his case.

SUBJECTS	—	Egg(s) Judge Persuaded By High-Flown Speech Justice	COUNTRY — Greece

MOTIFS	—	Humor Trickery Wit Prevails	TYPE OF FOLKLORE — Folk Tales

See also **0082** **Judge Not**
0206 **Wise Fool, The**
0322 **Mice That Ate Iron, The**

0012 ELEPHANTS AND THE MICE, THE (PANCHATANTRA TALE)

Reteller, Marilyn Hirsh
Illus. Marilyn Hirsh
N. Y., World Publishing Company, 1970. unp.

An elephant herd unknowingly crushes mice living in a ruined city. An emissary is sent to the elephant king who gladly changes his herd's route. A time comes when the mice return the favor to the elephant herd.

SUBJECTS	—	Cooperation Friendship Panchatantra Tale	COUNTRY — India

MOTIFS	—	Talking Animals	TYPE OF FOLKLORE — Fables

0524 ELVES AND THE SHOEMAKER

0398 Elves and the Shoemaker, The

By Grimm, The Brothers
Illus. Katrin Brandt
New York, Follett Publishing Company, 1967. unp.

The fairies help a poor shoemaker and his wife live comfortably by making shoes at night. Out of gratitude the shoemaker's wife makes clothes for them. They leave and never return again.

SUBJECTS	—	Elves Shoemaker Kindness Christmas	COUNTRY — Germany

Helpfulness
Grimm, The Brothers

MOTIFS   — Magic Objects   TYPE OF
             Supernatural   FOLKLORE — Folk Tales
             Creatures

0037 Shoemaker and the Elves, The

By Grimm, The Brothers, Trans. Wayne Andrews
Illus. Adrienne Adams
New York, Charles Scribner's Sons, 1960. unp.

> A kind but poor shoemaker is aided by naked elves in making shoes.
> In repayment the shoemaker and his wife make clothing for them.
> They dance happily away, and the shoemaker continues his success.

SUBJECTS — Elves   COUNTRY — Germany
             Shoemaker
             Kindness
             Christmas
             Helpfulness
             Grimm, The Brothers

MOTIFS   — Supernatural   TYPE OF
             Creatures   FOLKLORE — Folk Tales

0313 Elves and the Shoemaker, The

By Grimm, The Brothers, Reteller, Frances K. Pavel
Illus. Joyce Hewitt
New York, Holt, Rinehart, and Winston, Inc., 1961. 26p.

> Similar to title nos. 0398 Elves and the Shoemaker, The and 0037
> Shoemaker and the Elves, The. Different illus.

SUBJECTS — Elves   COUNTRY — Germany
             Shoemaker
             Kindness
             Helpfulness
             Grimm, The Brothers

MOTIFS   — Supernatural   TYPE OF
             Creatures   FOLKLORE — Folk Tales

0398 ELVES AND THE SHOEMAKER, THE
      See — 0524 Elves and the Shoemaker

0313 ELVES AND THE SHOEMAKER, THE
      See — 0524 Elves and the Shoemaker

0130 EMIR'S SON, THE

Reteller, Martin Ballard
Illus. Gareth Floyd
London, Constable Young Books Ltd., W. C. 2 N. Y., World Pub. Co.,
    1967. 32p.

> Selfish and vain Emir's son comes to understand the secret of true
> happiness after the old man said, "Others have planted and I have
> eaten. I, too, will plant that others may eat."

SUBJECTS	– Emir Precept Wisdom Selfishness	COUNTRY	– Nigeria
MOTIFS	– Realistic Events Wit Prevails	TYPE OF FOLKLORE	– Fables

0098 EMPEROR AND THE KITE, THE

By Jane Yolen
Illus. Ed Young
New York, World Publishing Company, 1967. unp.

The emperor's daughter weaves a long strong rope of her own hair, attaches it to a kite, and flies it to her imprisoned father so that he can escape from the high tower.

SUBJECTS	– Kite Love, Selfless Monk Royalty Emperor	COUNTRY	– China (Mainland)
MOTIFS	– Realistic Events Religion Wit Prevails	TYPE OF FOLKLORE	– Folk Tales

0186 EMPEROR'S BIG GIFT, THE

Reteller, Dell Britt
Illus. Jan Hogenbyl
Englewood Cliffs, N. J., Prentice-Hall, Inc., 1967. unp.

A small boy is the only one able to solve the problem of weighing a huge elephant when there are no scales in China big enough to weigh the animal.

SUBJECTS	– Elephant
	Emperor
	India
	Wisdom
	Weighing of Elephant
	  as Test of Resource-
	  fulness
		COUNTRY	– China
			(Mainland)

MOTIFS	– Wit Prevails	TYPE OF FOLKLORE	– Folk Tales

0550 EMPEROR'S NEW CLOTHES

0169 Emperor's New Clothes, The

By Hans Christian Andersen
Illus. Virginia Lee Burton
Boston, Houghton Mifflin Co., 1949. 44p.

Two imposters make clothes for the king and say they are visible only to those of noble birth. The king is afraid to admit he cannot see the clothes, and a child seeing the king naked reveals the imposture.

SUBJECTS	– Conformity Emperor	COUNTRY	– Denmark

Vanity
Clothes for King
  Imaginary
Andersen, Hans
  Christian

MOTIFS — Fools and   TYPE OF
            Simpletons   FOLKLORE — Folk Tales
          Trickery
          Wit Prevails
          Humor

0213 Emperor's New Clothes, The

By Hans Christian Andersen, Trans. By Erik Blegvad
Illus. Erik Blegvad
New York, Harcourt, Brace and Company, 1959. 32p.

> Reteller's version is similar to title no. 0169 Emperor's New Clothes, The.

SUBJECTS — Conformity   COUNTRY — Denmark
            Emperor
            Vanity
            Clothes for King
              Imaginary
            Andersen, Hans
              Christian

MOTIFS — Fools and   TYPE OF
            Simpletons   FOLKLORE — Folk Tales
          Trickery
          Wit Prevails
          Humor

0213 EMPEROR'S NEW CLOTHES, THE

See — 0550 Emperor's New Clothes

0169 EMPEROR'S NEW CLOTHES, THE

See — 0550 Emperor's New Clothes

0294 EPAMINONDAS AND HIS AUNTIE

See — 0547 Epaminondas and His Auntie

0547 EPAMINONDAS AND HIS AUNTIE

0294 Epaminondas and His Auntie

Reteller, Sara Cone Bryant
Illus. Inez Hogan
New York, Houghton Mifflin Co., 1938. 16p.

> Similar to the English lazy Jack tale, Epaminondas never properly carries home the things which his aunt gives him to take to his mother. Sterotyped illustrations.

SUBJECTS — Instructions of   COUNTRY — U.S.–Variants
            Mother Followed   of the
            Literally By Son   European
            Epaminondas   Stories

MOTIFS   —   Fools and   TYPE OF
               Simpletons   FOLKLORE   —   Folk Tales

See also   0256   Lazy Jack
            0145   Lazy Jack
            0199   Silly Simon

0347   EREC AND ENID

See — 0508 Erec and Enid

0508   EREC AND ENID

0347   Erec and Enid

Reteller, Barbara Schiller
Illus. Ati Forberg
New York, E. P. Dutton & Company, Inc., 1970. 47p.

To protect the honor of Guinevere and her attendant, the newly knighted Erec has a battle with the Knight of the Sparrow Hawk. He wins the battle and also the hand of Enid.

SUBJECTS   —   Arthurian Legend   COUNTRY   —   United
                   Chivalry   Kingdom
                   Christianity
                   Erec and Enid

MOTIFS   —   Legendary Heroes   TYPE OF
                                                 FOLKLORE   —   Epics

0369   Joy of the Court

Reteller, Constance Hieatt
Illus. Pauline Baynes
New York, Thomas Y. Crowell Company, 1971. 71p.

To prove his valor, Erec mades his wife Enid accompany him as he kills robber knights, giants, and breaks the spell in the garden. It is similar to title no. 0347 Erec and Enid. However, their adventures are expanded in this version.

SUBJECTS   —   Erec and Enid   COUNTRY   —   United
                   Arthurian Legend   Kingdom
                   Christianity
                   Chivalry
                   Giant(s)
                   Horn Wakes Knights
                       From Enchanted
                       Sleep

MOTIFS   —   Magic Objects   TYPE OF
                   Enchanted People   FOLKLORE   —   Epics
                   Legendary Heroes
                   Religion
                   Supernatural
                   Creatures

0359   ERIE CANAL, THE

Anonymous
Illus. Peter Spier
Garden City, New York, Doubleday & Company, Inc., 1970. unp.

This is a folksong often heard as the canal boats travel from Albany to Buffalo. Words and music plus historical notes are included.

SUBJECTS	– Canal Boats Folksong Erie Canal New York, Folksong	COUNTRY	– U.S.–Folk- songs
MOTIFS	– Humor	TYPE OF FOLKLORE	– Folk Songs, Ballads

0346 EVERY MAN HEART LAY DOWN

Reteller, Lorenz Graham
Illus. Colleen Browning
New York, Thomas Y. Crowell Company, 1970. unp.

When God looks down at the world and sees his people are not listening, he thinks about making a new world. His son offers to go down and tell the people.

SUBJECTS	– Christmas Christ Christianity	COUNTRY	– Liberia
MOTIFS	– Religion Legendary Heroes Pourquoi Stories	TYPE OF FOLKLORE	– Legends

0128 EXTRAORDINARY TUG-OF-WAR

Reteller, Letta Schatz
Illus. John Burningham
New York, Follett Publishing Company, 1968. 48p.

Hippopotamus and Elephant, the jungle giants, make life miserable for Hare by teasing him because he is so small and weak. He gets his revenge when he challenges his tormentors to a tug-of-war.

SUBJECTS	– Tug-of-War Elephant Hare Tricks Animals Hippopotamus	COUNTRY	– Nigeria
MOTIFS	– Humor Wit Prevails Trickery Talking Animals	TYPE OF FOLKLORE	– Folk Tales

See also   0385   Tortoise's Tug-of-War, The

0319 FALL FROM THE SKY: THE STORY OF DAEDALUS

See – 0534 Daedalus and Icarus

0298 FAST SOONER HOUND, THE

Retellers, Arna Bontemps and Jack Conroy
Illus. Virginia Lee Burton
Boston, Houghton Mifflin Company, 1942. 28p.

When Boomer is not allowed to take his dog in the train cab, he says Sooner will run alongside the train. When he does the railroad company is embarrassed and Sooner is permitted to ride in the cab.

STORIES BY TITLE

SUBJECTS	–	Railroads Sooner, Hound Dog Tall Tales	COUNTRY	–	U.S.–Native Tall Tales of the Paul Bunyan Variety
MOTIFS	–	Humor Local Legendary Heroes	TYPE OF FOLKLORE	–	Folk Tales

0329 FAT CAT, THE

Reteller, Jack Kent
Illus. Jack Kent
New York, Parents' Magazine Press, 1971. unp.

> This chain tale involves a cat which eats the porridge, pot, mistress, and other people and animals. Finally a woodcutter cuts the cat open when the cat threatens him. All the objects the cat has swallowed return to their ways. The woodcutter bandages the cat's stomach.

SUBJECTS	–	Cumulative Tale Chain Tale Cat Eats Pot, etc. Formula Tale	COUNTRY	–	Denmark
MOTIFS	–	Humor Talking Animals	TYPE OF FOLKLORE	–	Folk Tales

0052 FEATHER MOUNTAIN

Reteller, Elizabeth Olds
Illus. Elizabeth Olds
Boston, Houghton Mifflin Company, 1951. 33p.

> The birds of the world do not have any covering for their skins until the great spirit tells them that someone must go to Feather Mountain to secure a covering for all birds. The turkey buzzard brings back feathers for all.

SUBJECTS	–	Bird(s) Spirit Trees Feathers Cooperation	COUNTRY	–	U.S.–Tales From the North Ameri- can Indians
MOTIFS	–	Talking Animals Supernatural Creatures Pourquoi Stories	TYPE OF FOLKLORE	–	Folk Tales

0360 FIR TREE, THE

By Hans Christian Andersen, Reteller, H. W. Dulcken
Illus. Nancy Ekholm Burkert
New York, Harper & Row, Publishers, 1970. 36p.

> The little fir is unhappy with his lot, wanting to be taller and bigger, but when he is chosen as a Christmas tree his glory is shortlived for he is soon cut into firewood.

SUBJECTS	–	Christmas Tree, Fir Wishes for Unobtainable	COUNTRY	–	Denmark

Andersen, Hans
Christian

MOTIFS   –   Talking Animals   TYPE OF
FOLKLORE – Folk Tales

0555 FISHERMAN AND HIS WIFE

0084 Fisherman and His Wife, The

By Grimm, The Brothers
Illus. Madeleine Gekiere
New York, Pantheon Books, 1957. unp.

An enchanted fish, in return for his life, grants the wishes of a poor fisherman's wife, but her wishes become more and more extravagant and she loses all.

SUBJECTS   –   Fisherman (Men)   COUNTRY   –   Germany
Fish (Flounder)
Greediness
God
Grimm, The Brothers
Wishes, Fisherman
Given W. From
Fish

MOTIFS   –   Religion   TYPE OF
Wishes   FOLKLORE – Folk Tales
Talking Animals
Supernatural
Creatures

0179 Fisherman and His Wife, The

Reteller, Margot Zemach, Adapted from Grimm
Illus. Margot Zemach
New York, W. W. Norton & Company, Inc., 1966. unp.

This tale is similar to title no. 0084 Fisherman and His Wife, The Wife wishes for a cottage, and mansion and to become king, emperor, God.

SUBJECTS   –   Fisherman (Men)   COUNTRY   –   Germany
Fish (Flounder)
Greediness
God
Grimm, The Brothers
Wishes, Fisherman
Given W. From Fish

MOTIFS   –   Supernatural   TYPE OF
Creatures   FOLKLORE – Folk Tales
Wishes
Religion
Talking Animals

0084 FISHERMAN AND HIS WIFE, THE

See – 0555 Fisherman and His Wife

STORIES BY TITLE

0179 FISHERMAN AND HIS WIFE, THE

See – 0555 Fisherman and His Wife

0354 FISHERMAN AND THE GOBLET, THE

Reteller, Mark Taylor
Illus. Taro Yashima
San Carlos, California, Golden Gate Junior Books, 1971. unp.

The princess is shocked to find that the fisherman, whose flute music she loves, is ugly. Only when he dies does she realize faces are given to us but we fashion our own hearts.

SUBJECTS	–	Fate	COUNTRY	–	Vietnam
		Goblet (Unanswered Love)			
		Fisherman Plays Flute For Princess			
		Love			
		Mandarin			

| MOTIFS | – | Magic Objects | TYPE OF | | |
| | | Realistic Events | FOLKLORE | – | Folk Tales |

0090 FIVE CHINESE BROTHERS, THE

Reteller, Claire Huchet Bishop
Illus. Kurt Wiese
New York, Coward-McCann, Inc., 1938. unp.

Five identical brothers have unique characteristics. One can swallow the sea, one has an iron neck, one can stretch his legs to any height, one cannot be burned, and the fifth can hold his breath indefinitely.

SUBJECTS	–	Companions (Magic Wisdom Possessed by Extraordinary C.)	COUNTRY	–	China (Mainland)
		Burned, Cannot be B.			
		Drinking			
		Cooperation			
		Iron-Neck			
		Judge(s)			
		Stretching			

| MOTIFS | – | Wit Prevails | TYPE OF | | |
| | | Tasks and Trials | FOLKLORE | – | Folk Tales |

See also   0075   Fool of the World and the Flying Ship, The
           0115   Long, Broad and Quickeye
           0066   Seven Simeons
           0039   Four Clever Brothers, The

0110 FLYING CARPET, THE

Retold by Marcia Brown From Richard Burton's Trans. of the Arabian Nights
Illus. Marcia Brown
New York, Charles Scribner's Sons, 1956. unp.

The sultan's three sons love the same princess. He sets a task for each whereby the winner will gain her hand. Each does equally well so a shooting contest is held. Ali, the second son, wins.

SUBJECTS	— India Sultan Carpet Telescope (Magic) Arabian Nights Apple	COUNTRY	— Iran
MOTIFS	— Wishes Magic Objects Enchanted People Tasks and Trials	TYPE OF FOLKLORE	— Folk Tales

0075 FOOL OF THE WORLD AND THE FLYING SHIP, THE

Reteller, Arthur Ransome
Illus. Uri Shulevitz
New York, Farrar, Straus and Giroux, 1968. unp.

> The fool of the world, a peasant looked down on by his parents, wins the hand of the czar's daughter after overcoming enormous obstacles with the aid of an old wise man and seven supernaturally talented companions.

SUBJECTS	— Royalty Companions (Magic Wisdom Possessed by Extraordinary C.) Ship (Magic) Cooperation	COUNTRY	— U.S.S.R.
MOTIFS	— Magic Objects Tasks and Trials Supernatural Creatures	TYPE OF FOLKLORE	— Folk Tales

See also
0090	Five Chinese Brothers, The
0115	Long, Broad and Quickeye
0066	Seven Simeons
0039	Four Clever Brothers, The

0039 FOUR CLEVER BROTHERS, THE

By Grimm, The Brothers
Illus. Felix Hoffmann
New York, Harcourt, Brace & World, Inc., 1967. unp.

> Four brothers leave home to find a trade. One becomes a thief, one a hunter, one a tailor, and one a stargazer. They are called upon to save the princess from a dragon. As a reward, they are each given a quarter of the kingdom.

SUBJECTS	— Royalty Telescope (Magic) Needle Gun Cooperation Dragon Companions (Magic Wisdom Possessed By, Extraordinary C.) Grimm, the Brothers	COUNTRY	— Germany
MOTIFS	— Magic Objects Wit Prevails	TYPE OF FOLKLORE	— Folk Tales

Supernatural
Creatures

0525   FOX AND THE HORSE

0041   Horse, the Fox, and the Lion, The

By Grimm, The Brothers, Reteller, Paul Galdone
Illus. Paul Galdone
New York, The Seabury Press, 1968. unp.

An old horse is banished by the farmer he had served faithfully. The farmer tells him he may return if he brings home a lion. With the help of a fox the horse accomplishes the task.

SUBJECTS	–	Fox(es)	COUNTRY	–	Germany
		Horse			
		Lion(s)			
		Kindness			
		Farmer			
		Grimm, The Brothers			

MOTIFS	–	Humor	TYPE OF		
		Trickery	FOLKLORE	–	Folk Tales
		Wit Prevails			
		Talking Animals			

0187   FOX WEDDING, THE

Trans. Yasuo Segawa, Reteller, Miyoko Matsutani
Illus. Yasuo Segawa
New York, Encyclopaedia Britannica Press, 1963. unp.

Ojiisan, an old Japanese Miller, rescues an abandoned baby fox and raises it. The fox disappears but Ojiisan believes he sees her wedding procession in the rainbow. He is proved right and is rewarded for his guardianship.

| SUBJECTS | – | Fox(es) | COUNTRY | – | Japan |
| | | Miller | | | |

| MOTIFS | – | Friendly Animals | TYPE OF | | |
| | | | FOLKLORE | – | Folk Tales |

0320   FOX WENT OUT ON A CHILLY NIGHT, THE

Anonymous
Illus. Peter Spier
Garden City, New York, Doubleday & Company, Inc., 1961. unp.

Father Fox visits the barnyard and steals a duck and goose for his family. This folksong relates his journey to the barnyard in rollicking fashion.

SUBJECTS	–	Fox(es)	COUNTRY	–	U.S.–Folk-
		Farmer			songs
		Folksong			
		New England			

MOTIFS	—	Humor	TYPE OF	
		Talking Animals	FOLKLORE —	Folk Songs,
				Ballads

0561 FOX AND THE HARE

0225 Fox, and the Hare, The

Reteller, Mirra Ginsburg
Illus. Victor Nolden
New York, Crown Publishers, Inc., 1969. unp.

When Fox's ice house melts, he asks Hare, whose house is of wood, to take him in. Hare is driven out of his house by Fox and only regains his house with the aid of Rooster.

SUBJECTS	—	Fox(es)	COUNTRY	—	U.S.S.R.
		Hare(s)			
		Houses Made of			
		Wood and Ice			
		Rooster			
MOTIFS	—	Talking Animals	TYPE OF		
		Trickery	FOLKLORE —	Folk Tales	
		Friendly Animals			

0071 Neighbors, The

Reteller, Marcia Brown
Illus. Marcia Brown
New York, Charles Scribner's Sons, 1967. unp.

A hare befriends a homeless fox by inviting him to share his home. However, the fox gains control of the home and evicts the hare. After many failed, the cock succeeds in regaining the home for the hare.

SUBJECTS	—	Fox(es)	COUNTRY	—	U.S.S.R.
		Rabbit(s)			
		Rooster			
MOTIFS	—	Talking Animals	TYPE OF		
			FOLKLORE —	Folk Tales	

0225 FOX AND THE HARE, THE

See — 0561 Fox and the Hare

0244 FOX, THE DOG, AND THE GRIFFIN, THE

Adapted by Poul Anderson
Illus. Laszlo Kubinyi
Garden City, New York, Doubleday & Company, Inc., 1966. 62p.

Tricked by the fox who courts the cat, the dog finds his way into the griffin's lair. Faced with being eaten or serving as the griffin's guard, he serves faithfully and is helped to woo the cat.

SUBJECTS	—	Cat	COUNTRY	—	Denmark
		Dog(s)			
		Fox(es)			
		Griffin			
		Loyalty			
MOTIFS	—	Magic Transforma-	TYPE OF		
		tion	FOLKLORE —	Fables	
		Wit Prevails			
		Trickery			
		Talking Animals			
		Supernatural			
		Creatures			

0258 FROG WENT A-COURTIN'

Reteller, John Langstaff
Illus. Feodor Rojankovsky
New York, Harcourt, Brace & World, Inc., 1955. unp.

Frog goes a-courtin' and marries Miss Mouse. Many small animals and insects take part in their wedding. An American version of a Scottish ballad, the southern mountain song includes music.

SUBJECTS	–	Frog and Mouse	COUNTRY	–	U.S.–Folk-
		Appalachian Mountain Song			songs
		Animal Weddings (Frog and Miss Mouse)			
MOTIFS	–	Humor	TYPE OF		
		Talking Animals	FOLKLORE	–	Folk Songs,
		Friendly Animals			Ballads

0208 GILGAMESH: MAN'S FIRST STORY

Reteller, Bernarda Bryson
Illus. Bernarda Bryson
New York, Holt, Rinehart & Winston, 1966. 112p.

Written 3,000 years before the birth of Christ, this story tells of Gilgamesh, who, befriended by the gods, builds an ark and survives a great flood.

SUBJECTS	–	Dream(s)	COUNTRY	–	Iraq
		Friendship			
		Flood			
		Gods of Gilgamesh			
		Humbaba (Monster)			
		Immortality			
		Mankind, Story of			
		Sumerians (3000 B.C.)			
MOTIFS	–	Supernatural Creatures	TYPE OF		
		Religion	FOLKLORE	–	Epics
		Nature Calamities			
		Legendary Heroes			
		Tasks and Trials			

0361 GINGERBREAD BOY, THE

Reteller, Nova Nestrick
Illus. Bonnie & Bill Rutherford and Eulalie
New York, Platt & Munk, 1961. 28p.

A cumulative tale in which a gingerbread boy runs away but returns to the old man and woman who made him. The ending varies from the common version in which he is eaten by the last animal that talks to him.

SUBJECTS	–	Chain Tale	COUNTRY	–	United
		Cumulative Tale			Kingdom
		Gingerbread Boy			
		Formula Tale			
MOTIFS	–	Humor	TYPE OF		
		Magic Objects	FOLKLORE	–	Folk Tales
		Talking Animals			

STORIES BY TITLE

See also   0302   Journey Cake, Ho!
           0143   Johnny-Cake

0283 GOBLIN UNDER THE STAIRS, THE

Reteller, Mary Calhoun
Illus. Janet McCaffery
New York, William Morrow & Company, 1968. unp.

A pesky, unwelcome boggart plays havoc with the farmer's house and animals until the farmer's wife decides to become friends with the goblin.

SUBJECTS	—	Knothole, Elves Can Be Viewed Through It Boggart	COUNTRY	—	United Kingdom
MOTIFS	—	Humor Supernatural Creatures	TYPE OF FOLKLORE	—	Folk Tales

0074 GOLDEN COCKEREL, THE

Reteller, Alexander Pushkin, Trans. Elaine Pogany
Illus. Willy Pogany
N. Y., Thomas Nelson and Sons, 1938. unp.

The golden cockerel saves King Dadon's kingdom by killing the mighty magician who has everyone under his spell. The story ends with the cockerel being transformed into a prince who marries the princess of the enchanted forest.

SUBJECTS	—	Moon, Daughter Magician Royalty Cock (Golden)	COUNTRY	—	U.S.S.R.
MOTIFS	—	Supernatural Creatures Enchanted People Magic Transformation Trickery Talking Animals	TYPE OF FOLKLORE	—	Folk Tales

0093 GOLDEN CRANE, THE

Reteller, Tohr Yamaguchi
Illus. Marianne Yamaguchi
New York, Holt, Rinehart and Winston, 1963. unp.

When a sacred golden crane is injured, a small deaf, mute boy risks his life to save it from the avaricious noblemen who want it as a trophy.

SUBJECTS	—	Crane Fisherman (Men) Physically Handicapped Childless (Man) Greediness Kindness Sun	COUNTRY	—	Japan

39

MOTIFS   —   Supernatural   TYPE OF
                 Creatures   FOLKLORE — Folk Tales
                 Religion
                 Friendly Animals

0401 GOLDEN CUP, THE

Reteller, Marylou Reifsnyder
Illus. Marylou Reifsnyder
New York, Alfred A. Knopf, 1970. unp.

A band of raiders, plundering the village as the farmers' families prepare for St. Nicholas Day, kidnaps Basilio, the farmer's son. St. Nicholas rescues him. This tale explains winter solstice.

SUBJECTS   —   Christianity   COUNTRY   —   Saudi Arabia
                  Christmas
                  Sun
                  St. Nicholas Rescues
                   Basilio
                  Winter Solstice
                  New Year's Eve

MOTIFS   —   Religion   TYPE OF
                                   FOLKLORE — Legends

0526 GOLDEN GOOSE

0343 Grimm's Golden Goose

By Grimm, The Brothers
Illus. Charles Mikolaycak
New York, Random House, 1969. unp.

Only the youngest of three brothers divides his food with a hungry man. He receives a golden goose in return. Extraordinary companions help the hero in suitor tests.

SUBJECTS   —   Companions (Magic   COUNTRY   —   Germany
                  Wisdom Possessed
                  By Extraordinary C.)
                  Dummling (Simpleton)
                  Making Princess, Girl
                   Laugh
                  Suitor Tests
                  Sharing
                  Grimm, The Brothers

MOTIFS   —   Tasks and Trials   TYPE OF
                  Humor   FOLKLORE — Folk Tales
                  Supernatural
                   Creatures
                  Magic Objects

0222 Golden Goose, The

By Grimm, The Brothers, Reteller, William Stobbs
Illus. William Stobbs
New York, McGraw-Hill Book Company, First American Ed., 1967. 32p.

This account does not tell the complete Grimm version. It stops with the princess laughing and marrying the lowly hero. There are no suitor tests.

SUBJECTS	—	Simpleton	COUNTRY	—	Germany
		Sharing			
		Golden Goose			
		Making Princess, Girl			
		Laugh			
		Old Man (Magician)			
		Grimm, The Brothers			

MOTIFS	—	Humor	TYPE OF		
		Magic Objects	FOLKLORE	—	Folk Tales

0222 GOLDEN GOOSE, THE

See — 0526 Golden Goose

0053 GOLDEN SEED, THE

By Maria Konopnicka, Adapted by Catharine Fournier
Illus. Janina Domanska
New York, Charles Scribner's Sons, 1962. unp.

An old merchant tells a king to plant certain seeds if he wants his people to have gold. When the plants do not turn into gold, the king tries to destroy them. The merchant takes the remains and makes linen clothes for the people.

SUBJECTS	—	Gold	COUNTRY	—	Poland
		Royalty			
		Sharing			
		Cloth (Linen)			
		Flax			

MOTIFS	—	Wit Prevails	TYPE OF		
		Realistic Events	FOLKLORE	—	Folk Tales

0015 GOLDEN TOUCH, THE

See — 0537 Midas

0111 GONE IS GONE OR THE STORY OF A MAN WHO WANTED TO DO THE HOUSEWORK

See — 0501 Man Who Was Going To Mind the House

0167 GOOD LLAMA, THE

Reteller, Anne Rockwell
Illus. Anne Rockwell
New York, The World Publishing Company, 1968. unp.

The earth, angry because the sun shines night and day, begins to cry and floods its hills and valleys. Only when the sun agrees to let the moon shine at night does the earth stop crying.

SUBJECTS	—	Earth	COUNTRY	—	Peru
		Flood			
		Llama			
		Moon			
		Sun			
		Incas			

MOTIFS	—	Religion	TYPE OF		
		Nature Calamities	FOLKLORE	—	Folk Tales
		Talking Animals			
		Pourquoi Stories			

0031 GOOD-FOR-NOTHINGS, THE

By Grimm, The Brothers
Illus. Hans Fischer
N.Y., Harcourt, Brace, & Co., 1st Am. ed., 1957. Pub. Switz., 1945. unp.

Chanticleer and Parlet go to find nuts. On the way they meet a duck, a needle, and a pin. They trick the innkeeper into allowing them to stay at his inn.

SUBJECTS	–	Rooster	COUNTRY	–	Germany
		Duck			
		Rice			
		Needle			
		Pin			
		Grimm, The Brothers			
MOTIFS	–	Talking Animals	TYPE OF		
		Trickery	FOLKLORE	–	Folk Tales

0100 GOOD-LUCK HORSE

Reteller, Chih-Yi Chan
Illus. Plato Chan
New York, Whittlesey House, McGraw-Hill Book Company, Inc., 1943. unp.

A little Chinese boy's paper horse is transformed into a real horse by a magician. The horse obeys the little boy's commands and in the end helps to restore peace to his country.

SUBJECTS	–	Horse	COUNTRY	–	China
		Magician			(Mainland)
		War			
		China (Great Wall)			
MOTIFS	–	Friendly Animals	TYPE OF		
		Magic Objects	FOLKLORE	–	Legends

0034 GOOSE GIRL, THE

By Grimm, The Brothers, Reteller, Marguerite De Angeli
Illus. Marguerite De Angeli
Garden City, New York Doubleday & Company, 1964. 31p.

Through treachery the servant girl exchanges roles with the princess and marries the prince. The true princess tends the geese. The truth is learned and the servant girl proclaims her own doom and the real princess regains her rightful role.

SUBJECTS	–	Geese	COUNTRY	–	Germany
		Horse			
		Royalty			
		Grimm, The Brothers			
MOTIFS	–	Magic Objects	TYPE OF		
		Talking Animals	FOLKLORE	–	Folk Tales
		Trickery			

0044 GORGON'S HEAD: THE STORY OF PERSEUS, THE

See – 0538 Perseus

0009 GREAT BIG ENORMOUS TURNIP, THE

By Alexei Tolstoy
Illus. Helen Oxenbury
New York, Franklin Watts, Inc., 1968. unp.

In this cumulative tale the old man, old woman, granddaughter, dog, cat, and the mouse pull on the turnip.

SUBJECTS	– Cooperation Cumulative Tale Cat Dog(s) Formula Tale Mouse (Mice) Turnip(s) Chain Tale	COUNTRY	– U.S.S.R.
MOTIFS	– Humor Talking Animals	TYPE OF FOLKLORE	– Folk Tales

See also **0003**   **Turnip, The**

0364 GREEN CHILDREN, THE

Reteller, Kevin Crossley-Holland
Illus. Margaret Gordon
New York, The Seabury Press, 1968. unp.

The cotters find a green boy and girl from another land while working in the grain fields. When the boy and girl learn English, they tell how they came to be found in the field.

SUBJECTS	– Green Children	COUNTRY	– United Kingdom
MOTIFS	– Religion Supernatural Creatures	TYPE OF FOLKLORE	– Folk Tales

0405 GREEN NOSES

Reteller, William Wiesner
Illus. William Wiesner
New York, Four Winds Press, 1969. unp.

A poor farmer's son, Michael, leaves home to find work. He discovers a town where a rich farmer has a marriageable daughter. Using his wit, Michael overcomes obstacles to win the daughter's hand.

SUBJECTS	– Noses Painted Green Farmer Tricks Daughter's Suitors	COUNTRY	– France
MOTIFS	– Humor Wit Prevails Trickery	TYPE OF FOLKLORE	– Folk Tales

0158 GREYLING

Reteller, Jane Yolen
Illus. William Stobbs
N. Y., The World Publishing Company, 1968. unp.

Greyling, the adopted son of a kind fisherman, is really a selchie–a seal turned human. He is forbidden to swim lest he turn back into a seal, but when his father's ship sinks in a storm, Greyling must save him.

SUBJECTS	– Childless (Couple) Seal Selchie	COUNTRY	– United Kingdom
MOTIFS	– Magic Transforma- tion	TYPE OF FOLKLORE	– Folk Tales

Talking
Animals

0343 GRIMM'S GOLDEN GOOSE

See — 0526 Golden Goose

0085 GRINDSTONE OF GOD, THE

Reteller, Carl Withers
Illus. Bernarda Bryson
New York, Holt, Rinehart and Winston, 1970. unp.

Horse and fox live together peacefully until they run out of food. They cast lots to decide who should be slain to provide food. The horse loses and sends fox for a knife.

SUBJECTS	—	Fox(es)	COUNTRY	—	U.S.S.R.
		God			
		Grindstone			
		Formula Tale			
		Cumulative Tale			
		Horse			
		Chain Tale			
MOTIFS	—	Talking Animals	TYPE OF		
		Religion	FOLKLORE	—	Fables
		Humor			

0181 HANS IN LUCK

By Grimm, The Brothers, Reteller, David McKee
Illus. David McKee
New York, Abelard-Schuman, 1967. unp.

Hans gets his wage in a lump of silver when he goes to visit his mother. The silver becomes a burden as he travels and he is glad to exchange it. Finally he exchanges it for a rock and he is happy when it falls in a pool.

SUBJECTS	—	Bargaining From	COUNTRY	—	Germany
		Good to Bad			
		Chain Tale			
		Formula Tale			
		Cumulative Tale			
		Grimm, The Brothers			
MOTIFS	—	Humor	TYPE OF		
		Fools and	FOLKLORE	—	Folk Tales
		Simpletons			

0267 HANSEL AND GRETEL

See — 0527 Hansel and Gretel

0527 HANSEL AND GRETEL

0267 Hansel and Gretel
By Grimm, The Brothers
Illus. Arnold Lobel
New York, Delacorte Press, 1971. 38p.

Abandoned by their father and wicked stepmother, Hansel and Gretel find the wicked witch's house. They foil her plan to eat them and return home to find their stepmother gone and their father happy to have them home.

SUBJECTS	—	Gingerbread House	COUNTRY	—	Germany
		Pebbles As Clue			
		Witch(es)			
		Grimm, The			
		Brothers			

MOTIFS	—	Trickery	TYPE OF		
		Supernatural	FOLKLORE	—	Folk Tales
		Creatures			
		Wit Prevails			

0216 Nibble, Nibble Mousekin

By Grimm, The Brothers, Reteller, Joan Walsh Anglund
Illus. Joan Walsh Anglund
N. Y., Harcourt, Brace, & World, Inc., 1962. unp.

Similar to title no. 0267 Hansel and Gretel.

SUBJECTS	—	Gingerbread House	COUNTRY	—	Germany
		Pebbles As Clue			
		Witch(es)			
		Grimm, The Brothers			

MOTIFS	—	Trickery	TYPE OF		
		Supernatural	FOLKLORE	—	Folk Tales
		Creatures			
		Wit Prevails			

0251 HAPPY-GO-LUCKY

Reteller, William Wiesner
Illus. William Wiesner
New York, The Seabury Press, 1970. unp.

After selling his cow at the market, a farmer comes home with
nothing. He bets his neighbors his wife will not be furious and wins.

SUBJECTS	—	Chain Tale	COUNTRY	—	Poland
		Acceptance			
		Farmer			
		Married Bliss			
		Loyalty			
		Cumulative Tale			
		Formula Tale			

MOTIFS	—	Humor	TYPE OF		
		Realistic Events	FOLKLORE	—	Folk Tales

See also   **0308**   **What the Good Man Does Is Always Right**

0528 HARE AND THE HEDGEHOG

0219 Hedgehog and the Hare, The

By Grimm, The Brothers, Reteller, Wendy Watson, Trans. Margaret Hunt
Illus. Wendy Watson
New York, The World Publishing Company, 1969. 31p.

The hare boasts that he can easily beat the hedgehog but through a
deception the hedgehog wins the race.

SUBJECTS	–	Race (Speed Contest) Hare(s) Hedgehog Grimm, The Brothers	COUNTRY	–	Germany

MOTIFS	–	Humor Talking Animals Trickery Wit Prevails	TYPE OF FOLKLORE	–	Folk Tales

See also   **0157**   **Hare and the Tortoise, The**
              0081   **Hare and the Tortoise, The**

0546   HARE AND THE TORTOISE

0157   Hare and the Tortoise, The

By Aesop
Illus. Paul Galdone
N. Y., Whittlesey House, McGraw-Hill Book Company, Inc., 1962. unp.

The overconfident hare takes a nap during the race and loses to the slow, but persistent tortoise.

SUBJECTS	–	Hare(s) Tortoise Race (Speed Contest) Aesop	COUNTRY	–	Greece

MOTIFS	–	Humor Talking Animals	TYPE OF FOLKLORE	–	Fables

See also   **0219**   **Hedgehog and the Hare, The**
              0081   **Hare and the Tortoise, The**

0081   Hare and the Tortoise, The

Based on the Fable By La Fontaine
Illus. Brian Wildsmith
New York, Franklin Watts, Inc., 1966. unp.

The conceited hare learns a lesson after he dawdles during a race and loses to the tortoise which plodded along steadfastly.

SUBJECTS	–	Hare(s) Tortoise Vanity La Fontaine Race (Speed Contest)	COUNTRY	–	France

MOTIFS	–	Talking Animals	TYPE OF FOLKLORE	–	Fables

See also   **0219**   **Hedgehog and the Hare, The**
              0157   **Hare and the Tortoise, The**

0081   HARE AND THE TORTOISE, THE

See – 0546 Hare and the Tortoise

STORIES BY TITLE

0157 HARE AND THE TORTOISE, THE

See – 0546 Hare and the Tortoise

0377 HAVELOK THE DANE

Reteller, Ian Serraillier
Illus. Elaine Raphael
New York, Henry Z. Walck, Inc., 1967. 67p.

The long ago King of Denmark dies and leaves the kingdom to his
son Havelok. The wicked Earl Godard usurps the throne and Havelok
faces many dangers in regaining his kingdom.

SUBJECTS	–	Christianity	COUNTRY	–	United
		Bee			Kingdom
		Loyalty			
		Havelok			

MOTIFS	–	Religion	TYPE OF		
		Legendary Heroes	FOLKLORE	–	Epics

0047 HEART OF STONE: A FAIRY TALE

By Wilhelm Hauff, Reteller, Doris Orgel
Illus. David Levine
New York, MacMillan Company, 1964. unp.

Peter Munk seeks the aid of two forest spirits in order to become rich.
One offers sound advice and three wishes; the other offers the easy
life for Peter's soul. In the end Peter loses all material gains but regains a sense of values.

SUBJECTS	–	Forest Spirit	COUNTRY	–	Germany
		Glassman			
		Hollander Mike,			
		Lumberjack			
		Tall Tales			

MOTIFS	–	Magic Transforma- tion	TYPE OF FOLKLORE	–	Folk Tales
		Wishes			
		Trickery			
		Supernatural			
		Creatures			
		Local Legendary			
		Heroes			

0219 HEDGEHOG AND THE HARE, THE

See – 0528 Hare and the Hedgehog

0264 HEE HAW

See – 0520 Man, the Boy, and the Donkey, The

0358 HENNY PENNY

See – 0503 Chicken Little

0278 HENNY PENNY

See – 0503 Chicken Little

0348 HERACLES THE STRONG

See – 0535 Hercules and His Labors

0535 HERCULES AND HIS LABORS

0348 Heracles the Strong

Reteller, Ian Serraillier
Illus. Rocco Negri
New York, Henry Z. Walck Inc., 1970. 102p.

Heracles is famous for his strength but is hated by Hera, queen of the gods, who places a curse on him. He commits a crime and as penance must perform twelve difficult labors.

SUBJECTS	–	Courage	COUNTRY	–	Greece
		Fate			
		Gods			
		Hercules			

MOTIFS	–	Religion	TYPE OF	
		Legendary Heroes	FOLKLORE	– Myths
		Supernatural Creatures		
		Tasks and Trials		
		Magic Transformation		

0088 HILILI AND DILILI

Trans. Mrs. Neriman Hizir in Ankara, Turkey, Adpated By Barbara K. Walker
Illus. Bill Barss
Chicago, Follett Publishing Company, 1965. 32p.

A foolish old couple with the kindest of intentions goes to visit their married daughter and causes her problems.

SUBJECTS	–	Tar	COUNTRY	–	Turkey
		Parents			
		Poultry			

| MOTIFS | – | Fools and Simpletons | TYPE OF | |
| | | Humor | FOLKLORE | – Folk Tales |

0297 HIPPITY HOPPER, THE OR WHY THERE ARE NO INDIANS IN PENNSYLVANIA

Reteller, Lucille Wallower
Illus. Lucille Wallower
New York, David McKay Company, Inc., 1957. unp.

The Shawnee and Lenni Lenape Indians live in peace until a child from one tribe finds a grasshopper and a child from the other tribe wants it. This conflict develops into a fight between the children and the tribes finally leave Pennsylvania.

SUBJECTS	–	Grasshopper War	COUNTRY	–	U.S.–Tales
		Pennsylvania			From the
		Shawnee Indians			North Ameri-
		Lenni Lenape Indians			can Indians
MOTIFS	–	Religion	TYPE OF	
		Pourquoi Stories	FOLKLORE	– Folk Tales

0396 HOP O' MY THUMB

Reteller, Henry Matthew Brock
Illus. Henry Matthew Brock
London, Warne, n.d. unp.

Hop-O'-My Thumb and his brothers and sisters are left in the forest
by their poor parents. Taken in by an ogre's wife, Hop-O'-My Thumb
tricks the ogre so that his family can move into the ogre's house.

SUBJECTS	– Exchanged Neck Pieces Cause Giant To Kill Own Children Boots, Seven-League Famine, Children Abandoned in F. Ogre Hop O' My Thumb	COUNTRY	– United Kingdom
MOTIFS	– Supernatural Creatures Magic Objects Wit Prevails	TYPE OF FOLKLORE	– Folk Tales

0041 HORSE, THE FOX, AND THE LION, THE

See – 0525 Fox and the Horse

0557 HOUSE THAT JACK BUILT

0281 House That Jack Built, The

By Mother Goose
Illus. Joe Rogers
New York, Lothrop, Lee & Shepard Co., Inc., 1968.unp.

This cumulative tale involves "the farmer who sowed the corn, that fed
the cock that crowed in the morn, that waked the priest all shaven
and shorn. . . . that lay in the house that Jack built."

SUBJECTS	– Cumulative Tale Chain Tale Jack, The House That J. Built Mother Goose Formula Tale	COUNTRY	– United Kingdom
MOTIFS	– Humor	TYPE OF FOLKLORE	– Nursery Rhymes

0198 House That Jack Built, The

By Mother Goose
Illus. Paul Galdone
New York, Whittlesey House, McGraw-Hill Book Company, 1961. unp.

Same as title no. 0281 House That Jack Built, The. Different illus.

SUBJECTS	– Chain Tale Cumulative Tale Jack, The House That J. Built	COUNTRY	– United Kingdom

Mother Goose
Formula Tale

MOTIFS   —   Humor   TYPE OF
                       FOLKLORE — Nursery Rhymes

0150 House That Jack Built, The or Maison Que Jacques A Batie, La

By Mother Goose, Reteller, Antonio Frasconi
Illus. Antonio Frasconi
New York, Harcourt, Brace and Company, 1958. unp.

In two languages—French and English.

SUBJECTS   —   Chain Tale   COUNTRY   —   United
                    Cumulative Tale   Kingdom
                    Jack, The House
                      That J. Built
                    Mother Goose   TYPE OF
                    Formula Tale   FOLKLORE — Nursery Rhymes

0281 HOUSE THAT JACK BUILT, THE

See — 0557 House That Jack Built

0198 HOUSE THAT JACK BUILT, THE

See — 0557 House That Jack Built

0150 HOUSE THAT JACK BUILT, THE OR MAISON QUE JACQUES A BATIE, LA

See — 0557 House That Jack Built

0326 HOW OLD STORMALONG CAPTURED MOCHA DICK

See — 0561 Stormalong

0146 HUDDEN AND DUDDEN AND DONALD O'NEARY

Adapted by Joseph Jacobs
Illus. Doris Burn
New York, Coward-McCann, Inc., 1968. unp.

Donald O'Neary outwits his greedy neighbors Hudden and Dudden who scheme to take his meager holdings to make themselves richer.

SUBJECTS   —   Cowhide (Pseudo-   COUNTRY   —   United
                       Magic)   Kingdom
                    Peasant Outwits
                      Enemies
                    Greediness
                    Jacobs, Joseph

MOTIFS   —   Wit Prevails   TYPE OF
                 Humor   FOLKLORE — Folk Tales
                 Fools and
                   Simpletons
                 Trickery

0073 HUMPY

By P. Yershov, Trans. William C. White
Illus. Jacqueline Ayer
N. Y., Harcourt, Brace & World, Inc., 1966 (1931 c. Harper & Brothers), 72p.

With the help of Humpy, the magic humpbacked horse, the simple Ivan outwits his more clever older brothers.

SUBJECTS − Firebird
Horse
Royalty
Ring (From the
  Sea)
Moon, Daughter
Sun
Moon
God

COUNTRY − U.S.S.R.

MOTIFS − Magic Objects
Supernatural
  Creatures
Tasks and Trials
Talking Animals
Religion

TYPE OF
FOLKLORE − Folk Tales

0292 HUSH LITTLE BABY

Author, Anonymous
Illus. Aliki
Englewood Cliffs, New Jersey, 1968. unp.

"Hush, little baby, don't say a word. Papa's gonna buy you a mocking bird. If that mocking bird don't sing, papa's gonna buy you a diamond ring." Music and verses of the Appalachian song are included.

SUBJECTS − Music
Lullaby
Appalachian Moun-
  tain Song
Chain Tale
Cumulative Tale
Formula Tale

COUNTRY − U.S.–Folk-
     songs

MOTIFS − Humor

TYPE OF
FOLKLORE − Folk Songs,
    Ballads

0241 I AM YOUR MISFORTUNE

Reteller, Marguerita Rudolph
Illus. Imero Gobbato
New York, The Seabury Press, 1968. unp.

There are two brothers, one good-natured, the other stingy and mean. The good-natured one tricks Misfortune and places him in a snuff box. The mean brother releases him and Misfortune promises to always remain with him.

SUBJECTS − Monster
Misfortune (Monster)
Jealousy

COUNTRY − Lithuania

MOTIFS − Humor
Supernatural
  Creatures
Trickery
Wit Prevails

TYPE OF
FOLKLORE − Folk Tales

0171 ICE BIRD, THE

Reteller, Pauline Innis
Illus. Wesley Dennis
Cambridge, Maryland, Western Printing and Lithographing Co., 1965. unp.

News that the Christ child is born spreads throughout the world. The swans are chosen to give a word of welcome from all the birds of the world. The royal swans cannot sing; instead their tiny ice bird companion sings with beauty.

SUBJECTS	–	Christmas	COUNTRY	–	Norway
		Friendship			
		Swan(s)			
MOTIFS	–	Talking Animals	TYPE OF		
		Friendly Animals	FOLKLORE	–	Legends
		Religion			

0091 ISSUN BOSHI: THE INCHLINS.

Trans. Yone Mizuta, Reteller, Momoko Ishii
Illus. Fuko Akino
New York, Walker and Company, 1967. unp.

A childless couple prays to the sun for a child and one day a boy is born to them. Small as a thumb, he becomes a companion to the lord's daughter. He fights demons and wishes to be as tall as other men. His wish is fulfilled.

SUBJECTS	–	Little People	COUNTRY	–	Japan
		Mallet (Magic)			
		Royalty			
		Demons			
		Childless (Couple			
MOTIFS	–	Enchanted People	TYPE OF		
		Magic Objects	FOLKLORE	–	Folk Tales
		Supernatural			
		Creatures			

0023 IVANKO AND THE DRAGON

By Ivan Rudchenko, Trans. Marie Halun Bloch
Illus. Yaroslava
New York, Atheneum, 1969. unp.

A childless old couple substitutes a piece of wood for a child. In time the wood turns into a baby boy. When he is grown, he goes fishing and is captured by a she-dragon. His wit promotes his safe return home.

SUBJECTS	–	Dragon	COUNTRY	–	U.S.S.R.–
		Geese			Ukraine
		Kindness			
MOTIFS	–	Magic Transforma-			
		tion	TYPE OF		
		Wit Prevails	FOLKLORE	–	Folk Tales

0226 JACK AND THE BEANSTALK

See – 0551 Jack and the Beanstalk

0144 JACK AND THE BEANSTALK

See — 0551 Jack and the Beanstalk

0551 JACK AND THE BEANSTALK

0144 Jack and the Beanstalk

Adapted by William Stobbs
Illus. William Stobbs
New York, Delacorte Press, First American ed., 1966. unp.

Instead of selling the cow, Jack trades it for five magic beans that grow into the sky. Jack ascends the beanstalk and steals from the ogre whereby he gains the revenge for the ill-treatment of his father by the ogre.

SUBJECTS	—	Jack and the Beanstalk	COUNTRY	—	United Kingdom
		Cow			
		Beans			
		Hen Lays Golden Eggs			
		Harp (Golden)			
		Ogre			
MOTIFS	—	Magic Objects	TYPE OF		
		Magic Transformation	FOLKLORE	—	Folk Tales
		Supernatural Creatures			

0226 Jack and the Beanstalk

Reteller, Walter De La Mare
Illus. Joseph Low
New York, Alfred A. Knopf, 1927. 52p.

This version differs from title no. 0144 Jack and the Beanstalk in that an old man gives Jack seven beans, he meets an old woman at the top of the beanstalk, and he desires no revenge for his father.

SUBJECTS	—	Jack and the Beanstalk	COUNTRY	—	United Kingdom
		Cow			
		Beans			
		Hen Lays Golden Eggs			
		Harp (Golden)			
		Ogre			
MOTIFS	—	Magic Objects	TYPE OF		
		Supernatural Creatures	FOLKLORE	—	Folk Tales

0002 JACK AND THE THREE SILLIES

Reteller, Richard Chase
Illus. Joshua Tolford
Boston, Houghton Mifflin Co., 1950. 39p.

Jack starts out to sell a cow but through a series of exchanges he ends up with a stone. His irritated wife leaves home and vows not to return until she finds three people more foolish than Jack. She easily finds them.

| SUBJECTS | — | Shirt | COUNTRY | — | U.S.–Variants of the |
| | | Jack Tales | | | |

Tall Tales Moon Cow	European Stories

MOTIFS — Humor
Fools and
Simpletons TYPE OF
FOLKLORE — Folk Tales

See also **0001**   **Three Sillies, The**

0259 JACK SPRAT, HIS WIFE AND HIS CAT, THE LIFE OF
See — 0509 Jack Sprat, His Wife and the Cat

0509 JACK SPRAT, HIS WIFE AND THE CAT
0259 Jack Sprat, His Wife and His Cat, The Life of

From an 1820 Chapbook
Illus. Paul Galdone
New York, McGraw-Hill Book Company, 1969. unp.

A takeoff on the nursery rhyme about Jack Sprat and his wife, this version tells about his courtship, their accident-prone trip home from the church, and their many years of wedded bliss with their one-eared cat.

SUBJECTS — Jack Sprat   COUNTRY — United
Kingdom

MOTIFS — Humor   TYPE OF
FOLKLORE — Nursery
Rhymes

0109 JOCO AND THE FISHBONE (AN ARABIAN NIGHTS TALE)
Reteller, William Wiesner
Illus. William Wiesner
New York, Viking Press, 1966. unp.

When Joco is invited to supper with the tailor and his wife, he chokes on a fishbone and they think he is dead. Thus begins their humorous efforts to get rid of his body.

SUBJECTS — Arabian Nights
Fishbone
Truth
Chain Tale
Formula Tale
Judge(s)
Justice
Bagdad   COUNTRY — Iran

MOTIFS — Humor
Fools and
Simpletons
Religion   TYPE OF
FOLKLORE — Folk Tales

0296 Joe Magarac and His USA Citizen Papers
Reteller, Irwin Shapiro
Illus. James Daugherty
New York, Julian Messner, Inc., 1948. 64p.

Joe Magarac, who comes from the old country, faces many trials including discrimination in his quest for U.S. citizenship.

SUBJECTS	–	Industry	COUNTRY	–	U.S.–Native
		Joe Magarac, Steel			Tall Tales of
		Man			the Paul Bun-
		Steel			yan Variety
		Tall Tales			

MOTIFS	–	Humor	TYPE OF		
		Local Legendary	FOLKLORE	–	Folk Tales
		Heroes			

0544 JOHN HENRY

0017 John Henry, An American Legend

Reteller, Ezra Jack Keats
Illus. Ezra Jack Keats
New York, Random House (Pantheon Books), 1965. unp.

John Henry, who was born with a hammer in his hand, helps forge the railroads through the old West. He dies with the hammer in his hand after besting a steam drill in a contest.

SUBJECTS	–	Blacks	COUNTRY	–	U.S.–Native
		Railroads			Tall Tales of
		Tall Tales			the Paul Bun-
		John Henry			yan Variety
		Steam Driven Drill			

MOTIFS	–	Local Legendary	TYPE OF		
		Heroes	FOLKLORE	–	Folk Tales

0207 John Henry and His Hammer

Reteller, Harold W. Felton
Illus. Aldren A. Watson
New York, Alfred A. Knopf, 1950. 85p.

This version differs from title no. 0016 Steel Driving Man, The Legend of John Henry and 0017 John Henry. An American Legend in that music is included.

SUBJECTS	–	John Henry	COUNTRY	–	U.S.–Native
		Blacks			Tall Tales of
		Railroads			the Paul Bun-
		Steam Driven Drill			yan Variety
		Tall Tales			

MOTIFS	–	Local Legendary	TYPE OF		
		Heroes	FOLKLORE	–	Folk Tales

0016 Steel Driving Man, The Legend of John Henry

Reteller, R. Conrad Stein
Illus. Darrell Wiskur
Chicago, Children's Press, 1969. unp.

Similar to title no. 0017 John Henry, An American Legend.

SUBJECTS	–	Blacks	COUNTRY	–	U.S.–Native
		Railroads			Tall Tales of
		Tall Tales			the Paul

		John Henry		Bunyan
		Steam Driven Drill		Variety
MOTIFS	–	Local Legendary	TYPE OF	
		Heroes	FOLKLORE –	Folk Tales

0207 JOHN HENRY AND HIS HAMMER

See – 0544 John Henry

0017 JOHN HENRY, AN AMERICAN LEGEND

See – 0544 John Henry

0205 JOHN J. PLENTY AND FIDDLER DAN

See – 0531 Ant and the Grasshopper

0340 JOHN TABOR'S RIDE

Reteller, Blair Lent
Illus. Blair Lent
Boston, Little, Brown and Company, 1966. 48p.

Homesick John Tabor is carried by the whale from a South Sea Island where he has been shipwrecked. They travel over the ruins of a city beneath the sea, past the Cape of Good Hope, past a fog-shrouded lighthouse manned by an unexpected crew, and into the streets of Nantucket.

SUBJECTS	–	Nantucket Whalers	COUNTRY	–	U.S.–Native
		New England			Tall Tales of
		Neptune			the Paul Bun-
		Tall Tales			yan Variety
		Whale			
		John Tabor			
MOTIFS	–	Local Legendary	TYPE OF		
		Heroes	FOLKLORE –		Folk Tales
		Supernatural			
		Creatures			

0143 JOHNNY-CAKE

By Joseph Jacobs
Illus. Emma Brock
New York, G. P. Putnam's Sons, 1933. unp.

A woman makes a pancake which flees. Various people and animals try in vain to stop it, but finally the fox eats it.

SUBJECTS	–	Cumulative Tale	COUNTRY	–	United
		Chain Tale			Kingdom
		Fox(es)			
		Pancake			
		Formula Tale			
		Jacobs, Joseph			
MOTIFS	–	Trickery	TYPE OF		
		Talking Animals	FOLKLORE –		Folk Tales
		Magic Objects			
		Humor			

See also 0302 Journey Cake, Ho!
　　　　　0361 Gingerbread Boy, The

0033 JORINDA AND JORINGEL

By Grimm, The Brothers, Trans. Elizabeth Shub
Illus. Adrienne Adams
New York, Chares Scribner's Sons, 1968. unp.

Joringel, with the aid of a magic flower and love, frees Jorinda from the witch's spell which turned her into a nightingale.

SUBJECTS	–	Bird(s)	COUNTRY	–	Germany
		Dream(s)			
		Flower, Black Sun-			
		flower			
		Witch(es)			
		Grimm, The Brothers			
MOTIFS	–	Magic Objects	TYPE OF		
		Magic Transforma-	FOLKLORE	–	Folk Tales
		tion			
		Supernatural			
		Creatures			

0302 JOURNEY CAKE, HO!

Reteller, Ruth Sawyer
Illus. Robert McCloskey
New York, The Viking Press and The Junior Literary Guild, 1953. 45p.

A cumulative tale in which Johnny is forced to leave the old couple's impoverished home with a journey cake in his bag. The journey cake bounces out of his bag and the tale begins.

SUBJECTS	–	Pancake	COUNTRY	–	U.S.–Variants
		Cumulative Tale			of the Euro-
		Chain Tale			pean Stories
		Formula Tale			
MOTIFS	–	Humor	TYPE OF		
		Magic Objects	FOLKLORE	–	Folk Tales

See also 0143 **Johnny-Cake**
0361 **Gingerbread Boy, The**

0369 JOY OF THE COURT

See – 0508 Erec and Enid

0188 JUAN BOBO AND THE QUEEN'S NECKLACE

Reteller, Pura Belpre
Illus. Christine Price
New York, Frederick Warne and Company, Inc., 1962. unp.

Juan Bobo is laughed at when he tries to find the queen's stolen necklace. By listening to the nightingale he learns three servants stole the necklace. He helps them return the necklace without the king's knowledge.

SUBJECTS	–	Goose Swallows	COUNTRY	–	U.S.–Puerto
		Necklace			Rico
		Necklace			
		Royalty			
		Theft			
MOTIFS	–	Humor	TYPE OF		
		Trickery	FOLKLORE	–	Folk Tales
		Wit Prevails			

0082 JUDGE NOT

Reteller, John Faulkner
Illus. John Faulkner
Chicago, Albert Whitman and Company, 1968. unp.

A man journeys to Mecca and leaves his money with a judge whom he believes he can trust. When he returns, the judge refuses to give him his money but a wise lady recovers the money for him through cleverness.

SUBJECTS	–	Judge(s)	COUNTRY	–	Middle East
		Pilgrimage			
		Weaver			
		Forgetting (Forget-fulness)			
		Justice			

MOTIFS	–	Trickery	TYPE OF		
		Wit Prevails	FOLKLORE	–	Folk Tales
		Religion			
		Humor			

See also 0156   Eggs, The
0206   Wise Fool, The
0322   Mice That Ate Iron, The

0260 JUDGE, THE

Author Anonymous
Illus. Margot Zemach
New York, Farrar, Straus and Giroux, 1969. unp.

The fiery old judge, impatient with the prisoners' nonsense, calls them scoundrels and throws them back in jail. Justice is finally done.

SUBJECTS	–	Cumulative Tale	COUNTRY	–	France
		Chain Tale			
		Judge(s)			
		Formula Tale			

| MOTIFS | – | Humor | TYPE OF | | |
| | | | FOLKLORE | – | Nursery Rhymes |

0083 JUST SAY HIC!

Trans. Mrs. Neriman Hizir in Ankara, Turkey, Adapted by Barbara
K. Walker
Illus. Don Bolognese
Chicago, Follett Publishing Company, 1965. 32p.

Sent by his master to buy salt, a forgetful boy repeats the word for salt, "hic." Along the way he is told to change what he is saying for something more appropriate. Finally he says the word he started with and buys the salt.

| SUBJECTS | – | Forgetting (For-getfulness) | COUNTRY | – | Turkey |
| | | Salt | | | |

| MOTIFS | – | Fools and Simpletons | TYPE OF | | |
| | | Humor | FOLKLORE | – | Folk Tales |

0094 KAP AND THE WICKED MONKEY

Reteller, Betty Jean Lifton
Illus. Ellchi Mitsui
New York, W. W. Norton and Company, Inc., 1968. unp.

Kap, a mischievous water elf, tries to find a cure for his father who has over-moon-sickness. Without the help of Crane, Kap succeeds.

SUBJECTS	—	Crane	COUNTRY	—	Japan
		Kappa-Water Spirit			
		Kindness			
		Moon			
		Monkey			
MOTIFS	—	Trickery	TYPE OF		
		Talking Animals	FOLKLORE	—	Folk Tales
		Friendly Animals			
		Supernatural			
		Creatures			

0021 KAPPA'S TUG-OF-WAR WITH BIG BROWN HORSE: THE STORY OF A JAPANESE WATER IMP

Reteller, Dorothy W. Baruch
Illus. Sanryo Sakai
Rutland, Vermont, Charles E. Tuttle Company, 1964. 36p.

Sly, slippery Kappa tries to steal old farmer Shiba's horse and stirs up so much excitement in the process that his life is never the same again.

SUBJECTS	—	Kappa–Water Spirit	COUNTRY	—	Japan
		Water Spirit (Sprite)			
		Horse			
		Monkey			
MOTIFS	—	Supernatural Creatures	TYPE OF		
		Trickery	FOLKLORE	—	Folk Tales
		Friendly Animals			

0275 KELLYBURN BRAES

Adapted by Sorche Nic Leodhas
Illus. Evaline Ness
New York, Holt, Rinehart and Winston, 1968. unp.

In this Scottish folksong the farmer wants to get rid of his terrible wife and the devil offers to take her. She proves too much even for the devil who ships her back to her husband.

SUBJECTS	—	Devil	COUNTRY	—	United Kingdom
		Farmer's Wife			
		Music			
MOTIFS	—	Humor	TYPE OF		
		Supernatural Creatures	FOLKLORE	—	Folk Songs, Ballads

0309 KING CARLO OF CAPRI

See – **0521 Riquet With the Tuft**

0549 KING OF THE GOLDEN RIVER

0152 King of the Golden River, The or The Black Brothers

Adapted by John Ruskin
Illus. John C. Johansen
New York, Rand McNally and Company, 1903. 82p.

> Gluck, a cinder lad, is mistreated by his two older brothers. Gluck befriends the King of the Golden River. His selfish brothers are turned to stone and Gluck shares his inheritance with all people.

SUBJECTS	–	Black Brothers Dwarf Holy Water Kindness South-west Wind	COUNTRY	–	United Kingdom
MOTIFS	–	Religion Supernatural Creatures Magic Objects Magic Transforma- tion	TYPE OF FOLKLORE	–	Folk Tales

0201 King of the Golden River, The or The Black Brothers

Adapted by John Ruskin
Illus. Sandro Nardini
New York, The MacMillan Company, 1962. 42p.

> Similar to title nos. 0152 King of the Golden River, The or the Black Brothers and 0284 King of the Golden River, The or The Black Brothers. Different illus.

SUBJECTS	–	Black Brothers Dwarf Holy Water Kindness South-west Wind	COUNTRY	–	United Kingdom
MOTIFS	–	Religion Supernatural Creatures Magic Objects Magic Transforma- tion	TYPE OF FOLKLORE	–	Folk Tales

0284 King of the Golden River, The or The Black Brothers

Adapted by John Ruskin
Illus. Charles Stewart
New York, Franklin Watts, Inc., 1958. 60p.

> Similar to title nos. 0152 King of the Golden River, The or The Black Brothers and 0201 King of the Golden River, The or The Black Brothers.

SUBJECTS	–	Black Brothers Dwarf	COUNTRY	–	United Kingdom

Holy Water
Kindness
South-west Wind

MOTIFS   — Legendary Heroes   TYPE OF
                      Supernatural   FOLKLORE — Folk Tales
                       Creatures
                      Magic Objects
                      Magic Transforma-
                      tion

0284 KING OF THE GOLDEN RIVER, THE OR THE BLACK BROTHERS

See — 0549 King of the Golden River

0152 KING OF THE GOLDEN RIVER, THE OR THE BLACK BROTHERS

See — 0549 King of the Golden River

0201 KING OF THE GOLDEN RIVER, THE OR THE BLACK BROTHERS

See — 0549 King of the Golden River

0095 KING THRUSHBEARD

By Grimm, The Brothers
Illus. Felix Hoffmann
New York, Harcourt, Brace and World, Inc., First American ed., 1970, unp.

The arrogant princess refuses all suitors. To her dismay the king marries her to a minstrel. The many tasks her husband sets for her lead to humiliation, and finally, happiness.

SUBJECTS — Character Forming   COUNTRY — Germany
                   Royalty
                   Snobbishness
                   Courtship
                   Grimm, The Brothers

MOTIFS   — Trickery   TYPE OF
                   Tasks and Trials   FOLKLORE — Folk Tales
                   Wit Prevails

See also   **0055**   **Swineherd, The**

0042 KING THRUSHBEARD

Reteller, Kurt Werth
Illus. Kurt Werth
New York, Viking Press, 1968. unp.

Similar to title no. 0095 King Thrushbeard.

SUBJECTS — Royalty   COUNTRY — Germany
                   Character Forming
                   Snobbishness
                   Courtship
                   Grimm, The Brothers

MOTIFS   — Tasks and Trials   TYPE OF
                   Trickery   FOLKLORE — Folk Tales
                   Wit Prevails
                   Humor

See also   **0055**   **Swineherd, The**

0153 KITCHEN KNIGHT, THE

Adapted and Retold by Barbara Schiller
Illus. Nonny Hogrogian
New York, Holt, Rinehart and Winston, 1965. 64p.

Gareth of Orkney, dubiously dubbed the Kitchen Knight, sets out to save the Lady Lyoness in distress. He overcomes the Indigo, Red and Green knights, and wins the respect of Lynet, sister of Lyoness.

SUBJECTS	—	Arthurian Legend Chivalry Knighthood	COUNTRY	—	United Kingdom
MOTIFS	—	Legendary Heroes Religion Tasks and Trials Humor	TYPE OF FOLKLORE	—	Epics

0378 KNIGHT OF THE CART, THE

Reteller, Constance Hieatt
Illus. John Gretzer
New York, Thomas Y. Crowell Company, 1969. 85p.

Sir Lancelot goes to rescue Queen Guinevere from Sir Malagant, his horse is wounded and he is forced to travel in a lowly farm wagon. Tricked by Malagant, he almost loses Guinevere.

SUBJECTS	—	Arthurian Legend Christianity Chivalry Dwarf Lancelot Sword Bridge	COUNTRY	—	United Kingdom
MOTIFS	—	Religion Legendary Heroes Tasks and Trials	TYPE OF FOLKLORE	—	Epics

0367 KNIGHT OF THE LION, THE

Reteller, Constance Hieatt
Illus. Joseph Low
New York, Thomas Y. Crowell Company, 1968. 69p.

With the help of his faithful lion, Ywain of King Arthur's Court defeats Harpin the monster and rescues his lady's handmaiden.

SUBJECTS	—	Arthurian Legend Christianity Lion Helps Man In Gratitude Ywain	COUNTRY	—	United Kingdom
MOTIFS	—	Religion Legendary Heroes Friendly Animals Supernatural Creatures	TYPE OF FOLKLORE	—	Epics

0362 LAIRD OF COCKPEN, THE

Reteller, Sorche Nic Leodhas

Illus. Adrienne Adams
New York, Holt, Rinehart and Winston, 1969. unp.

The Laird of Cockpen chooses a penniless lass with a long pedigree to
be his wife. She refuses and the Laird is dumbfounded. At last she
reconsiders, and they marry. Music and words are included.

SUBJECTS	—	Scotland, Folksong	COUNTRY	—	United
		Laird			Kingdom
		Courtship			
		Music			
MOTIFS	—	Humor	TYPE OF		
			FOLKLORE	—	Folk Songs,
					Ballads

0256 LAZY JACK

See — 0510 Lazy Jack

0510 LAZY JACK

0256 Lazy Jack

By Joseph Jacobs
Illus. Barry Wilkinson
New York, The World Publishing Company, First American Edition,
1970. unp.

When a son literally follows his mother's instructions all sorts of
humorous events occur. Objects in the story are a coin, milk, cream
cheese, cat, leg of mutton and a donkey.

SUBJECTS	—	Lazy Jack	COUNTRY	—	United
		Instructions of			Kingdom
		Mother Followed			
		Literally By Son			
		Simpleton			
		Jacobs, Joseph			
MOTIFS	—	Humor	TYPE OF		
		Fools and	FOLKLORE	—	Folk Tales
		Simpletons			

See also **0294** **Epaminondas and His Auntie**

0145 Lazy Jack

Reteller, Kurt Werth
Illus. Kurt Werth
New York, The Viking Press, 1970. unp.

Similar to title no. 0256 Lazy Jack.

SUBJECTS	—	Lazy Jack	COUNTRY	—	United
		Instructions of			Kingdom
		Mother Followed			
		Literally By Son			
		Making Princess, Girl			
		Laugh			
		Jacobs, Joseph			
MOTIFS	—	Humor	TYPE OF		
		Fools and Simpletons	FOLKLORE	—	Folk Tales

STORIES BY TITLE

See also **0294**   **Epaminondas and His Auntie**

0199 Silly Simon

Reteller, Mollie Clarke
Illus. Eccles
New York, Follett Publishing Company, First American Edition, 1967. 32p.

> This version is similar to title no. 0145 Lazy Jack and 0256 Lazy Jack. There is a slight modification in objects—a penny, jug of milk, cream cheese, log of wood, leg of mutton, and a donkey.

SUBJECTS	–	Instructions of Mother Followed Literally By Son Lazy Jack Making Princess, Girl Laugh Jacobs, Joseph	COUNTRY	–	United Kingdom

MOTIFS	–	Humor Fools and Simpletons	TYPE OF FOLKLORE	–	Folk Tales

See also **0294**   **Epaminondas and His Auntie**

0145 LAZY JACK

See – 0510 Lazy Jack

0307 LION AND THE RAT, THE

By La Fontaine, Jean De
Illus. Brian Wildsmith
New York, Franklin Watts, Inc., First American Edition, 1963. unp.

> The lion spares the rat and later the rat repays the kindness by releasing the lion from the net.

SUBJECTS	–	Friendship Kindness Lion(s) Rat La Fontaine	COUNTRY	–	France

MOTIFS	–	Friendly Animals Talking Animals	TYPE OF FOLKLORE	–	Fables

0160 LITTLE COCK, THE

Reteller, Jeanne B. Hardendorff
Illus. Joseph Domjan
New York, J. B. Lippincott Company, 1969. unp.

> When Cock finds a diamond half-penny, a Turkish sultan demands the coin. Cock's magic power aids him in his efforts to get the coin back.

SUBJECTS	–	Swallows, Cock S. Water and Bees Cock (Golden) Diamond Half-Penny Turkish Sultan	COUNTRY	–	Hungary

STORIES BY TITLE

MOTIFS   – Humor   TYPE OF
                  Supernatural   FOLKLORE – Folk Tales
                  Creatures
                  Talking Animals

0079 LITTLE JUGGLER, THE

Adapted From An Old French Legend by Barbara Cooney
Illus. Barbara Cooney
New York, Hastings House, Publishers, 1961. 47p.

A monk befriends Barnaby the juggler by giving him a home in the monastery. At Christmas time, the monks give gifts to the Virgin Mary and Christ Child. Barnaby gives the only gift he has–the act of juggling.

SUBJECTS – God   COUNTRY – France
                  Christmas
                  Juggler
                  Sharing

MOTIFS   – Religion   TYPE OF
                  Supernatural   FOLKLORE – Legends
                  Creatures

0059 LITTLE MATCH GIRL, THE

By Hans Christian Andersen
Illus. Blair Lent
Boston, Houghton Mifflin Company, 1968. 43p.

This story ends in the gentle death of a little match girl who sees a vision of her dead grandmother taking her to heaven in the last flicker of her matches.

SUBJECTS – New Year's Eve   COUNTRY – Denmark
                  Matches
                  Poverty
                  Dreaming, Day
                  Andersen, Hans
                    Christian

MOTIFS   – Realistic Events   TYPE OF
                  Religion   FOLKLORE – Folk Tales

0058 LITTLE MERMAID, THE

By Hans Christian Andersen
Illus. Dorothy P. Lathrop
New York, The MacMillan Company, 1939. unp.

To gain human form a mermaid loses her power to speak to humans. She never wins the prince's love, but gains immortality.

SUBJECTS – Christianity   COUNTRY – Denmark
                  Mermaid Rescues
                   Hero From
                   Shipwreck
                  Royalty
                  Witch(es)
                  Love, Selfless
                  Andersen, Hans
                   Christian

| MOTIFS | — Religion
Magic Objects
Magic Transforma-
tion
Supernatural
Creatures | TYPE OF
FOLKLORE — Folk Tales |

0380 LITTLE MERMAID, THE

By Hans Christian Andersen, Reteller Eva Le Gallienne
Illus. Edward Frascino
New York, Harper & Row, Publishers, 1971. 50p.

The mermaid sells her voice for a chance to join the upper world of
human beings, especially that of the prince. She dies when the prince
marries someone else, but gains immortality for having been loved by
a human.

| SUBJECTS | — Christianity
Love, Selfless
Mermaid Rescues
  Hero From Ship-
  wreck
Witch(es)
Andersen, Hans
  Christian | COUNTRY — Denmark |

| MOTIFS | — Supernatural
  Creatures
Religion
Magic Objects
Magic Transforma-
tion | TYPE OF
FOLKLORE — Folk Tales |

0387 LITTLE MERMAID, THE

Reteller, M. R. James
Illus. Pamela Bianco
New York, Holiday House, 1935. 55p.

Similar to title nos. 0380 Little Mermaid, The and 0058 Little Mermaid,
The.

| SUBJECTS | — Christianity
Love, Selfless
Mermaid Rescues
  Hero From Ship-
  wreck
Witch(es)
Andersen, Hans
  Christian | COUNTRY — Denmark |

| MOTIFS | — Supernatural
  Creatures
Religion
Magic Objects
Magic Transforma-
tion | TYPE OF
FOLKLORE — Folk Tales |

0368 LITTLE RED HEN

See — 0511 Little Red Hen and The Grain of Wheat

0511 LITTLE RED HEN AND THE GRAIN OF WHEAT

0368 Little Red Hen

Anonymous
Illus. William Curtis Holdsworth
New York, Farrar, Straus & Giroux, 1969. unp.

Only after little red hen sows the wheat, reaps it, and makes it into flour for bread, do the dog, cat, pig, and turkey offer to help her eat it. She refuses their help.

| SUBJECTS | – | Chain Tale
Cumulative Tale
Little Red Hen (Asks
  Animals To Help
  Her)
Industrious
Formula Tale | COUNTRY | – | United
Kingdom |
| MOTIFS | – | Humor
Talking Animals | TYPE OF
FOLKLORE | – | Folk Tales |

0255 Little Red Hen, The

Reteller, Tony Palazzo
Illus. Tony Palazzo
Garden City, N.Y., Doubleday & Company, Inc., 1958. unp.

Little Red Hen plants the grain, harvests it, takes wheat to miller, and bakes the cookies. She eats them, too. Moral: Those who don't work, don't eat.

| SUBJECTS | – | Cat
Cumulative Tale
Chain Tale
Dog(s)
Duck
Little Red Hen (Asks
  Animals To Help
  Her)
Industrious
Formula Tale | COUNTRY | – | United
Kingdom |
| MOTIFS | – | Humor
Talking Animals | TYPE OF
FOLKLORE | – | Folk Tales |

0255 LITTLE RED HEN, THE

See – 0511 Little Red Hen and The Grain of Wheat

0519 LITTLE RED RIDING HOOD

0180 Little Red Riding Hood

By Grimm, The Brothers
Illus. Harriet Pincus
New York, Harcourt, Brace & World, 1968. unp.

On the way to her ill grandmother's, Red Riding Hood meets a treacherous wolf, who eats the grandmother and Red Riding Hood. A hunter cuts open the wolf and rescues both of them.

| SUBJECTS | – | Red Riding Hood
Wolf
Grimm, The Brothers | COUNTRY | – | Germany |
| MOTIFS | – | Talking Animals
Trickery | TYPE OF
FOLKLORE | – | Folk Tales |

0211 Little Red Riding Hood

By Grimm, The Brothers
Illus. Bernadette
New York, The World Publishing Company, First American Edition,
1969. unp.

Similar to title no. 0180 Little Red Riding Hood. Different illus.

SUBJECTS	–	Wolf	COUNTRY	–	Germany
		Red Riding Hood			
		Grimm, The Brothers			
MOTIFS	–	Talking Animals	TYPE OF		
		Trickery	FOLKLORE	–	Folk Tales

0043 Little Red Riding Hood, The Renowned History of

By Charles Perrault
Illus. Nonny Hogrogian
New York, Thomas Y. Crowell, 1967. unp.

Little Red Riding Hood tells wolf she is going to her grandmother's
house to give her cake and a pot of butter. Wolf tricks grandmother
and little Red Riding Hood, eating both of them.

SUBJECTS	–	Wolf	COUNTRY	–	France
		Red Riding Hood			
		Perrault, Charles			
MOTIFS	–	Trickery	TYPE OF		
		Talking Animals	FOLKLORE	–	Folk Tales

0180 LITTLE RED RIDING HOOD

See – 0519 Little Red Riding Hood

0211 LITTLE RED RIDING HOOD

See – 0519 Little Red Riding Hood

0043 LITTLE RED RIDING HOOD, THE RENOWNED HISTORY OF

See – 0519 Little Red Riding Hood

0257 LITTLE TOM TUCKER, THE HISTORY OF

By Mother Goose
Illus. Paul Galdone
New York, McGraw-Hill Book Company, n.d. unp.

Little Tom Tucker didn't like school but after playing hooky one
day he gets into trouble and changes his attitude. He learns to read
and grows up to be a fine young man. Didactic.

SUBJECTS	–	Little Tom Tucker	COUNTRY	–	United
		School			Kingdom
		Mother Goose			
MOTIFS	–	Humor	TYPE OF		
			FOLKLORE	–	Nursery
					Rhymes

0168 LITTLE TUPPEN

STORIES BY TITLE

Author Unknown
Illus. Paul Galdone
New York, The Seabury Press, 1967. unp.

Chain story in which Little Tuppen chokes on a seed and her mother, Cluck-Cluck goes to get water for her.

SUBJECTS — Cumulative Tale   COUNTRY — Scandinavia
Chain Tale
Dwarf
Helpfulness
Tuppen
Formula Tale

MOTIFS — Humor   TYPE OF
Supernatural   FOLKLORE — Nursery
Creatures   Rhymes
Talking Animals
Friendly Animals

0310 LITTLE WHITE HEN

Reteller, Hajime Kijima
Illus. Setsuko Hane
New York, Harcourt, Brace & World, Inc., 1969. 27p.

The little white hen outwits the fox who sets out to catch her. After he puts her in the bag, she cuts her way out, fills the bag with stones, and sews it up.

SUBJECTS — Hen   COUNTRY — Japan
Fox(es)

MOTIFS — Talking Animals   TYPE OF
Humor   FOLKLORE — Folk Tales
Wit Prevails
Trickery

0282 LONDON BRIDGE IS FALLING DOWN

By Mother Goose, Reteller, Ed Emberley
Illus. Ed Emberley
Boston, Little, Brown and Company, 1967. 32p.

This picture book has three parts: picture book, instructions for the singing game, and music. It is the familiar "London bridge is falling down, falling down, falling down, London bridge is falling down, my fair lady" with many verses.

SUBJECTS — Music   COUNTRY — United
Mother Goose   Kingdom
Singing Games
London Bridge

MOTIFS — Humor   TYPE OF
FOLKLORE — Nursery
Rhymes

0197 LONDON BRIDGE IS FALLING DOWN

By Mother Goose
Illus. Peter Spier
Garden City, New York, Doubleday & Company, Inc., 1967. unp.

London bridge has had its ups and downs since the early history of England. Peter Spier's illus. show in vivid form the many materials used over the years to repair and rebuild the bridge. Music is included.

SUBJECTS	– London Bridge Mother Goose Music	COUNTRY	– United Kingdom
MOTIFS	– Humor	TYPE OF FOLKLORE	– Nursery Rhymes

0115 LONG, BROAD AND QUICKEYE

Adapted by Evaline Ness From the Andrew Lang Version
Illus. Evaline Ness
New York, Charles Scribner's Sons, 1969. unp.

A handsome prince is required to do certain tasks before he can marry the beautiful princess. Together with three companions with extraordinary powers, he rescues the imprisoned princess from a mysterious castle.

SUBJECTS	– Royalty
	Ring (From the Sea)
	Key (Gold)
	Wizard
	Companions (Magic
	  Wisdom Possessed
	  By Extraordinary C.)
	Acorn
	Jewel (Precious
	  Stone)
		COUNTRY	– Czechoslovakia

MOTIFS	– Enchanted People Tasks and Trials Magic Transforma- tion Magic Objects	TYPE OF FOLKLORE	– Folk Tales

See also	0090	Five Chinese Brothers, The
	0075	Fool of the World and the Flying Ship, The
	0066	Seven Simeons
	0039	Four Clever Brothers, The

0529 LONGNOSE THE DWARF

0371 Dwarf Long-Nose

By Wilhelm Hauff, Reteller Doris Orgel
Illus. Maurice Sendak
New York, Random House, 1960. 62p.

The wicked fairy gives Jacob, the shoemaker's son, a potion which transforms him into an ugly dwarf. After seven years her prisoner, he returns home and a bewitched goose helps him finally regain his former appearance.

SUBJECTS	– Dwarf Longnose Fairy Changes Boy To Dwarf Herb Enchantment	COUNTRY	– Germany

MOTIFS	–	Talking Animals	TYPE OF		
		Supernatural	FOLKLORE	–	Folk Tales
		Creatures			
		Magic Transforma-			
		tion			
		Magic Objects			

0051 LOOK, THERE IS A TURTLE FLYING

Reteller, Janina Domanska
Illus. Janina Domanska
New York, The MacMillan Company, 1968. unp.

A talkative turtle must fly with a stick in his mouth in order to learn when to keep quiet.

SUBJECTS	–	Vanity	COUNTRY	–	Greece
		Turtle			
		Royalty			
		Herons			
		Poland			

MOTIFS	–	Humor	TYPE OF		
		Talking Animals	FOLKLORE	–	Folk Tales
		Wit Prevails			

0032 LUCK CHILD, THE

By Grimm, The Brothers, Reteller, Gaynor Chapman
Illus. Gaynor Chapman
New York, Atheneum, 1968. unp.

Good fortune always follows Luck Child. He grows up to marry the king's daughter.

SUBJECTS	–	Astrologer	COUNTRY	–	Germany
		Eyes			
		Royalty			
		Grimm, The Brothers			

| MOTIFS | – | Trickery | TYPE OF | | |
| | | Wit Prevails | FOLKLORE | – | Folk Tales |

0133 LULLABY: WHY THE PUSSY-CAT WASHES HIMSELF SO OFTEN

Adapted By Josephine B. Bernhard
Illus. Irena Lorentowicz
New York, Roy Publishers, 1944. unp.

After all the people arrive with gifts and best wishes for the Christ Child, the excitement keeps him awake. With the help of a purring cat the Christ Child falls asleep. Thereafter, the Christ Child wants the purring cat's lullaby.

SUBJECTS	–	Christmas	COUNTRY	–	Poland
		Cat			
		Sharing			
		Lullaby			

MOTIFS	–	Religion	TYPE OF		
		Pourquoi Stories	FOLKLORE	–	Folk Tales
		Friendly Animals			
		Talking Animals			

0271 MAGIC FLUTE, THE

By Wolfgang Mozart, Reteller, Stephen Spender
Illus. Beni Montresor
New York, G. P. Putnam's Sons, 1966. unp.

A young prince goes in search of a princess with the help of a bird-man. His magic flute and silver bells, which have the power to create harmony in man and nature, protect him on his travels.

SUBJECTS	–	Opera	COUNTRY	–	Austria
		Mozart			
		Flute and Silver			
		Bells (Magic)			
		Queen of the Night			
		Music			

MOTIFS	–	Humor	TYPE OF		
		Supernatural	FOLKLORE	–	Folk Tales
		Creatures			
		Magic Objects			
		Magic Transforma-			
		tion			

0103 MAGIC MONKEY, THE

Adapted From An Old Chinese Legend By Christina Chan
Illus. Plato Chan
New York, McGraw-Hill Book Company, Inc., 1944. 51p.

A curious monkey finds many ways to perform magic after attending the school of magic. His monkey friends proclaim him king monkey and he finds the way to have eternal life and save his kingdom from the demon of havoc.

SUBJECTS	–	Monkey	COUNTRY	–	China
		Magician			(Mainland)
		Magic Wand			
		Milky Way			
		Curiosity			
		Life, Eternal			
		Invisibility			
		Demons			

MOTIFS	–	Magic Objects	TYPE OF		
		Magic Transforma-	FOLKLORE	–	Fables
		tion			
		Supernatural			
		Creatures			
		Talking Animals			
		Humor			

0116 MAGIC RING, THE

Retellers, Matija Valjavec and Cene Vipotnik
Illus. Marlenka Stupica
New York, World Publishing Company, First American ed., 1968. unp.

A boy receives a magic ring for saving the life of a snake. He uses the ring to successfully complete the tasks the king presents to him before he may wed the princess. Before the wedding the ring is stolen. His cat and dog retrieve it for him.

SUBJECTS   –   Snake   COUNTRY – Yugoslavia
                       Ring (From the Sea)
                       Emperor
                       Maharajah
                       Kindness
                       Fish
                       Dog(s)
                       Cat

MOTIFS   –   Magic Objects   TYPE OF
                       Tasks and Trials   FOLKLORE – Folk Tales
                       Trickery
                       Talking Animals
                       Friendly Animals

0240 MAGIC SACK, THE

Reteller, Marguerita Rudolph
Illus. Ralph Pinto
New York, McGraw-Hill Book Company, 1967. unp.

The poor peasant boy gives his meager wages to three beggars. In return he receives a sack, a stick and the power to have his wishes fulfilled from the last beggar.

SUBJECTS – Beggar(s) (Super-   COUNTRY – Lithuania
                       natural Creature)
                       Magic Fiddle, Stick,
                       Sack
                       Sharing

MOTIFS   –   Magic Objects   TYPE OF
                       Humor   FOLKLORE – Folk Tales
                       Supernatural
                       Creatures

0249 MAGNIFICENT HOUSE OF MAN ALONE, THE

Reteller, Helen Rushmore
Illus. Frank Vaughn
Champaign, Illinois, Garrard Publishing Company, 1968. 64p.

When the white man finds oil on the Osage Indians' land, the Indians buy luxuries with their new-found wealth. Man Alone builds a magnificient house but continues to live in his lodge.

SUBJECTS – Osage Indians   COUNTRY – U.S.–Tales
                       (Oklahoma's)   From the
                       Oil   North Ameri-
                       Oklahoma   can Indians

MOTIFS   –   Local Legendary   TYPE OF
                       Heroes   FOLKLORE – Folk Tales
                       Humor
                       Realistic Events

0245 MAI-LING AND THE MIRROR

Reteller, Roz Abish
Illus. Boche Kaplan
Englewood Cliffs, New Jersey, Prentice-Hall, Inc., 1969. unp.

Choy loves working in his rice fields so much that he thinks of nothing else—not even his pretty wife Mai-Ling. When she asks him to bring home a comb from the city, he brings home a mirror. Mai-Ling is taught a lesson when the villagers, who had never seen a mirror, react to it in a humorous way.

SUBJECTS	–	Farmer	COUNTRY	–	China
		Mirror			(Mainland)

MOTIFS	–	Humor	TYPE OF		
		Realistic Events	FOLKLORE	–	Folk Tales

0315 MAID AND HER PAIL OF MILK, THE

See – 0536 Milkmaid and Her Pail of Milk

0501 MAN WHO WAS GOING TO MIND THE HOUSE

0111 Gone is Gone or the Story of a Man Who Wanted To Do the Housework

Reteller, Wanda Gag
Illus. Wanda Gag
New York, Coward-McCann, Inc., 1935. unp.

A husband who believes his work harder than his wife's learn a lesson after they exchange jobs. She performs his chores with ease while he struggles through many amusing incidents performing her tasks.

SUBJECTS	–	Cow	COUNTRY	–	Czechoslovakia
		Housework			
		Exchange, Man and			
		Wife E. Duties			

MOTIFS	–	Humor	TYPE OF		
		Fools and	FOLKLORE	–	Folk Tales
		Simpletons			

0520 MAN, THE BOY, AND THE DONKEY, THE

0010 Donkey Ride, The

By Aesop, Reteller, Jean B. Showalter
Illus. Tomi Ungerer
Garden City, N. Y., Doubleday and Company, Inc., 1967. unp.

After following literally the advice of the people, the Miller comes to the conclusion: "My son," he says, "Always remember two things: you can't please everybody, and some people are never satisfied!"

SUBJECTS	–	Donkey	COUNTRY	–	Greece
		Farmer			
		Individuality,			
		Expressing			
		Aesop			

MOTIFS	–	Humor	TYPE OF		
		Fools and	FOLKLORE	–	Fables
		Simpletons			

0176 Miller, The Boy, and the Donkey, The

By La Fontaine, Adapted by Brian Wildsmith
Illus. Brian Wildsmith
New York, Franklin Watts, Inc., 1969, unp.

The miller becomes a wiser man through his encounters as he and his son take their donkey to market to sell.

SUBJECTS – Donkey   COUNTRY – France
               Farmer
               Individuality,
                 Expressing
               La Fontaine

MOTIFS   – Humor   TYPE OF
             Fools and   FOLKLORE – Fables
             Simpletons

0005 Miller, His Son, and Their Donkey, The

By Aesop
Illus. Roger Duvoisin
New York, McGraw-Hill Book Company, Inc., 1962. 32p.

Similar to title nos. 0176 Miller, the Boy, and the Donkey, The and 0010 Donkey Ride, The.

SUBJECTS – Individuality,   COUNTRY – Greece
                 Expressing
               Donkey
               Miller
               Aesop

MOTIFS   – Humor   TYPE OF
             Fools and   FOLKLORE – Fables
             Simpletons

0264 Hee Haw

By Aesop, Reteller, Ann McGovern
Illus. Eric Von Schmidt
Boston, Houghton Mifflin Company, 1969. unp.

An old man and a boy going to market to trade a donkey for three hens are given much advice on how to treat the donkey. The donkey runs away. Ending is different from title nos. 0010 Donkey Ride, The, 0176 Miller, the Boy, and the Donkey, The, and 0005 Miller, His Son, and Their Donkey, The.

SUBJECTS – Individuality,   COUNTRY – Greece
                 Expressing
               Donkey
               Farmer
               Aesop

MOTIFS   – Humor   TYPE OF
             Fools and   FOLKLORE – Fables
             Simpletons

0266 MAZEL AND SHIMAZEL OR THE MILK OF A LIONESS

Reteller, Isaac Bashevis Singer, Yiddish Trans. By Singer & Elizabeth Shub
Illus. Margot Zemach
New York, Farrar, Straus, & Giroux, 1967. 43p.

The good spirit Mazel and the bad spirit Shimazel make a wager. Mazel says Shimazel can bring only bad luck through mishap, sickness, famine or war, and challenges him to find another way to do it.

SUBJECTS	– Contest Between Good Spirit and Bad Spirit Mazel and Shimazel	COUNTRY	– Israel
MOTIFS	– Humor Tasks and Trials Supernatural Creatures Trickery Wit Prevails	TYPE OF FOLKLORE	– Folk Tales

0322 MICE THAT ATE IRON, THE

Reteller, Katherine Evans
Illus. Katherine Evans
Chicago, Albert Whitman and Co., 1963. unp.

Pablo loses his ship and money by flittering away his time. When he gives his anchor to a friend for safekeeping and the friend sells it, a dispute erupts. The mayor is called in to settle the dispute.

SUBJECTS	– Iron-eating Mice Justice Spain	COUNTRY	– India
MOTIFS	– Trickery Wit Prevails	TYPE OF FOLKLORE	– Fables

See also   **0082**   **Judge Not**
            0206   **Wise Fool, The**
            0156   **Eggs, The**

0537 MIDAS

0015 Golden Touch, The

Reteller, Nathaniel Hawthorne, Forward By Anne Thaxter Eaton
Illus. Paul Galdone
New York, McGraw-Hill Book Company, Inc., 1959. 61p.

King Midas has the power to turn everything he touches into gold. He soon finds it to be a curse, especially when he touches his daughter. He regains happiness after he loses his magic power.

SUBJECTS	– Allegory–Myth Type Greediness Gold Royalty Wealth, Curse of	COUNTRY	– Greece
MOTIFS	– Supernatural Creatures Wishes	TYPE OF FOLKLORE	– Myths

0536 MILKMAID AND HER PAIL OF MILK

0315 Maid and Her Pail of Milk, The

By Aesop, Reteller, Katherine Evans
Illus. Katherine Evans
Chicago, Albert Whitman & Company, 1959. unp.

Anna becomes so engrossed in what she will buy with the money from the milk she is going to sell that she spills the milk.

SUBJECTS	–	Dreaming, Day	COUNTRY	–	Greece
		Woman and Pail of			
		Milk			
		Aesop			

MOTIFS	–	Humor	TYPE OF		
			FOLKLORE	–	Fables

See also 0285 **Don't Count Your Chicks**

0005 MILLER, HIS SON, AND THEIR DONKEY, THE

See – 0520 **Man, the Boy, and the Donkey, The**

0176 MILLER, THE BOY, AND THE DONKEY, THE

See – 0520 **Man, the Boy, and the Donkey, The**

0077 MITTEN, THE

Adapted by E. Rachev, Reteller, Alvin Tresselt
Illus. Yaroslava
New York, Lothrop, Lee & Shepard Co., Inc., 1964. unp.

A mouse, frog, owl, rabbit, fox, wolf, boar and a bear try to make a home in a mitten dropped by a boy. When a black cricket tries to join them, it pops apart.

SUBJECTS	–	Animals, Wild	COUNTRY	–	U.S.S.R.–
		Forest			Ukraine
		Mitten(s)			
		Formula Tale			
		Cumulative Tale			
		Chain Tale			

MOTIFS	–	Humor	TYPE OF		
		Talking Animals	FOLKLORE	–	Folk Tales

0392 MOLLY WHUPPIE

By Joseph Jacobs
Illus. Pelagie Doane
New York, Oxford University Press, n.d., unp.

The youngest of three sisters saves their lives from a giant and brings about their marriages to three princes by using her wit.

SUBJECTS	–	Molly Whuppie	COUNTRY	–	United
		Exchanged Neck			Kingdom
		Pieces Cause Giant			
		To Kill Own Chil-			
		dren			
		Bag, Giant's Wife			
		Tricked In Taking			
		Prisoner's Place in			
		B.			

Royalty
Punishment, Chooses
  Type of
Jacobs, Joseph

MOTIFS	—	Supernatural	TYPE OF	
		Creatures	FOLKLORE	— Folk Tales
		Tasks and Trials		
		Wit Prevails		
		Trickery		

0306 MOMMY, BUY ME A CHINA DOLL

Reteller, Harve Zemach
Illus. Margot Zemach
New York, Follett Publishing Company, 1966. 32p.

A cumulative Ozark children's song with music included is presented.
"Mommy, buy me a china doll, do Mommy do! What could we buy it
with, Eliza Lou. Trade our daddy's featherbed. . . .'

SUBJECTS	—	Cumulative Tale	COUNTRY	— U.S.–Folk-
		Chain Tale		songs
		Lullaby		
		Ozark Mountain		
		Song		
		Formula Tale		
		Music		

MOTIFS	—	Humor	TYPE OF	
			FOLKLORE	— Folk Songs,
				Ballads

0195 MONKEY AND THE CROCODILE, THE

Reteller, Paul Galdone
Illus. Paul Galdone
New York, The Seabury Press, 1969. unp.

A young monkey constantly outwits a crocodile which tries to
catch him.

SUBJECTS	—	Crocodile	COUNTRY	— India
		Buddha as Monkey		
		(Built Temple)		
		Jataka		
		Monkey		

MOTIFS	—	Religion	TYPE OF	
		Humor	FOLKLORE	— Fables
		Wit Prevails		
		Trickery		
		Talking Animals		

0393 MONKEY SEE, MONKEY DO

Reteller, Ellis Credle
Illus. Ellis Credle
Camden, New Jersey, Thomas Nelson & Sons, 1968. unp.

A sad lonely family's life is made livelier by a monkey given them
by their uncle sailor Bill.

STORIES BY TITLE

SUBJECTS	– Monkey Makes Frontier Life Exciting Frontier and Pioneer Life	COUNTRY	– U.S.–Native Folk Tales
MOTIFS	– Humor	TYPE OF FOLKLORE	– Folk Tales

0220 MONKEY, THE LION, AND THE SNAKE, THE

Reteller, Kurt Werth
Illus. Kurt Werth
New York, The Viking Press, 1967. 32p.

When a peasant rescues a monkey, lion, snake and nobleman from a pit, all reward him but the nobleman who denies knowing him. Justice is served when the peasant is awarded the nobleman's castle.

SUBJECTS	– Grateful Animals Justice Judge(s) Italy Lion(s) Monkey Snake Rescue From Pit	COUNTRY	– Saudi Arabia
MOTIFS	– Trickery Wit Prevails	TYPE OF FOLKLORE	– Fables

0318 MONKEY'S WHISKERS, THE

Adapted by Anne Rockwell
Illus. Anne Rockwell
New York, Parents' Magazine Press, 1971. unp.

This is a cumulative tale in which a monkey, after he has been shaved, wants to get his whiskers back. The chain consists of razor, fish, coffee beans, flour, and little girl.

SUBJECTS	– Chain Tale Cumulative Tale Monkey Formula Tale	COUNTRY	– Brazil
MOTIFS	– Humor Wit Prevails Trickery Talking Animals	TYPE OF FOLKLORE	– Folk Tales

0341 MONTH BROTHERS, THE

See – 0562 Twelve Months

0163 MOURKA, THE MIGHTY CAT

Reteller, Lee Wyndham
Illus. Charles Mikolaycak
New York, Parent's Magazine Press, 1969. unp.

After Mourka the cat rids the village of all the mice, he has to pilfer food from the villagers. The villagers drive him out but realize their mistake and invite him back.

SUBJECTS	– Cat Mouser Bear(s) Fox(es) Boar Wolf	COUNTRY	– U.S.S.R.
MOTIFS	– Wit Prevails Humor Talking Animals	TYPE OF FOLKLORE	– Folk Tales

0139 MR. MIACCA

Reteller, Evaline Ness
Illus. Evaline Ness
New York, Holt, Rinehart and Winston, 1967. unp.

Tommy Grimes is told Mr Miacca will eat him if he leaves his street. Tommy is almost eaten twice before he learns his lesson.

SUBJECTS	– Disobedience	COUNTRY	– United Kingdom
MOTIFS	– Humor Supernatural Creatures	TYPE OF FOLKLORE	– Folk Tales

0355 MUNACHAR AND MANACHAR

By Joseph Jacobs
Illus. Anne Rockwell
New York, Thomas Y. Crowell Company, 1970. unp.

Manachar promptly eats as many raspberries as Munachar can pick. But when poor Munachar decides to punish his greedy friend, this cumulative tale begins.

SUBJECTS	– Cumulative Tale Chain Tale Leprechaun Greediness Formula Tale Jacobs, Joseph	COUNTRY	– United Kingdom
MOTIFS	– Humor Supernatural Creatures	TYPE OF FOLKLORE	– Folk Tales

0072 MY MOTHER IS THE MOST BEAUTIFUL WOMAN IN THE WORLD

Reteller, Becky Reyher
Illus. Ruth Gannett
New York, Howell, Soskin, Publishers, 1945. unp.

A lost little girl looks for her mother whom she describes as the most beautiful woman in the world. The astonished villagers discover that her mother is the homely Marfa.

SUBJECTS	– Mother Love	COUNTRY	– U.S.S.R.– Ukraine

MOTIFS	— Realistic Events	TYPE OF FOLKLORE	— Folk Tales

0027 NAIL SOUP

Reteller, Harve Zemach
Illus. Margot Zemach
New York, Follett Publishing Company, 1964. 32p.

A tramp tricks an old lady into helping him make nail soup. The old lady actually supplies all of the ingredients in the soup and is the kinder for it.

SUBJECTS	— Friendship Tramp Cooperation Soup	COUNTRY	— Sweden

MOTIFS	— Wit Prevails Humor	TYPE OF FOLKLORE	— Folk Tales

See also **0028** **Stone Soup, An Old Tale**

0071 NEIGHBORS, THE

See — **0561 Fox and the Hare**

0127 NEVER—EMPTY

Reteller, Letta Schatz
Illus. Sylvie Selig
New York, Follett Publishing Company, 1969. 48p.

When hare finds Never-Empty, giver of food aplenty from the bottom of the pond, he knows his food worries are over but he fails to reckon with greedy elephant. He gets his revenge, however, with the aid of Swing and Sting.

SUBJECTS	— Famine Food Hare(s) Elephant Greediness	COUNTRY	— Africa

MOTIFS	— Magic Objects Talking Animals Trickery	TYPE OF FOLKLORE	— Folk Tales

0216 NIBBLE, NIBBLE MOUSEKIN

See — **0527 Hansel and Gretel**

0204 NIGHTINGALE, THE

See — **0554 Nightingale, The**

0060 NIGHTINGALE, THE
See – 0554 Nightingale, The

0554 NIGHTINGALE, THE

0204 Nightingale, The

By Hans Christian Andersen
Illus. Harold Berson
New York, J. B. Lippincott Company, 1962. 32p.

All the court is impressed by the nightingale's song until the emperor of Japan gives the emperor of China a mechanical nightingale. They realize true values only after the artificial bird wears out and the emperor approaches death.

SUBJECTS	– China	COUNTRY	– Denmark
	Nightingale		
	Royalty		
	Kindness		
	Andersen, Hans		
	Christian		
MOTIFS	– Talking Animals	TYPE OF	
		FOLKLORE	– Folk Tales

0060 Nightingale, The

By Hans Christian Andersen, Trans. Eva Le Gallienne
Illus. Nancy Ekholm Burkert
New York, Harper & Row, Publishers, 1965. 33p.

Similar to title no. 0204 Nightingale, The. Different illus.

SUBJECTS	– China	COUNTRY	– Denmark
	Nightingale		
	Royalty		
	Kindness		
	Andersen, Hans		
	Christian		
MOTIFS	– Talking Animals	TYPE OF	
		FOLKLORE	– Folk Tales

0108 NINE IN A LINE

Arabic By Leila Leonard, Reteller, Ann Kirn
Illus. Ann Kirn
New York, W. W. Norton and Company, 1966. unp.

Amin is convinced the "Evil One" has stolen one of his camels when he counts eight instead of nine. He forgets to include the camel he is riding.

SUBJECTS	– Camels	COUNTRY	– Saudi Arabia
	Counting Wrong By		
	Not Counting		
	Oneself		

MOTIFS	— Humor	TYPE OF	
	Fools and	FOLKLORE —	Folk Tales
	Simpletons		

See also **0149**   **Six Foolish Fishermen**

0106 NINE(9) CRY-BABY DOLLS

Adapted By Josephine B. Bernhard
Illus. Irena Lorentowicz
New York, Roy Publishers, 1945. unp.

A crisis is created when Mrs. Bartosh makes 9 crying dolls to stop her baby's crying and distributes them to her neighbors. Ol Granny helps them solve the problem.

SUBJECTS	— Dolls	COUNTRY	— Poland
	Crying		

MOTIFS	— Magic Objects	TYPE OF	
	Humor	FOLKLORE —	Folk Tales
	Enchanted People		

0070 NO ROOM, AN OLD STORY RETOLD

Reteller, Rose Dobbs
Illus. Fritz Eichenberg
New York, David McKay Company, Inc., 1944. unp.

An old selfish peasant comes to appreciate what he has with the help of a wise man. He is instructed to fill his house with many animals after her complains about his poor daughter, her husband, and baby who have come to stay.

SUBJECTS	— Animals, Farm	COUNTRY	— U.S.S.R.
	Wise Man		
	Sharing		
	Advice (Counsel–		
	Precept)		

MOTIFS	— Humor	TYPE OF	
	Realistic Events	FOLKLORE —	Folk Tales

0080 NORTH WIND AND THE SUN

By La Fontaine
Illus. Brian Wildsmith
New York, Franklin Watts Incorporated, 1964. unp.

The sun wins a contest with the wind.

SUBJECTS	— Contest Between	COUNTRY	— France
	Sun and Wind		
	Sun		
	Wind		
	La Fontaine		

MOTIFS	— Supernatural	TYPE OF	
	Creatures	FOLKLORE —	Fables
	Humor		

0390 NUTCRACKER

See — **0530** Nutcracker and the Mouse King

0530 NUTCRACKER AND THE MOUSE KING

0390 Nutcracker

Reteller, Daniel Walden
Illus. Harold Berson
New York, J. B. Lippincott Company, 1959. 48p.

Maria receives an iron soldier nutcracker for Christmas. In her dreams the nutcracker and other soldiers defeat the mouse king and his army, and the nutcracker changes into a handsome prince.

SUBJECTS	– Dream, Nutcracker, and Sugar Plum Fairy Christmas Mouse King	COUNTRY	– Germany
MOTIFS	– Magic Objects Magic Transformation Supernatural Creatures	TYPE OF FOLKLORE	– Folk Tales

0232 Nutcracker, The

By E. T. A. Hoffmann
Illus. Dagmar Berkova
New York, Franklin Watts, Inc., 1968. 64p.

In her dreams Clara saves the nutcracker's life when he fights the mouse king. He tells Clara how he was transformed from a young man to a nutcracker. He takes her to his country where he meets his Princess Pirlipate whom he weds.

SUBJECTS	– Dream, Nutcracker, and Sugar Plum Fairy Mouse King Nutcracker Music	COUNTRY	– Germany
MOTIFS	– Magic Transformation Supernatural Creatures	TYPE OF FOLKLORE	– Folk Tales

0231 Nutcracker, The

Based on Alexandre Dumas Version By E. T. A. Hoffmann, Ret., Warren Chappell
Illus. Warren Chappell
New York, Alfred A. Knopf, 1958. unp.

Similar to title no. 0232 Nutcracker, The.

SUBJECTS	– Dream, Nutcracker, and Sugar Plum Fairy Mouse King Nutcracker Music	COUNTRY	– Germany
MOTIFS	– Magic Transformation	TYPE OF FOLKLORE	– Folk Tales

Supernatural
Creatures

0231 NUTCRACKER, THE

See — 0530 Nutcracker and the Mouse King

0232 NUTCRACKER, THE

See — 0530 Nutcracker and the Mouse King

0261 OL' DAN TUCKER

Reteller, John Langstaff
Illus. Joe Krush
New York, Harcourt, Brace & World, Inc., 1963. unp.

A singing game is presented in which "Ol' Dan Tucker came to town,
riding a billy goat, leadin' a hound. The hound gave a yelp, the goat
gave a jump and threw ol' Dan A-straddle of a stump....!"

SUBJECTS	–	Abraham Lincoln	COUNTRY	–	U.S.–Folk-
		Ol' Dan Tucker			songs
		Singing Games			
MOTIFS	–	Humor	TYPE OF		
			FOLKLORE	–	Folk Songs,
					Ballads

0512 OLD MOTHER HUBBARD

0254 Old Mother Hubbard and Her Dog

By Mother Goose
Illus. Paul Galdone
New York, McGraw-Hill Book Company, 1960. 32p.

Old Mother Hubbard did many things for her dog. She "went to the
cupboard to get her poor dog a bone, but when she got there the
cupboard was bare, and so the poor dog had none...."

SUBJECTS	–	Old Mother	COUNTRY	–	United
		Hubbard			Kingdom
		Dog(s)			
		Mother Goose			
MOTIFS	–	Humor	TYPE OF		
			FOLKLORE	–	Nursery
					Rhymes

0254 OLD MOTHER HUBBARD AND HER DOG

See — 0512 Old Mother Hubbard

0209 OLD SATAN

Reteller, Lucille Wallower
Illus. Lucille Wallower
New York, David McKay Company, Inc., 1956. unp.

Old Satan is the most ornery mule until the day he drinks a
barrel of soft-soap. A changed congenial animal, he supplies soap
lather to men when it is needed. That's why mules wear shaving-brush
tails today.

SUBJECTS	–	Mule	COUNTRY	–	U.S.–Native
		Soap, Soft			Tall Tales of
		Shaving Brush Tails			the Paul Bun-
		Tall Tales			yan Variety
MOTIFS	–	Humor	TYPE OF		
		Pourquoi Stories	FOLKLORE	–	Folk Tales

0276 OLD WOMAN AND HER PIG, THE

Anonymous
Illus. Paul Galdone
N.Y., Whittlesey House, Division of McGraw-Hill Book Co., Inc., 1960.
  32p.

An old woman finally gets her pig to jump a stile so she can go home.
Several objects form the chain story: cow, cat, rat, rope, butcher, ox,
water, fire, stick, dog, and pig.

SUBJECTS	–	Cumulative Tale	COUNTRY	–	United
		Chain Tale			Kingdom
		Old Woman and Pig			
		Formula Tale			
MOTIFS	–	Humor	TYPE OF		
		Talking Animals	FOLKLORE	–	Folk Tales

0140 OLD WOMAN AND THE PEDLAR, THE

Reteller, Mark Taylor
Illus. Graham Booth
San Carlos, California, Golden Gate Junior Books, 1969. unp.

A peddler uses trickery to convince a very self-sufficient woman
she should marry him.

SUBJECTS	–	Old Woman Who	COUNTRY	–	United
		Does Not Know			Kingdom
		Herself			
		Peddler			
MOTIFS	–	Humor	TYPE OF		
		Trickery	FOLKLORE	–	Folk Tales
		Fools and			
		Simpletons			

0323 ONCE A MOUSE

Reteller, Marcia Brown
Illus. Marcia Brown
New York, Charles Scribner's Sons, 1961. unp.

A kind hermit, adept at magic, turns a mouse into a cat, a dog and
finally into a tiger. When the tiger becomes vain and proud, the hermit transforms him back into a mouse.

SUBJECTS	–	Hitopadesa	COUNTRY	–	India
		Mouse (Mice)			
		Pride			
		Hermit Trans. Mouse			
MOTIFS	–	Magic Transforma-	TYPE OF		
		tion	FOLKLORE	–	Fables
		Talking Animals			
		Religion			

0382 ONE FINE DAY

Reteller, Nonny Hogrogian
Illus. Nonny Hogrogian
New York, The MacMillan Company, 1971. unp.

The cumulative tale begins when the miller gives grain to the fox and ends when the old woman sews the fox's tail in place.

SUBJECTS	–	Cumulative Tale	COUNTRY	–	Turkey
		Chain Tale			
		Fox Regains His Tail			
		Formula Tale			
MOTIFS	–	Talking Animals	TYPE OF		
		Humor	FOLKLORE	–	Folk Tales

0202 ONE GOOD DEED DESERVES ANOTHER

Reteller, Katherine Evans
Illus. Katherine Evans
Chicago, Ill., Albert Whitman & Company, 1964. unp.

A family who helps a robber to safety is robbed by him. They believe it is an unjust repayment and ask a boy to decide who is right.

SUBJECTS	–	Justice	COUNTRY	–	Mexico
		Judge(s)			
		Robber(s)			
MOTIFS	–	Humor	TYPE OF		
		Trickery	FOLKLORE	–	Fables
		Wit Prevails			

See also **0119**   **Tiger, the Brahman, and the Jackal, The**

0288 ONE-LEGGED GHOST, THE

Reteller, Betty Jean Lifton
Illus. Fuku Akino
New York, Atheneum, 1968. unp.

The headman declares a one-legged creature a god, and the villagers build a shrine to it. The headman soon decides its purpose is to keep people dry from the rain so the villagers construct many like it.

SUBJECTS	–	Umbrella	COUNTRY	–	Japan
MOTIFS	–	Humor	TYPE OF		
		Realistic Events	FOLKLORE	–	Folk Tales

0099 ONIROKU AND THE CARPENTER

Trans. By Masako Matsuno, Reteller, Tadashi Matsui
Illus. Suekichi Akaba
Englewood Cliffs, N. J., Prentice-Hall, Inc., 1963. unp.

An ogre builds a bridge and in repayment asks for the carpenter's eyes. The carpenter will be free of the debt if he can correctly guess the ogre's name.

SUBJECTS	–	Eyes	COUNTRY	–	Japan
		Carpenter			
		Ogre			

Name of Helper
Discovered

| MOTIFS | — Supernatural Creatures | TYPE OF FOLKLORE — Folk Tales |

See also   **0287**   **Rumpelstiltskin**
            0142   **Tom Tit Tot**

0384 ORANGE PRINCESS, THE LEGEND OF THE

Reteller, Mehlli Gobhai
Illus. Mehlli Gobhai
New York, Holiday House, Inc., 1971. unp.

When the queen gives birth to an orange, the king treats it as his child. One day a prince asks for the orange in marriage and it turns into a beautiful maiden.

| SUBJECTS | — Orange Transf. Into Princess By Night Love, Selfless | COUNTRY — India |

| MOTIFS | — Magic Objects Magic Transformation | TYPE OF FOLKLORE — Folk Tales |

0273 OTE

Reteller, Pura Belpre
Illus. Paul Galdone
New York, Random House, Inc., 1969. unp.

In southeastern Puerto Rico, Ote is plagued by the devil. The old woman tells him what he must do to get rid of the devil but he disobeys and his son must save him.

| SUBJECTS | — Forgetting (Forgetfulness) Devil (Nearsighted) | COUNTRY — U.S.–Puerto Rico |

| MOTIFS | — Humor Trickery Wit Prevails Supernatural Creatures | TYPE OF FOLKLORE — Folk Tales |

0242 OTWE

Reteller, Verna Aardema
Illus. Elton Fax
New York, Coward-McCann, Inc., 1960. unp.

Otwe saves a small snake from a large snake and is rewarded with a magic feather which enables him to hear what the animals are saying. He is not permitted to reveal his power, however. When Otwe has to choose between revealing his power or losing his wife, he tells and dies. The tribe is remorseful at his death and the snake returns him to life.

| SUBJECTS | — Snake Kindness | COUNTRY — Africa |

| MOTIFS | — Supernatural Creatures | TYPE OF FOLKLORE — Folk Tales |

Talking Animals
Humor

0391 OWL AND THE PUSSY-CAT, THE

By Edward Lear
Illus. William Pene Du Bois
Garden City, New York, Doubleday & Company, Inc., n. d. unp.

The owl and the pussycat go to sea in a pea green boat. After sailing a year and a day they meet a pig who sells them the ring at the end of his nose for their wedding.

SUBJECTS	–	Owl and Pussycat	COUNTRY	–	United
		Lear, Edward			Kingdom
MOTIFS	–	Humor	TYPE OF		
		Talking Animals	FOLKLORE	–	Nursery
		Friendly Animals			Rhymes

0351 PAINTING THE MOON

Reteller, Carl Withers
Illus. Adrienne Adams
New York, E. P. Dutton & Co., 1970. 31p.

Old Father creates the world with his helpers working on the moon and stars. Only the devil is unhappy. His scheme to blot out the moon is foiled by Old Father and the devil's helper is forced to remain on the moon as punishment.

SUBJECTS	–	Moon	COUNTRY	–	Estonia
		God			
		Devil			
MOTIFS	–	Religion	TYPE OF		
		Humor	FOLKLORE	–	Folk Tales
		Supernatural			
		Creatures			
		Pourquoi Stories			

0410 PALM TREE, THE LEGEND OF THE

Reteller, Margarida Estrela Bandeira Duarte
Illus. Paulo Werneck
New York, Grosset & Dunlap, 1968, unp.

Drought forces a couple and their child to leave their home. Their prayers to god Tupan are answered by the emergence of a woman's spirit from a palm tree. The palm tree spirit tells the family how to obtain food, clothing, and shelter for themselves and all the people of Brazil.

SUBJECTS	–	Palm Tree	COUNTRY	–	Brazil
		Drought			
MOTIFS	–	Religion	TYPE OF		
		Nature Calamities	FOLKLORE	–	Legends
		Magic Transforma-			
		tion			

0545 PAUL BUNYAN

0290 Paul Bunyan

Reteller, Maurice Dolbier
Illus. Leonard Everett Fisher
New York, Random House, 1959. 54p.

Paul Bunyan makes the Great Lakes, the Rocky Mountains, the Appalachian Mountains, and the Mississippi River.

SUBJECTS	–	Bunyan, Paul	COUNTRY	–	U.S.–Native
		Babes, The Blue Ox			Tall Tales of
		Tall Tales			the Paul Bun-
					yan Variety

MOTIFS	–	Pourquoi Stories	TYPE OF		
		Local Legendary	FOLKLORE	–	Folk Tales
		Heroes			
		Humor			

0291 Paul Bunyan, The Story of

Reteller, Barbara Emberley
Illus. Ed Emberley
Englewood Cliffs, N. J., Prentice-Hall, Inc., 1963. unp.

Paul Bunyan is a lumberjack who squeezes water out of boulders and drives stumps into the ground with his bare fists. With his companion Babe, the Blue Ox, he digs the Mississippi, and also clears Iowa and Kansas.

SUBJECTS	–	Bunyan, Paul	COUNTRY	–	U.S.–Native
		Babes, The Blue Ox			Tall Tales of
		Tall Tales			the Paul Bun-
					yan Variety

MOTIFS	–	Pourquoi Stories	TYPE OF		
		Local Legendary	FOLKLORE	–	Folk Tales
		Heroes			
		Humor			

0290 PAUL BUNYAN

See – 0545 Paul Bunyan

0291 PAUL BUNYAN, THE STORY OF

See – 0545 Paul Bunyan

0113 PEACOCK AND THE CROW, THE

Reteller, Ann Kirn
Illus. Ann Kirn
New York, Four Winds Press, 1969. unp.

A peacock is a false friend. This is proven by Peacock who becomes magnificent to behold and makes sure that Crow will not outdazzle him at Lord Tiger's wedding.

SUBJECTS	–	Bird(s)	COUNTRY	–	China
		Crow (Paints Pea-			(Mainland)
		cock Feathers)			
		Flowers			
		Jealousy			
		Peacock			
		Painting (Feathers)			

STORIES BY TITLE

| MOTIFS | — | Pourquoi Stories
Trickery
Talking Animals | TYPE OF
FOLKLORE | — | Folk Tales |

0019 PECOS BILL AND THE MUSTANG

Reteller, Harold W. Felton
Illus. Leonard Shortall
Englewood Cliffs, N. J., Prentice-Hall, Inc., 1965. unp.

When Pecos Bill was small, he was befriended and raised by coyotes. As a man he tames a mountain lion, a rattlesnake, and a wild mustang and becomes the first cowboy.

| SUBJECTS | — | Cowboys
Tall Tales | COUNTRY | — | U.S.—Native
Tall Tales
of the Paul
Bunyan
Variety |

| MOTIFS | — | Friendly Animals
Humor
Local Legendary
Heroes | TYPE OF
FOLKLORE | — | Folk Tales |

0403 PEDLAR OF SWAFFHAM, THE

Reteller, Kevin Crossley-Holland
Illus. Margaret Gordon
New York, The Seabury Press, 1971. unp.

A peddler is directed by a dream to London Bridge where a scornful shopkeeper tells his dream of a treasure buried in the peddler's backyard. The peddler keeps some of the money and gives the rest to the building of the church.

| SUBJECTS | — | Dream, Advice to
Peddler
Peddler Finds Gold | COUNTRY | — | United
Kingdom |

| MOTIFS | — | Religion
Humor | TYPE OF
FOLKLORE | — | Folk Tales |

0165 PEREZ AND MARTINA

Reteller, Pura Belpre
Illus. Carlos Sanchez. M.
New York, Frederick Warne & Company, Inc., 1932. 79p.

Martina, a Spanish cockroach, is very refined and proud of her descent. She has many suitors, but the mouse's voice is most pleasing to her. She marries him but he falls into a Christmas treat she is making for him and dies.

| SUBJECTS | — | Spain
Cockroach
Animal Weddings
(Cockroach and
Mouse)
Christmas
Courtship
Death | COUNTRY | — | U.S.—Puerto
Rico |

| MOTIFS | – | Humor
Friendly Animals
Talking Animals | TYPE OF
FOLKLORE – Folk Tales |

0538 PERSEUS

0044 Gorgon's Head: The Story of Perseus, The

Reteller, Ian Serraillier
Illus. William Stobbs
New York, Henry Z. Walck, Inc., 1962. 71p.

Perseus promises to bring the king the head of the Gorgon, Medusa, who turns anyone who looks at her into stone. With Athena's help, and his own courage, he slays the monster.

| SUBJECTS | – | Sandals, Winged
Shield, Magic
Invisibility
Gods
Courage
Fate | COUNTRY – Greece |

| MOTIFS | – | Magic Objects
Tasks and Trials
Supernatural
  Creatures
Wit Prevails
Religion | TYPE OF
FOLKLORE – Myths |

0229 PETER AND THE WOLF

By Serge Prokofieff
Illus. Warren Chappell
New York, Alfred A. Knopf, Inc., 1940. unp.

When Peter wanders into the meadow, he is scolded because a wolf might come. When the wolf swallows a duck, Peter and his friend bird devise a way to catch the wolf.

| SUBJECTS | – | Cat
Duck
Music
Peter and the Wolf
Wolf | COUNTRY – U.S.S.R. |

| MOTIFS | – | Talking Animals
Wit Prevails
Trickery | TYPE OF
FOLKLORE – Folk Tales |

0265 PIGS AND PIRATES

Reteller, Barbara Walker
Illus. Harold Berson
New York, David White, 1969. unp.

Three Greek swineherds teach their pigs to do tricks. When the pirates steal them, the boys blow a whistle and the pigs' weight tips over the pirates' boat. The pigs swim to shore, but the pirates drown.

| SUBJECTS | – | Pig(s)
Pirates
Swineherds | COUNTRY – Greece |

MOTIFS	– Humor	TYPE OF	
	Trickery	FOLKLORE	– Folk Tales
	Wit Prevails		

0138 PIXY AND THE LAZY HOUSEWIFE, THE

Reteller, Mary Calhoun
Illus. Janet McCaffery
New York, William Morrow & Company, 1969. unp.

Bessy is repaid in kind after she tricks the pixies into cleaning her house.

SUBJECTS	– Housework	COUNTRY	– United
	Lazy Woman		Kingdom
	Pixies		
MOTIFS	– Humor	TYPE OF	
	Trickery	FOLKLORE	– Folk Tales
	Supernatural		
	Creatures		

0065 PRINCE IVAN, THE FIREBIRD, AND THE GRAY WOLF, THE STORY OF

Trans. From the Russian By Thomas P. Whitney
Illus. Nonny Hogrogian
New York, Charles Scribner's Sons, 1968. unp.

Prince Ivan seeks to find the firebird that ate the golden apples from the royal tree. With the help of a gray wolf, he wins the firebird, a great steed, and a beautiful wife.

SUBJECTS	– Wolf	COUNTRY	– U.S.S.R.
	Firebird		
	Royalty		
	Loyalty		
	Horse		
MOTIFS	– Trickery	TYPE OF	
	Talking Animals	FOLKLORE	– Folk Tales
	Magic Objects		
	Tasks and Trials		
	Supernatural		
	Creatures		

0129 PRINCESS OF THE FULL MOON

Reteller, Frederic Guirma, Trans. John Garrett
Illus. Frederic Guirma
New York, The MacMillan Company, 1970. unp.

Kiugu Peulgo, Princess of the Full Moon, marries the perfect man but on the way to her husband's home, the prince is transformed into a monster, the Devil Prince of Midnight. Through the power of selfless love, a shepherd kills the monster and is returned to his original self, Prince of the Noonday Sun. The sun, day, and night are also in title no. 0352, Vasilisa the Beautiful.

SUBJECTS	– Royalty	COUNTRY	– Upper Volta
	Physically		
	Handicapped		

Flute
Monster
Love, Selfless
Invisibility
Vanity
Snobbishness

MOTIFS	— Supernatural Creatures Trickery Magic Transforma- tion Magic Objects	TYPE OF FOLKLORE — Folk Tales

0304 PUNIA AND THE KING OF THE SHARKS

Reteller, Beverly Mohan
Illus. Don Bolognese
Chicago, Follett Publishing Company, 1964. unp.

Punia outwits the Shark King in order to get lobsters for his mother's cooking pot.

SUBJECTS	— Hawaii Lobsters Sharks Punishment, Chooses Type of	COUNTRY — U.S.—Variants of the African Tales
MOTIFS	— Wit Prevails Trickery Talking Animals Humor	TYPE OF FOLKLORE — Folk Tales

See also **0191   Beeswax Catches a Thief**
       0193   Clever Turtle, The

0007 PUSS IN BOOTS

See — 0553 Puss In Boots

0011 PUSS IN BOOTS

See — 0553 Puss In Boots

0183 PUSS IN BOOTS

See — 0553 Puss In Boots

0553 PUSS IN BOOTS

0183 Puss In Boots

By Charles Perrault
Illus. Barry Wilkinson
New York, The World Publishing Company, First American Edition, 1969. unp.

Through Puss' ingenuity his master becomes owner of a castle and much land, and marries the king's daughter. Puss only asks for boots and a plumed hat in return.

SUBJECTS	— Loyalty Cat Ogre	COUNTRY — France

Royalty
Puss in Boots
Perrault, Charles

MOTIFS	— Magic Transformation	TYPE OF
	Wit Prevails	FOLKLORE — Folk Tales
	Trickery	
	Talking Animals	
	Supernatural	
	Creatures	

0007 Puss In Boots

By Charles Perrault—Free Translated Version
Illus. Marcia Brown
New York, Charles Scribner's Sons, 1952. unp.

Same as title no. 0183 Puss In Boots. Different illus.

SUBJECTS	— Loyalty	COUNTRY — France
	Cat	
	Ogre	
	Royalty	
	Puss In Boots	
	Perrault, Charles	

MOTIFS	— Talking Animals	TYPE OF
	Trickery	FOLKLORE — Folk Tales
	Supernatural	
	Creatures	
	Wit Prevails	
	Magic Transformation	

0011 Puss In Boots

By Charles Perrault, Reteller, Hans Fischer
Illus. Hans Fischer
New York, Harcourt, Brace and Company, 1959. unp.

Slightly different from title no. 0183 Puss In Boots. Different illus.

SUBJECTS	— Loyalty	COUNTRY — France
	Cat	
	Royalty	
	Giant(s)	
	Puss In Boots	
	Perrault, Charles	

MOTIFS	— Talking Animals	TYPE OF
	Trickery	FOLKLORE — Folk Tales
	Supernatural	
	Creatures	
	Wit Prevails	

0243 RABBIT AND THE TURNIP, THE

Translated From the German by Richard Sadler
Illus. Roswitha Gruttner
Garden City, New York, Doubleday & Company, Inc., 1968. unp.

When little rabbit finds two turnips, he eats one and gives the other to his friend the donkey who might be hungry. And so the chain begins. Finally the turnip comes back to little rabbit after many acts of kindness.

SUBJECTS	–	Rabbit(s)	COUNTRY	–	China
		Turnip(s)			(Mainland)
		Kindness			
		Cumulative Tale			
		Chain Tale			
		Formula Tale			
MOTIFS	–	Talking Animals	TYPE OF		
		Friendly Animals	FOLKLORE	–	Fables

0126 RAKOTO AND THE DRONGO BIRD

Reteller, Robin McKown
Illus. Robert Quackenbush
New York, Lothrop, Lee & Shepard Co., Inc., 1966. 52p.

Rakoto warns the people when slave traders land on Madagascar (now known as Malagasy Republic). The Drongo bird tricks the traders by imitating a baby's cry causing them to take a wrong route.

SUBJECTS	–	Drongo Bird	COUNTRY	–	Malagasy Re-
		Slavery			public
MOTIFS	–	Wit Prevails	TYPE OF		
		Supernatural	FOLKLORE	–	Folk Tales
		Creatures			
		Friendly Animals			

0272 RAMAYANA, THE

Adapted From the English Trans. of Hari Prasad Shastri By Elizabeth Seeger
Illus. Gordon Laite
New York, William R. Scott, Inc., 1969. 244p.

Rama, son of the king of Ayoudhya, is banished from his home by his stepmother's trickery. Sita, his wife, is kidnapped, and with the aid of a tribe of monkeys, he locates her and eventually rightfully inherits his kingdom.

SUBJECTS	–	Reincarnation	COUNTRY	–	India
		Fate			
		Hindu Trinity			
		(Brahma, Vishnu,			
		and Shiva)			
		Obedience			
MOTIFS	–	Magic Objects	TYPE OF		
		Magic Transforma-	FOLKLORE	–	Epics
		tion			
		Religion			
		Legendary Heroes			
		Supernatural			
		Creatures			

0078 RAMINAGROBIS AND THE MICE

Reteller, Harold Berson
Illus. Harold Berson
New York, The Seabury Press, 1965. unp.

Raminagrobis the cat gets in the tower where a family of mice lives and the story begins.

SUBJECTS	– Cat Mouse (Mice)	COUNTRY	– France
MOTIFS	– Talking Animals Wit Prevails Trickery	TYPE OF FOLKLORE	– Folk Tales

0040 RAPUNZEL

By Grimm, The Brothers
Illus. Felix Hoffmann
New York, Harcourt, Brace and Company, First American ed., 1961.
unp.

A childless couple promises a witch their first child. When the child is grown, the witch locks the girl in a tower with no doors. A prince tries to rescue her.

SUBJECTS	– Tower Royalty Witch(es) Childless (Couple) Rapunzel Grimm, The Brothers	COUNTRY	– Germany
MOTIFS	– Supernatural Creatures	TYPE OF FOLKLORE	– Folk Tales

0182 Rich Man and the Shoe-maker, The

By La Fontaine
Illus. Brian Wildsmith
New York, Franklin Watts, Inc., 1965. unp.

Is it better to be poor and happy, or rich and care-worn? The poor but cheerful shoemaker tries both ways and makes a decision.

SUBJECTS	– Gold Shoemaker Character Forming La Fontaine	COUNTRY	– France
MOTIFS	– Humor	TYPE OF FOLKLORE	– Fables

0376 Rip Van Winkle

Reteller, Washington Irving
Illus. Leonard Everett Fisher
New York, Franklin Watts, Inc., 1966. 45p.

While serving drink to strangely dressed men playing ninepins, Rip occasionally takes a drink, falls asleep and doesn't awaken for 18 years. Upon awakening he finds a war is over and his wife and friends are dead.

SUBJECTS	– Rip Van Winkle Sleep Extended Over Many Years New York	COUNTRY	– U.S.–Variants of the Euro- pean Stories

MOTIFS	— Enchanted People Humor Local Legendary Heroes	TYPE OF FOLKLORE — Legends

0521 RIQUET WITH THE TUFT

0309 King Carlo of Capri

Reteller, Warren Miller from Riquet With Tuft-of-Hair By Charles Perrault
Illus. Edward Sorel
New York, Harcourt, Brace and Company, 1958. unp.

The wise wizard casts a spell on the ugly baby Prince Carlo making
him full of generosity and wisdom. And to the woman the prince
will love would go the greatest gift—wisdom and love. Through her
eyes, he becomes the handsomest of men.

SUBJECTS	— Love Royalty Wizard Riquet With the Tuft-of-Hair Perrault, Charles	COUNTRY — France

MOTIFS	— Supernatural Creatures	TYPE OF FOLKLORE — Folk Tales

0325 ROOSTER, MOUSE, AND LITTLE RED HEN, THE

See — 0506 Cock, the Mouse, and the Little Red Hen

0324 ROOSTER, THE MOUSE, AND THE LITTLE RED HEN, THE

See — 0506 Cock, the Mouse, and the Little Red Hen

0287 RUMPELSTILTSKIN

By Grimm, the Brothers
Illus. Jacqueline Ayer
New York, Harcourt, Brace & World, Inc., 1967. unp.

A bragging miller tells the king his daughter can spin gold out of
straw. The king commands the daughter to spin gold. With the help
of a little man she succeeds. As payment she must give him her first
born child if she cannot guess his name.

SUBJECTS	— Name of Helper Discovered Spinning Rumpelstiltskin Grimm, the Brothers	COUNTRY — Germany

MOTIFS	— Supernatural Creatures Fools and Simpletons Humor	TYPE OF FOLKLORE — Folk Tales

See also   0099   **Oniroku and the Carpenter**
            0142   **Tom Tit Tot**

0068 SALT

By Alexei Afanasev, Trans. By Benjamin Zemach, Adapted By Harve
Zemach

Illus. Margot Zemach
Chicago, Follett Publishing Company, 1965. unp.

> Ivan the Fool makes a fortune by bringing salt to a country where it is unknown. His jealous brothers take his wealth and princess and throw him into the sea. With the help of a kind giant he regains everything.

SUBJECTS	–	Royalty Giant(s) Salt	COUNTRY	–	U.S.S.R.
MOTIFS	–	Supernatural Creatures Wit Prevails	TYPE OF FOLKLORE	–	Folk Tales

0252 SERGEANT O'KEEFE AND HIS MULE, BALAAM

Reteller, Harold W. Felton
Illus. Leonard Everett Fisher
New York, Dodd, Mead & Company, 1962. 94p.

> Sgt. John Timothy O'Keefe and his army mule man the Army Signal Corps weather station atop Pikes Peak in 1881. This is based on a true life character.

SUBJECTS	–	Mule (Balaam) Pike's Peak Sergeant O'Keefe Tall Tales	COUNTRY	–	U.S.–Native Tall Tales of Paul Bunyan Variety
MOTIFS	–	Humor Local Legendary Heroes	TYPE OF FOLKLORE	–	Folk Tales

0203 SEVEN RAVENS, THE

By Grimm, the Brothers
Illus. Felix Hoffmann
New York, Harcourt, Brace and World, Inc., First American ed., 1963.
unp.

> When seven brothers fail to return from getting water, they are turned into ravens at their father's wish. Only their sister is able to remove the curse.

SUBJECTS	–	Ravens Glass Mountain Dwarf Love, Selfless Sister Seeks Brothers Grimm, the Brothers	COUNTRY	–	Germany
MOTIFS	–	Magic Objects Magic Transformation Tasks and Trials Supernatural Creatures	TYPE OF FOLKLORE	–	Folk Tales

See also   0057   Wild Swans, The

0172 SEVEN SILLY WISE MEN

Retellers, James Cloyd Bowman and Margery Bianco, Trans. Aili
Kolehmainen
Illus. John Faulkner
Chicago, Albert Whitman & Co., Text 1964, Illus. 1965. unp.

A certain group of Finns are said to deliberate their every move. Their
deliberations lead them into some unusual situations.

SUBJECTS	–	Porridge	COUNTRY	–	Finland
		Grain Harvesting			
		Sunlight Trapped In			
		a Bag, House			

MOTIFS	–	Fools and Simpletons	TYPE OF		
		Humor	FOLKLORE	–	Folk Tales

0066 SEVEN SIMEONS

Reteller, Boris Artzybasheff
Illus. Boris Artzybasheff
New York, The Viking Press, 1937. unp.

King Douda wants to find a princess who is as beautiful as he is
handsome. He employs the Seven Simeon Brothers who use their
talents to find the beautiful princess.

SUBJECTS	–	Royalty	COUNTRY	–	U.S.S.R.
		Tower			
		Cooperation			
		Gun			
		Ship (Magic)			
		Companions (Magic			
		Wisdom Possessed			
		By Extraordinary C.)			

MOTIFS	–	Magic Transformation	TYPE OF		
		Trickery	FOLKLORE	–	Folk Tales
		Wit Prevails			
		Magic Objects			
		Tasks and Trials			

See also	0090	Five Chinese Brothers, The
	0075	Fool of the World and the Flying Ship, The
	0115	Long, Broad and Quickeye
	0039	Four Clever Brothers, The

0037 SHOEMAKER AND THE ELVES, THE

See – 0524 Elves and the Shoemaker

0199 SILLY SIMON

See – 0510 Lazy Jack

0277 SIMON'S SONG

By Mother Goose, Reteller, Barbara Emberley
Illus. Ed Emberley
Englewood Cliffs, N. J., Prentice-Hall, Inc., 1969. unp.

The folksong, based on the nursery rhyme Simple Simon in which
Simon asks to sample the pieman's wares, includes many verses and
music.

SUBJECTS	– Music Simple Simon Mother Goose	COUNTRY	– United Kingdom
MOTIFS	– Humor	TYPE OF FOLKLORE	– Nursery Rhymes

0154 SIR GAWAIN AND THE GREEN KNIGHT

See – 0513 Sir Gawain and the Green Knight

0513 SIR GAWAIN AND THE GREEN KNIGHT

0366 Challenge of the Green Knight, The

Reteller, Ian Serraillier
Illus. Victor G. Ambrus
New York, Henry Z. Walck, Incorporated, 1967. 56p.

New Year's Day festivities are interrupted when a stranger bursts in on King Arthur and his court. The Green Knight challenges the court knights to the beheading game and Gawain accepts.

SUBJECTS	– Knighthood Morgan Le Fay, Sorceress Arthurian Legend Chivalry Christmas Game Green Knight Christianity	COUNTRY	– United Kingdom
MOTIFS	– Supernatural Creatures Tasks and Trials Religion Legendary Heroes	TYPE OF FOLKLORE	– Epics

0154 Sir Gawain and the Green Knight

Reteller, Constance Hieatt
Illus. Walter Lorraine
New York, Thomas Y. Crowell, 1967. unp.

Similar to title no. 0366 Challenge of the Green Knight, The. Christmas season is a time of great festivals at King Arthur's court. Sir Gawain and the Green Knight play a beheading Christmas game. Chivalry and honesty are the winning keys for Sir Gawain.

SUBJECTS	– Chivalry Christmas Game Arthurian Legend Green Knight Morgan Le Fay, Sorceress Knighthood	COUNTRY	– United Kingdom
MOTIFS	– Supernatural Creatures Legendary Heroes Religion Tasks and Trails	TYPE OF FOLKLORE	– Epics

Magic Transforma-
tion

0149 SIX FOOLISH FISHERMEN

Based on Ashton's Chap-book, Reteller, Benjamin Elkin
Illus. Katherine Evans
New York, Children's Press, 1957. unp.

Six brothers, fearing they may drown while fishing, count heads only
to find there are only five of them. Each one forgets to count himself.

SUBJECTS	– Counting Wrong	COUNTRY	– United
	By Not Counting		Kingdom
	Oneself		
	Fisherman (Men)		
MOTIFS	– Humor	TYPE OF	
	Fools and Simpletons	FOLKLORE	– Folk Tales

See also   **0108**   **Nine in a line**

0238 SIX WHO WERE LEFT IN A SHOE

Reteller, Padraic Colum
Illus. Joseph Schindelman
New York, McGraw-Hill Book Company Inc., 1968. unp.

Six animals set out to find another mistress when the old woman who
lives in the shoe leaves them to brush the cobwebs off the sky.

SUBJECTS	– Animals Who Lived	COUNTRY	– United
	In a Shoe		Kingdom
	Loneliness		
MOTIFS	– Humor	TYPE OF	
	Talking Animals	FOLKLORE	– Folk Tales
	Friendly Animals		

0087 SIXTY AT A BLOW

Reteller, Christine Price
Illus. Christine Price
New York, E. P. Dutton & Co., Inc., 1968. 48p.

Mocked by his wife for his timidity, Mustafa kills 60 in a swarm of
flies with a single sweep of his knife. A second sweep kills 70 and he
confidently sets out to seek his fortune.

SUBJECTS	– Knife	COUNTRY	– Turkey
	Giant(s)		
	Tall Tales		
	Fly (Flies)		
MOTIFS	– Wit Prevails	TYPE OF	
	Humor	FOLKLORE	– Folk Tales
	Tasks and Trials		
	Supernatural		
	Creatures		
	Fools and Simpletons		

See also   **0013**   **Valiant Tailor, The**

0303 SLAPPY HOOPER THE WONDERFUL SIGN PAINTER

Retellers, Arna Bontemps and Jack Conroy
Illus. Ursula Koering
Boston, Houghton Mifflin Company, 1946. 44p.

Slappy Hooper is such a good painter that whatever he paints appears very real. Unfortunately, it causes him many problems.

SUBJECTS	–	Tall Tales Slappy Hooper, Sign Painter	COUNTRY	–	U.S.–Native Tall Tales of the Paul Bunyan Variety
MOTIFS	–	Humor Local Legendary Heroes	TYPE OF FOLKLORE	–	Folk Tales

0563 SLEEPING BEAUTY

0029 Sleeping Beauty, The

By Grimm, the Brothers
Illus. Felix Hoffmann
N. Y., Harcourt, Brace and World, 1959. First American ed., 1960. unp.

All the fairies of the court wish the newly born princess well but for one who wishes her death. One of the fairies counteracts the spell. The girl sleeps for one hundred years and is awakened by a prince who marries her.

SUBJECTS	–	Spindle Wise Women Frog Grimm, the Brothers	COUNTRY	–	Germany
MOTIFS	–	Magic Objects Supernatural Creatures Enchanted People	TYPE OF FOLKLORE	–	Folk Tales

0030 Sleeping Beauty, The

By Charles Perrault, Reteller, Warren Chappell
Illus. Warren Chappell
New York, Alfred A. Knopf, 1961. unp.

Similar to title no. 0029 Sleeping Beauty, The.

SUBJECTS	–	Ballet Dwarf Fairy Boots, Magic Royalty Music Perrault, Charles	COUNTRY	–	France
MOTIFS	–	Magic Objects Supernatural Creatures Enchanted People	TYPE OF FOLKLORE	–	Folk Tales

0030 SLEEPING BEAUTY, THE

See – 0563 Sleeping Beauty

0029 SLEEPING BEAUTY, THE

See — 0563 Sleeping Beauty

0166 SNOW AND THE SUN, THE

Reteller, Antonio Frasconi
Illus. Antonio Frasconi
New York, Harcourt, Brace & World, Inc., 1961. unp.

This cumulative tale begins when the man, whose feet are hurt by snow, corrals the ox.

SUBJECTS	—	Cumulative Tale	COUNTRY	—	South America
		Chain Tale			
		Snow			
		Formula Tale			
MOTIFS	—	Humor	TYPE OF		
		Talking Animals	FOLKLORE	—	Nursery Rhymes

0049 SNOW QUEEN, THE

By Hans Christian Andersen, Trans. R. P. Keigwin
Illus. June Atkin Corwin
New York, Atheneum, 1968. 95p.

One day a bit of the Snow Queen's magic mirror, broken by imps, lodges in Kay's eye and heart. He can no longer see the good and true. Carried away by the wicked queen, he is rescued by his friend Gerda.

SUBJECTS	—	Christianity	COUNTRY	—	Denmark
		Snow Queen			
		Gerda and Kay			
		Escape the Snow Queen			
		Loyalty			
		Andersen, Hans Christian			
MOTIFS	—	Magic Objects	TYPE OF		
		Supernatural Creatures	FOLKLORE	—	Folk Tales
		Talking Animals			

0397 SNOW QUEEN, THE

By Hans Christian Andersen, Reteller, Naomi Lewis
Illus. Toma Bogdanovic
New York, Scroll Press, Inc., First American ed., 1968. unp.

The Snow Queen has Kay attach his sled to hers, and they glide to her home beyond Lapland and Finland. Kay's friend Gerda searches for him and finally is able to break the Snow Queen's spell.

SUBJECTS	—	Christianity	COUNTRY	—	Denmark
		Snow Queen			
		Gerda and Kay			
		Escape the Snow Queen			
		Loyalty			
		Andersen, Hans Christian			

MOTIFS	–	Religion Supernatural Creatures Friendly Animals	TYPE OF FOLKLORE	– Folk Tales

0560 SNOW WHITE AND ROSE RED

0008 Snow-White and Rose-Red

By Grimm, the Brothers, Reteller, Barbara Cooney
Illus. Barbara Cooney
New York, Delacorte Press, 1965. 47p.

Two sisters and their mother befriend a bear. They also help a dwarf who never appreciates it. The bear kills the dwarf and breaks the spell cast on him.

SUBJECTS	–	Kindness Sharing Dwarf Bear(s) Prince Trans. Into Bear Grimm, the Brothers	COUNTRY	– Germany

MOTIFS	–	Supernatural
		  Creatures
		Magic Transforma-
		  tion
		Talking Animals
			TYPE OF
			FOLKLORE
				– Folk Tales

0006 Snow White and Rose Red

By Grimm, the Brothers
Illus. Adrienne Adams
New York, Charles Scribner's Sons, 1964. unp.

Similar to title no. 0008 Snow-White and Rose-Red. Different illus.

SUBJECTS	–	Kindness Sharing Dwarf Bear(s) Prince Transf. Into Bear Grimm, the Brothers	COUNTRY	– Germany

MOTIFS	–	Supernatural
		  Creatures
		Magic Transforma-
		  tion
		Talking Animals
			TYPE OF
			FOLKLORE
				– Folk Tales

0006 SNOW WHITE AND ROSE RED

See – 0560 Snow White and Rose Red

0008 SNOW-WHITE AND ROSE-RED

See – 0560 Snow White and Rose Red

0036 SNOW WHITE AND THE SEVEN DWARFS

By Grimm, the Brothers, Trans. Wanda Gag
Illus. Wanda Gag
New York, Coward-McCann, Inc., 1938. 43p.

Jealous of Snow White's beauty, a wicked queen attempts to destroy her. Seven dwarfs try to protect her. In the end a prince saves and marries her.

SUBJECTS	–	Witch(es)	COUNTRY	–	Germany
		Mirror			
		Royalty			
		Apple			
		Dwarf			
		Grimm, the Brothers			
MOTIFS	–	Magic Objects	TYPE OF		
		Enchanted People	FOLKLORE	–	Folk Tales
		Supernatural			
		Creatures			

0135 SORCERER'S APPRENTICE

See – 0564 Sorcerer's Apprentice

0564 SORCERER'S APPRENTICE

0134 Sorcerer's Apprentice, The

Reteller, Richard Rostron
Illus. Frank Lieberman
New York, William Morrow and Company, 1941. unp.

The sorcerer's apprentice is tempted to try magic which is more exciting than the menial tasks he is assigned to do. One trick results in a catastrophe. Chaos rules until the sorcerer returns.

SUBJECTS	–	Apprentice	COUNTRY	–	Germany
		Broom			
		Sorcerer(s)			
		Switzerland			
MOTIFS	–	Magic Objects	TYPE OF		
		Supernatural	FOLKLORE	–	Folk Tales
		Creatures			
		Humor			

0135 Sorcerer's Apprentice

Reteller, Donald E. Cooke
Illus. Donald E. Cooke
Philadelphia, The John C. Winston Company, 1947. 56p.

Similar to title no. 0134 Sorcerer's Apprentice, The.

SUBJECTS	–	Apprentice	COUNTRY	–	Germany
		Broom			
		Sorcerer(s)			
MOTIFS	–	Magic Objects	TYPE OF		
		Supernatural	FOLKLORE	–	Folk Tales
		Creatures			
		Humor			

0269 Sorcerer's Apprentice, The

Reteller, Lisl Weil
Illus. Lisl Weil
Boston, Little, Brown and Company, 1962. 32p.

The ending is different from title no. 0134 Sorcerer's Apprentice, and title no. 0135 Sorcerer's Apprentice. In these two stories the Apprentice is sent away. In title no. 0269 Sorcerer's Apprentice, the Apprentice stays.

SUBJECTS — Apprentice Broom Sorcerer(s)	COUNTRY — Germany
MOTIFS — Magic Objects Supernatural Creatures Humor	TYPE OF FOLKLORE — Folk Tales

0134 SORCERER'S APPRENTICE, THE

See — 0564 Sorcerer's Apprentice

0269 SORCERER'S APPRENTICE, THE

See — 0564 Sorcerer's Apprentice

0069 SPECKLED HEN

Adapted by Harve Zemach
Illus. Margot Zemach
New York, Holt, Rinehart and Winston, 1966. unp.

A speckled egg laid by a little speckled hen causes window panes to shatter, geese to scatter, water buckets to spill, and the father of the family to stand on his head in a haystack.

SUBJECTS — Formula Tale Chain Tale Cumulative Tale Egg(s)	COUNTRY — U.S.S.R.
MOTIFS — Humor Fools and Simpletons	TYPE OF FOLKLORE — Nursery Rhymes

0155 ST. GEORGE AND THE DRAGON

Adapted and Retold By Alice Dalgliesh
Illus. Lois Maloy
New York, Charles Scribner's Sons, 1941. unp.

George is kidnapped by the evil enchantress Kalyb but she shares her magic powers with him. With them St. George destroys the dragon and wins the hand of the King of Egypt's daughter.

SUBJECTS — Christianity Egypt Dragon Knighthood Chivalry Sorceress Saints	COUNTRY — United Kingdom
MOTIFS — Legendary Heroes Tasks and Trials Magic Objects Supernatural Creatures Religion	TYPE OF FOLKLORE — Legends

0089 STARGAZER TO THE SULTAN

Retellers, Barbara K. Walker and Mine Sumer

Illus. Joseph Low
New York, Parents' Magazine Press, 1967. unp.

A humble woodcutter who wants no more than a roof over his head, a bit of food and the blessings of Allah, is driven by his wife to aspire to the position of stargazer to the Sultan.

SUBJECTS	– Prophesying	COUNTRY	– Turkey
	Theft		
	Woodcutter		
	Greediness		

MOTIFS	– Humor	TYPE OF	
	Wit Prevails	FOLKLORE	– Folk Tales

0056 STEADFAST TIN SOLDIER, THE

By Hans Christian Andersen, Trans. M. R. James
Illus. Marcia Brown
New York, Charles Scribner's Sons, 1953. unp.

For his birthday a little boy gets a box of tin soldiers, one of which has only one leg. This soldier falls in love with a toy ballerina. After surviving many difficulties, the soldier is reunited with the dancer. However, the story ends in sadness.

SUBJECTS	– Ballet Dancer	COUNTRY	– Denmark
	Soldier(s)		
	Andersen, Hans		
	Christian		

MOTIFS	– Magic Objects	TYPE OF	
		FOLKLORE	– Folk Tales

0016 STEEL DRIVING MAN, THE LEGEND OF JOHN HENRY

See – 0544 John Henry

0328 STEEL FLEA, THE

Retellers, Babette Deutsch and Avrahm Yarmolinsky
Illus. Janina Domanska
New York, Harper & Row, Publishers, Rev. Ed. 1964. 56p.

When the Russians defeat Napoleon, the Emperor takes his Chief Platov visiting. The English show him a microscopic steel dancing flea. Russian gunsmiths in turn do the English one better by providing shoes for the flea.

SUBJECTS	– English	COUNTRY	– U.S.S.R.
	Flea		
	Nationalism		
	Originality		
	Russians		

MOTIFS	– Humor	TYPE OF	
	Realistic Events	FOLKLORE	– Folk Tales

0118 STOLEN NECKLACE, THE

Reteller, Anne Rockwell
Illus. Anne Rockwell
New York, The World Publishing Company, 1968. unp.

Based on a tale from the Jataka, a collection of stories over 2,000 years old, this amusing story tells how a vain little monkey is caught after he steals a pearl necklace from a princess.

SUBJECTS	—	Buddha as Gardener	COUNTRY	—	India
		Jataka			
		Monkey			
		Necklace			
		Stealing			
		Vanity			

MOTIFS	—	Religion	TYPE OF		
		Talking Animals	FOLKLORE	—	Folk Tales
		Trickery			
		Wit Prevails			
		Humor			

0028 STONE SOUP, AN OLD TALE

Reteller, Marcia Brown
Illus. Marcia Brown
New York, Charles Scribner's Sons, 1947. unp.

Three weary soldiers are turned away by everyone they approach for food and lodging. By using their wits the soldiers entice the villagers into sharing with each other. Their solution is to make stone soup.

SUBJECTS	—	Soldier(s)	COUNTRY	—	France
		Friendship			
		Cooperation			
		Soup			

| MOTIFS | — | Wit Prevails | TYPE OF | | |
| | | Humor | FOLKLORE | — | Folk Tales |

See also **0027**   **Nail Soup**

0561 STORMALONG

0326 How Old Stormalong Captured Mocha Dick

Reteller, Irwin Shapiro
Illus. Donald McKay
Eau Claire, Wisconsin, E. M. Hale and Company, 1942. 48p.

When Stormalong fails to capture the great white whale, he tries farming and ranching. Finally he returns to the sea and is successful.

SUBJECTS	—	New England	COUNTRY	—	U.S.–Native
		Nantucket Whalers			Tall Tales of
		Stormalong			the Paul Bun-
		Sailor			yan Variety
		Tall Tales			
		Whale			

MOTIFS	—	Humor	TYPE OF		
		Local Legendary	FOLKLORE	—	Folk Tales
		Heroes			

0389 STORY OF JOHNNY APPLESEED

Reteller, Aliki

Illus. Aliki
Englewood Cliffs, N. J., Prentice-Hall, 1963. unp.

Johnny Chapman carries a large sack full of appleseeds and his cook pan when he goes west. He plants the seeds everywhere and becomes friends with the Indians, settlers, and animals in the forest.

SUBJECTS	–	Johnny Appleseed Frontier and Pioneer Life	COUNTRY	–	U.S.–Native Tall Tales of the Paul Bunyan Variety
MOTIFS	–	Local Legendary Heroes Friendly Animals	TYPE OF FOLKLORE	–	Legends

0379 STORY, A STORY, A

Reteller, Gail E. Haley
Illus. Gail E. Haley
New York, Atheneum, 1970. unp.

Ananse, the spider man, meets the tasks required to buy the stories for children belonging to Nyame, the sky god. When he gets back with the box containing the stories, he opens it and they scatter over all the earth.

SUBJECTS	–	Ananse Bargains With Sky God Ladder to Heaven Made of Spider Web Sky God Invisibility	COUNTRY	–	Africa
MOTIFS	–	Tasks and Trials Pourquoi Stories Humor Wit Prevails Religion	TYPE OF FOLKLORE	–	Folk Tales

0054 SUCH IS THE WAY OF THE WORLD

Reteller, Benjamin Elkin
Illus. Yoko Mitsuhashi
New York, Parents' Magazine Press, 1968. unp.

A chain tale is started when Desta loses his monkey when a dog chases it up a tree. Then begins a series of exchanges–dog–gameboard –pot–feathers–knife–rope–and finally spear–for monkey.

SUBJECTS	–	Chain Tale Formula Tale Monkey Cumulative Tale	COUNTRY	–	Ethiopia
MOTIFS	–	Fools and Simpletons Humor	TYPE OF FOLKLORE	–	Folk Tales

0086 SUHO AND THE WHITE HORSE

By Yuzo Otsuka, Trans. Yasuko Hirawa
Illus. Suekichi Akaba
New York, Bobbs-Merrill Company, Inc., 1969. unp.

Suho, a shepherd, raises a horse. The governor offers his daughter's hand in marriage to the winner of a great race, but when Suho wins, he is not only deprived of his rightful prize, but of his horse as well. It is the origin of the horse-head fiddle.

SUBJECTS	– Horse	COUNTRY	– Mongolian
	Horse-Head Fiddle		People's
	Cruelty		Republic
	Governor		
	Shepherd(s)		

MOTIFS	– Realistic Events	TYPE OF	
	Pourquoi Stories	FOLKLORE –	Folk Tales

0131 SUNDIATA, THE EPIC OF THE LION KING

Reteller, Roland Bertol
Illus. Gregorio Prestopino
New York, Thomas Y. Crowell Company, 1970. 81p.

Ugly, crippled baby Sundiata, Sword of Islam, rises to challenge the accursed Sumanguru and becomes the reknown king of Mali. completing a prophecy foretold during the 13th century.

SUBJECTS	– Afreets–Demons	COUNTRY	– Mali
	Allah		
	Djinns		
	Dwarf		
	Sorcerer(s)		
	Soothsayer		

MOTIFS	– Supernatural	TYPE OF	
	Creatures	FOLKLORE –	Epics
	Religion		
	Magic Transforma-		
	tion		
	Magic Objects		

0262 SWAPPING BOY, THE

Reteller, John Langstaff
Illus. Beth and Joe Krush
New York, Harcourt, Brace & World, Inc., 1960. unp.

This is an Appalachian Mountain trading song. Swapping Boy trades wheelbarrow for mare, for cow, for calf, for mule, for sheep, for goat, for pig, for hen, for cat, for mole respectively.

SUBJECTS	– Appalachian Moun-	COUNTRY	– U.S.–Folk-
	tain Song		songs
	Chain Tale		
	Trading (Swapping		
	Song)		
	Music		
	Cumulative Tale		
	Formula Tale		

MOTIFS	– Humor	TYPE OF	
		FOLKLORE –	Folk Songs,
			Ballads

0055 SWINEHERD, THE

By Hans Christian Andersen, Trans. Erik Blegvad
Illus. Erik Blegvad
New York, Harcourt, Brace and Company, 1958. 32p.

> When the prince offers simple gifts to the princess, she refuses. However, she gladly gives kisses to the swineherd, the disguised prince, for a magic pot and musical instrument. Because of her choice the prince will not marry her.

SUBJECTS	– Royalty	COUNTRY	– Denmark
	Snobbery		
	Andersen, Hans		
	Christian		
	Character Forming		
	Courtship		
	Swineherds		

MOTIFS	– Trickery	TYPE OF	
	Magic Objects	FOLKLORE	– Folk Tales

See also   **0095**   **King Thrushbeard**
           0042   **King Thrushbeard**

0286 SWORD OF SIEGFRIED, THE

Reteller, Katherine Scherman
Illus. Douglas Gorsline
New York, Random House, 1959. 51p.

> Siegfried is unbeatable in battle with the sword forged from parts of one given to his father by Odin, greatest of the Norse gods. He is killed, however, by Hagen after coming out from under a spell.

SUBJECTS	– Siegfried	COUNTRY	– Germany
	Dragon		
	Gods		
	Fate		
	Brynhild		
	Norsemen		
	Odin		
	Vikings		

MOTIFS	– Magic Objects	TYPE OF	
	Enchanted People	FOLKLORE	– Epics
	Legendary Heroes		
	Religion		
	Supernatural		
	Creatures		

0177 TALE OF A PIG

Adapted by Wallace Tripp
Illus. Wallace Tripp
New York, McGraw-Hill Book Company, 1968. 32p.

> The prince is astonished to see the pig picking berries turn into a pretty maiden. He persuades the woodsman to sell the pig and he marries her.

SUBJECTS	– Childless (Couple)	COUNTRY	– U.S.S.R.
	Pig(s)		
	Royalty		
	Woodcutter		

MOTIFS	–	Humor	TYPE OF
		Magic Transforma- tion	FOLKLORE – Folk Tales
		Supernatural Creatures	
		Friendly Animals	

0067 TALE OF STOLEN TIME, A

Reteller, Evgeny Schwartz, Trans. Lila Pargment and Estelle Titiev
Illus. Nonny Hogrogian
Englewood Cliffs, N. J., Prentice-Hall, 1966. unp.

> Four sorcerers steal time from children so they can be young. Suddenly time becomes important to the children who try to regain their stolen years.

SUBJECTS	–	Cooperation	COUNTRY – U.S.S.R.
		Clock	
		Sorcerer(s)	
		Time	

MOTIFS	–	Magic Objects	TYPE OF
		Supernatural Creatures	FOLKLORE – Folk Tales
		Magic Transforma- tion	
		Tasks and Trials	

0514 TALIESEN

0372 Taliesin and King Arthur

Reteller, Ruth Robbins
Illus. Ruth Robbins
Berkeley, California, Parnassus Press, 1970. unp.

> Taliesen, a famous poet in Welsh legend, wins the contest of the bards at King Arthur's court. He wins by singing the riddle of his birth.

SUBJECTS	–	Arthurian Legend	COUNTRY – United
		Christmas	Kingdom
		Herb Enchantment	
		Taliesin, Poet	

MOTIFS	–	Legendary Heroes	TYPE OF
		Magic Objects	FOLKLORE – Epics
		Magic Transforma- tion	

0372 TALIESIN AND KING ARTHUR

See – 0514 Taliesen

0539 THESEUS

0046 Way of Danger: The Story of Theseus, The

Reteller, Ian Serraillier
Illus. Nonny Hogrogian
New York, Henry Z. Walck, Inc., 1963. 86p.

> This is the story of Theseus' triumphs and his rise to greatness as the far-sighted ruler of Athens, his later misfortunes and unmourned death in exile.

SUBJECTS	– Gods Courage Fate	COUNTRY	– Greece
MOTIFS	– Enchanted People Tasks and Trials Wit Prevails Religion Supernatural Creatures	TYPE OF FOLKLORE	– Myths

0215 THIEVING DWARFS, THE

Reteller, Mary Calhoun
Illus. Janet McCaffery
New York, William Morrow & Company, 1967. unp.

In German dwarf lore, Karl the farmer finds a way to stop the invisible dwarfs from stealing his wheat and begins a long friendship with them.

SUBJECTS	– Theft Dwarf Friendship Invisibility	COUNTRY	– Germany
MOTIFS	– Supernatural Creatures Trickery Wit Prevails Magic Objects Humor	TYPE OF FOLKLORE	– Folk Tales

0151 THIRTEEN DAYS OF YULE, THE

Author, Anonymous
Illus. Nonny Hogrogian
New York, Thomas Y. Crowell Company, 1968. unp.

In this Scottish version of The Twelve Days of Christmas, the King sends his lady three of everything. Music is included.

SUBJECTS	– Cumulative Tale Chain Tale Christmas Counting Music Formula Tale	COUNTRY	– United Kingdom
MOTIFS	– Humor	TYPE OF FOLKLORE	– Folk Songs, Ballads

0132 THIRTY GILT PENNIES, THE

Reteller, Alice Geer Kelsey
Illus. Gordon Laite
New York, Abington Press, 1968. 64p.

The money which was given to the Christ Child becomes the link in the chain connecting the old testament and new testament history. The final figure touched is Judas as he receives the thirty pieces of silver for betraying Christ.

SUBJECTS   –   Middle East   COUNTRY – Germany
Christmas
Astrologer
Christ
Judas
New Testament
Old Testament
Thirty Pieces of
  Silver (Gold)

MOTIFS   –   Religion   TYPE OF
FOLKLORE – Legends

0263 THOUSAND AND ONE BUDDHAS, A

Reteller, Louise Lee Floethe
Illus. Richard Floethe
New York, Farrar, Straus & Giroux, 1967. unp.

In the year 1164 the Emperor of Japan built a beautiful temple
to Buddha in the hope of inspiring his countrymen to live in peace.
The temple of a thousand and one buddhas in Kyoto still stands.

SUBJECTS   –   Buddha as Gardener   COUNTRY – Japan
Peace
War

MOTIFS   –   Supernatural   TYPE OF
               Creatures   FOLKLORE – Legends
               Religion

0515 THREE BEARS

0212 Three Bears, The Story of

Reteller, Eleanor Mure
Illus. Eleanor Mure
New York, Henry Z. Walch, Inc., 1967. unp.

A nosey old woman searches the three bears' house while they are
out. Catching her they are unable to burn or drown her so they
throw her to the top of St. Paul Church Steeple.

SUBJECTS   –   Bear(s)   COUNTRY – United
Old Woman   Kingdom

MOTIFS   –   Talking Animals   TYPE OF
FOLKLORE – Folk Tales

0137 Three Bears, The Story of

Reteller, William Stobbs
Illus. William Stobbs
N. Y., Whittlesey House, McGraw-Hill Book Co., 1st American ed.,
1965. 32p.

While the three bears are out, Goldilocks enters their home. She
tastes their porridge, tries their chairs and their beds. The bears return to find her asleep. She flees never to return again.

SUBJECTS   –   Bear(s)   COUNTRY – United
Goldilocks   Kingdom

MOTIFS   –   Talking Animals   TYPE OF
FOLKLORE – Folk Tales

0233 Three Bears, The Story of

Author Unknown
Illus. Leslie Brooks
New York, Frederick Warne & Co., Ltd., 1904. unp.

> Similar to title no. 0137 Three Bears, The Story of.

SUBJECTS	– Bear(s) Goldilocks	COUNTRY	– United Kingdom

MOTIFS	– Talking Animals

0137 THREE BEARS, THE STORY OF

See – 0515 Three Bears

0212 THREE BEARS, THE STORY OF

See – 0515 Three Bears

0233 THREE BEARS, THE STORY OF

See – 0515 Three Bears

0548 THREE BILLY GOATS GRUFF

0200 Three Billy Goats Gruff, The

By P. C. Asbjornsen and J. E. Moe, Trans. G. W. Dasent, Reteller, Marcia Brown
Illus. Marcia Brown
New York, Harcourt, Brace & World, Inc., 1957. unp.

> Three billy goats gruff cross a bridge every day to go to their grazing ground. A troll threatens the first two billy goats. However, the troll is no match for the biggest billy goat.

SUBJECTS	– Goat(s) Troll Asbjornsen, P. C. and Moe, J. E.	COUNTRY	– Norway

MOTIFS	– Humor Supernatural Creatures Talking Animals	TYPE OF FOLKLORE	– Folk Tales

0214 Three Billy Goats Gruff, The

By P. C. Asbjornsen and J. E. Moe, Reteller, William Stobbs
Illus. William Stobbs
New York, McGraw-Hill Book Company, First American Edition, 1968. unp.

> Similar to title no. 0200 Three Billy Goats Gruff, The. Different illus.

SUBJECTS	– Goat(s) Troll Asbjornsen, P. C. and Moe, J. E.	COUNTRY	– Norway

MOTIFS	– Humor Supernatural Creatures Talking Animals	TYPE OF FOLKLORE	– Folk Tales

0200 THREE BILLY GOATS GRUFF, THE
See – 0548 Three Billy Goats Gruff

0214 THREE BILLY GOATS GRUFF, THE
See – 0548 Three Billy Goats Gruff

0400 THREE BROTHERS, THE
Reteller, Mollie Clarke
Illus. William Stobbs
New York, Follett Publishing Company, 1965. 32p.

Three brothers are granted their wishes when they offer an old woman two pears, but when she returns to ask for some food and is refused by two of the brothers, those two lose their wishes. The youngest son's wife is rewarded when she shows kindness to the old woman.

SUBJECTS	– Wishes, Brothers Given Three W. Woman, Old W. With Magic Powers Kindness Serbia	COUNTRY	– Yugoslavia

MOTIFS	– Wishes Supernatural Creatures Magic Transformation	TYPE OF FOLKLORE	– Folk Tales

0112 THREE FEATHERS, THE
Reteller, Mollie Clarke
Illus. Graham Oakley
New York, Follett Publishing Company, First American ed., 1968. 32p.

To decide who shall get his kingdom, the king throws three feathers in the air and tells his three sons to each follow the feathers and perform a task.

SUBJECTS	– Carpet Frog Ring (From the Sea) Royalty	COUNTRY	– Germany

MOTIFS	– Supernatural Creatures Talking Animals Tasks and Trials Magic Transformation Friendly Animals	TYPE OF FOLKLORE	– Folk Tales

0189 THREE GOLD PIECES
Reteller, Aliki
Illus. Aliki
New York, Pantheon Books, 1967. unp.

A poor man is given his wages of three gold pieces after 10 years of work but exchanges them for advice which enables him to live happily every after.

SUBJECTS — Advice (Counsel–   COUNTRY — Greece
                    Precept)
                  Gold Pieces
                  Poverty
                  Earthquake

MOTIFS   — Realistic Events   TYPE OF
                  Nature Calamities   FOLKLORE — Folk Tales

0516 THREE LITTLE PIGS

0147 Three Little Pigs, The Story of the

By J. O. Halliwell, Reteller, William Stobbs
Illus. William Stobbs
New York, McGraw-Hill Book Company, 1965. unp.

> The three little pigs each build a house. The wolf blows down the
> houses of the first two and eats them but he is unable to destroy
> the brick house of the third. He is killed when he tries to trick the
> little pig.

SUBJECTS — Pigs Build Houses   COUNTRY — United
                  Wolf   Kingdom

MOTIFS   — Talking Animals   TYPE OF
                  Trickery   FOLKLORE — Folk Tales
                  Wit Prevails

0223 Three Little Pigs, The

Reteller, Paul Galdone
Illus. Paul Galdone
New York, The Seabury Press, 1970. unp.

> Similar to title no. 0147 Three Little Pigs, The Story of the.

SUBJECTS — Pigs Build Houses   COUNTRY — United
                  Wolf   Kingdom

MOTIFS   — Talking Animals   TYPE OF
                  Trickery   FOLKLORE — Folk Tales
                  Wit Prevails

0234 Three Little Pigs, The Story of the

Author Unknown
Illus. Leslie Brooke
New York, Frederick Warne & Co. Ltd., 1904. unp.

> Similar to title no. 0147 Three Little Pigs, The Story of the.

SUBJECTS — Pigs Build Houses   COUNTRY — United
                  Wolf   Kingdom

MOTIFS   — Talking Animals   TYPE OF
                  Trickery   FOLKLORE — Folk Tales
                  Wit Prevails

0224 Three Little Pigs, The

Author, Unknown
Illus. William Pene Du Bois
New York, The Viking Press, 1962. 32p.

Similar to title no. 0147 Three Little Pigs, The Story of the. This version is in verse.

SUBJECTS – Pigs Build Houses   COUNTRY – United
                Wolf   Kingdom

MOTIFS – Talking Animals   TYPE OF
            Trickery   FOLKLORE – Folk Tales
            Wit Prevails

0224 THREE LITTLE PIGS

See – 0516 Three Little Pigs

0223 THREE LITTLE PIGS, THE

See – 0516 Three Little Pigs

0234 THREE LITTLE PIGS, THE STORY OF THE

See – 0516 Three Little Pigs

0147 THREE LITTLE PIGS, THE STORY OF THE

See – 0516 Three Little Pigs

0161 THREE POOR TAILORS, THE

Reteller, Victor G. Ambrus
Illus. Victor G. Ambrus
New York, Harcourt, Brace & World, Inc., First American ed., 1966. unp.

Three naive tailors beat a hasty retreat when they find they have no money to pay the innkeeper's bill.

SUBJECTS – Goat(s)   COUNTRY – Hungary
              Tailor(s)

MOTIFS – Humor   TYPE OF
            Fools and Simpletons   FOLKLORE – Folk Tales

0001 THREE SILLIES, THE

By Joseph Jacobs
Illus. Margot Zemach
New York, Holt, Rinehart and Winston, 1963. unp.

While drawing beer, the poor couple's daughter predicts that if she has a son he might be killed by an ax on the ceiling when he goes to draw beer. Her suitor says he will not marry her until he finds three people as silly as she. He finds them.

SUBJECTS – Cow   COUNTRY – United
              Moon   Kingdom
              Trousers
              Jacobs, Joseph

MOTIFS – Humor   TYPE OF
            Fools and Simpletons   FOLKLORE – Folk Tales

See also **0002** **Jack and the Three Sillies**

0101 THREE STRONG WOMEN

Reteller, Claus Stamm

Illus. Kazue Mizumura
New York, Viking Press, 1962. 47p.

A daughter, mother, and grandmother teach a strong wrestler a thing or two before he goes to a wrestling contest at court. It was easy for the women to pick up a tree and toss it over a mountain.

SUBJECTS	–	Boasting Tall Tales Contest (Wrestling)	COUNTRY	–	Japan
MOTIFS	–	Humor Local Legendary Heroes	TYPE OF FOLKLORE	–	Folk Tales

0148 THREE WISHES, THE

Adapted By Joseph Jacobs
Illus. Paul Galdone
N. Y., McGraw-Hill Book Company, Whittlesey House, 1961. 32p.

A fairy promises a woodcutter three wishes for not cutting down a giant tree. His first wish for a sausage infuriates his wife who wishes the sausage on his nose. It is removed with the third wish.

SUBJECTS	–	Fairy Woodcutter Jacobs, Joseph Wishes, Woodcutter Given Three W.	COUNTRY	–	United Kingdom
MOTIFS	–	Wishes Humor Fools and Simpletons	TYPE OF FOLKLORE	–	Folk Tales

0048 THUMBELINA

By Hans Christian Andersen, Trans. R. P. Keigwin
Illus. Adrienne Adams
New York, Charles Scribner's Sons, 1961. unp.

Thumbelina is an inch tall girl who has many adventures. She is nearly married to a toad and a mole. Through the help of a bird she befriends she meets the King Guardian Spirit of the flowers and marries him.

SUBJECTS	–	Flower King Little People Witch(es) Swallows Thumbelina Andersen, Hans Christian	COUNTRY	–	Denmark
MOTIFS	–	Magic Transforma- tion Talking Animals Wit Prevails	TYPE OF FOLKLORE	–	Folk Tales

0394 THUMBELINA

By Hans Christian Andersen, Reteller, Paul Leyssac
Illus. Oscar Fabres
New York, The Hyperion Press, 1943. unp.

Similar to title no. 0048 Thumbelina.

SUBJECTS	– Thumbelina Little People Flower King Witch(es) Swallows Andersen, Hans Christian	COUNTRY	– Denmark
MOTIFS	– Magic Transforma- tion Talking Animals Wit Prevails	TYPE OF FOLKLORE	– Folk Tales

0119 TIGER, THE BRAHMAN, AND THE JACKAL, THE

See – 0541 Brahman

0102 TIKKI TIKKI TEMBO

Reteller, Arlene Mosel
Illus. Blair Lent
New York, Holt, Rinehart and Winston, 1968. unp.

This is a humorous tale of how the Chinese came to give all their children short names. Two mischievous brothers convince the ancient Chinese that grand names can be very dangerous indeed.

SUBJECTS	– Well Name Choosing	COUNTRY	– China (Mainland)
MOTIFS	– Humor Pourquoi Stories Realistic Events	TYPE OF FOLKLORE	– Folk Tales

0210 TIKTA'LIKTAK, AN ESKIMO LEGEND

Reteller, James Houston
Illus. James Houston
New York, Harcourt, Brace & World, Inc., 1965. 63p.

Tikta'Liktak, an eskimo hunter, is carried to sea one day on an ice floe. He never expects to see home again but he shows great courage against the grim realities of survival.

SUBJECTS	– Eskimos Arctic Animals Night Spirits Sea Spirits Survival	COUNTRY	– North America
MOTIFS	– Religion Realistic Events Legendary Heroes	TYPE OF FOLKLORE	– Legends

0184 TIMIMOTO'S GREAT ADVENTURES

Reteller, Frank Francis
Illus. Frank Francis
New York, Holiday House, 1969. unp.

Four inches tall, but of great wit, Timimoto attacks the terrifying ogre who carries off everyone in his sight. No magic exists as in title no. 0091, Issun Boshi: The Inchlins.

SUBJECTS	– Little People Ogre	COUNTRY	– Japan
MOTIFS	– Supernatural Creatures Wit Prevails	TYPE OF FOLKLORE	– Folk Tales

0247 TINDER BOX, THE

By Hans Christian Andersen
Illus. Cyril Satorsky
Englewood Cliffs, N. J., Prentice-Hall, Inc., 1970. unp.

A witch asks a soldier to retrieve a magic tinderbox from under a tree. He kills the witch and keeps the tinderbox. He uses its power to marry the princess.

SUBJECTS	– Candle (Magic) Dream(s) Dog(s) Royalty Soldier(s) Tinder Box (Magic) Witch(es) Andersen, Hans Christian	COUNTRY	– Denmark
MOTIFS	– Wit Prevails Magic Objects Supernatural Creatures	TYPE OF FOLKLORE	– Folk Tales

0230 TOM THUMB

See – 0517 Tom Thumb

0517 TOM THUMB

0280 Diverting Adventures of Tom Thumb, The

Reteller, Barry Wilkinson
Illus. Barry Wilkinson
New York, Harcourt, Brace and World, Inc., First American ed., 1969. 29p.

Disguised as a beggar, Merlin the Magician is treated kindly by a childless couple. In return he grants them a child as big as a thumb. The child's size gets him into many predicaments.

SUBJECTS	– Little People King Arthur Childless (Couple) Merlin, Magician Tom Thumb	COUNTRY	– United Kingdom
MOTIFS	– Humor Magic Transforma- tion Supernatural Creatures	TYPE OF FOLKLORE	– Folk Tales

STORIES BY TITLE

0230 Tom Thumb

Author Unknown
Illus. Leslie Brooke
New York, Frederick Warne & Co. Ltd., n.d. unp.

Merlin the Magician grants a couple their wish for a child. The child's size gets him into many predicaments. He spends most of his life at King Arthur's court in this version.

SUBJECTS	–	Little People	COUNTRY	–	United
		Elves			Kingdom
		Giant(s)			
		King Arthur			
		Merlin, Magician			
		Tom Thumb			

MOTIFS	–	Supernatural	TYPE OF		
		Creatures	FOLKLORE	–	Folk Tales
		Humor			
		Magic Transformation			

0142 TOM TIT TOT

By Joseph Jacobs
Illus. Evaline Ness
New York, Charles Scribner's Sons, 1965. unp.

The king vows to make a woman's daughter his bride if the girl can spin five skeins of flax a day during the last month of the year. In order to meet the test she bargains with a scheming creature whose name she must guess.

SUBJECTS	–	Name of Helper	COUNTRY	–	United
		Discovered			Kingdom
		Spinning			
		Jacobs, Joseph			

MOTIFS	–	Supernatural	TYPE OF		
		Creatures	FOLKLORE	–	Folk Tales
		Fools and Simpletons			
		Humor			

See also **0099 Oniroku and the Carpenter**
          0287 Rumpelstiltskin

0317 TOM, TOM THE PIPER'S SON

Reteller, Paul Galdone
Illus. Paul Galdone
New York, McGraw-Hill Book Company, Whittlesey House, 1964. 32p.

Tom, Tom the piper's son has many misadventures as he wanders down the road playing his pipe.

SUBJECTS	–	Pipe	COUNTRY	–	United
		Tom, Tom the			Kingdom
		Piper's Son			

MOTIFS	–	Humor	TYPE OF		
			FOLKLORE	–	Nursery
					Rhymes

123

0311 TOO MUCH NOSE

Reteller, Harve Zemach
Illus. Margot Zemach
New York, Holt, Rinehart and Winston, 1967. unp.

A dying father gives valuable gifts to his three sons. The second son is tricked by the queen into giving up the three possessions, but he finally finds a way to get them back.

SUBJECTS	—	Hat, Horn, Coin Purse Invisibility Figs and Cherries (Magic)	COUNTRY	—	Italy
MOTIFS	—	Trickery Wit Prevails Humor Magic Objects Magic Transformation	TYPE OF FOLKLORE	—	Folk Tales

0239 TOPS AND BOTTOMS

Reteller, Lesley Conger
Illus. Imero Gobbato
New York, Four Winds Press, 1970. unp.

A farmer outwits a lazy goblin who says he will take the crop from the field the farmer is plowing.

SUBJECTS	—	Farmer Goblin Harvesting	COUNTRY	—	United Kingdom
MOTIFS	—	Supernatural Creatures Humor Trickery	TYPE OF FOLKLORE	—	Folk Tales

See also **0190**   **Why the Jackal Won't Speak to the Hedgehog**

0385 TORTOISE'S TUG OF WAR, THE

Reteller, Giulio Maestro
Illus. Giulio Maestro
Scarsdale, New York, Bradbury Press, 1971. unp.

This is another version of the Extraordinary Tug of War in which the tortoise tricks the whale and tapir into thinking he is stronger.

SUBJECTS	—	Tug-of-War Tortoise Tricks Animals Tapir and Whale	COUNTRY	—	South America
MOTIFS	—	Trickery Humor Wit Prevails Talking Animals	TYPE OF FOLKLORE	—	Folk Tales

See also **0128**   **Extraordinary Tug-of-War**

STORIES BY TITLE

0038 TRAVELING MUSICIANS, THE

See — 0523 Bremen Town Musicians

0289 TROJAN HORSE, THE

See — 0540 Wooden Horse

0064 TSAR'S RIDDLE OR THE WISE LITTLE GIRL

Reteller, Guy Daniels
Illus. Paul Galdone
New York, McGraw-Hill Book Company, 1967. 32p.

In an attempt to help her father win a legal suit, a seven-year-old daughter challenges the tsar in a riddle contest. The father regains his colt.

SUBJECTS	—	Royalty	COUNTRY	—	U.S.S.R.
		Horse			
		Riddle(s)			
		Colt			
		Tsar			
		Judge Persuaded By			
		High-Flown Speech			
		Justice			
MOTIFS	—	Wit Prevails	TYPE OF		
		Fools and Simpletons	FOLKLORE	—	Folk Tales
		Trickery			
		Humor			

0003 TURNIP, THE

Reteller, Janina Domanska
Illus. Janina Domanska
New York, The MacMillan Company, 1969. unp.

This cumulative tale tells how Grandfather and Grandmother with the help of animals and their grandson pull the turnip from the ground.

SUBJECTS	—	Turnip(s)	COUNTRY	—	Yugoslavia
		Cooperation			
		Cumulative Tale			
		Animals, Farm			
		Formula Tale			
		Chain Tale			
MOTIFS	—	Humor	TYPE OF		
		Talking Animals	FOLKLORE	—	Folk Tales

See also   0009   Great Big Enormous Turnip, The

0178 TWELVE DANCING PRINCESSES

See — 0559 Twelve Dancing Princesses, The

0004 TWELVE DANCING PRINCESSES, THE

See — 0559 Twelve Dancing Princesses, The

0559 TWELVE DANCING PRINCESSES, THE

0004   Twelve Dancing Princesses, The

Reteller, Adrienne Adams
Illus. Adrienne Adams
New York, Holt, Rinehart and Winston, 1966. unp.

By following directions given in dreams, a cowherder solves the mystery of the twelve princesses and their dancing slippers. As a reward, he marries the youngest princess.

SUBJECTS	– Dream(s) Invisibility Unselfishness Ogre Cloak (Invisibility) Princess, Twelve Dancing P.	COUNTRY	– France
MOTIFS	– Magic Objects Enchanted People Supernatural Creatures	TYPE OF FOLKLORE	– Folk Tales

0178 Twelve Dancing Princesses

By Grimm, The Brothers, Trans. Elizabeth Shub
Illus. Uri Shulevitz
New York, Charles Scribner's Sons, 1966. unp.

The king declares that any man who discovers how his twelve daughters spend their nights will inherit the throne. With the aid of an old woman, a soldier discovers what they do and the king keeps his promise.

SUBJECTS	– Cloak (Invisibility) Invisibility Soldier(s) Old Woman Grimm, The Brothers Princesses, Twelve Dancing P.	COUNTRY	– Germany
MOTIFS	– Magic Objects Enchanted People Supernatural Creatures	TYPE OF FOLKLORE	– Folk Tales

0562 TWELVE MONTHS

0341 Month Brothers, The

Reteller, Dorothy Nathan
Illus. Uri Shulevitz
New York, E. P. Dutton & Co., Inc., 1967. 95p.

According to Russian legend one can meet the 12 months of the year as brothers around a New Year's Eve campfire. The brothers help Katya deal with her stepmother and stepsister.

SUBJECTS	– Flowers (Snowdrop) Month Brothers Ring (Magic)	COUNTRY	– U.S.S.R.

MOTIFS	– Magic Objects
	Magic Transforma-
	  tion
	Friendly Animals
	Supernatural
	  Creatures
		TYPE OF
		FOLKLORE
			– Folk Tales

0096 TWO STONECUTTERS, THE

Adapted by Eve Titus
Illus. Yoko Mitsuhashi
Garden City, New York, Doubleday & Company, Inc., 1967. unp.

Two brothers are stonecutters. The younger is happy with his work; the older longs to be rich. The brothers are granted seven wishes by the goddess of the forest for their kindness.

SUBJECTS	–	Stonecutters	COUNTRY	–	Japan
		Sun			
		Stormcloud			
		Wind			
		Wealth			
		Goddess of the Forest			
		Kindness			
		Wishes, Brothers Given			
		Seven W.			

MOTIFS	–	Religion	TYPE OF		
		Supernatural Creatures	FOLKLORE	–	Folk Tales
		Wishes			
		Magic Transformation			

0552 UGLY DUCKLING

0246 Ugly Duckling, The

By Hans Christian Andersen, Trans. R. P. Keigwin
Illus. Johannes Larsen
New York, The MacMillan Company, 1955. 54p.

Hatched by a duck, the ugly duckling is considered to be the ugliest member of the farmyard. He flees into the world only to find it equally harsh. Finally, he realizes his true identity as a swan.

SUBJECTS	–	Duckling	COUNTRY	–	Denmark
		Swan(s)			
		Allegory–Myth Type			
		Andersen, Hans Christian			

MOTIFS	–	Talking Animals	TYPE OF		
			FOLKLORE	–	Folk Tales

0061 Ugly Duckling, The

By Hans Christian Andersen, Trans. R. P. Keigwin
Illus. Adrienne Adams
New York, Charles Scribner's Sons, 1965. unp.

Similar to title no. 0246 Ugly Duckling, The. Different illus.

SUBJECTS	–	Duckling	COUNTRY	–	Denmark
		Swan(s)			
		Allegory–Myth Type			
		Andersen, Hans Christian			

MOTIFS	–	Talking Animals	TYPE OF		
			FOLKLORE	–	Folk Tales

0061 UGLY DUCKLING, THE

See – **0552 Ugly Duckling**

0246 UGLY DUCKLING, THE

See – **0552 Ugly Duckling**

0122 USHA THE MOUSE-MAIDEN

Reteller, Mehlli Gobhai
Illus. Mehlli Gobhai
New York, Hawthorne Books, Inc., 1969. unp.

A holy man and his wife want a child, so he changes a little mouse
into a lovely little baby. When the baby is grown, she is offered the
sun, clouds, winds and mountains for a husband but she chooses a
mouse, so the holy man changes her back into a mouse.

SUBJECTS	–	Cloud	COUNTRY	–	India
		Holy Man			
		Mouse (Mice)			
		Mountain			
		Wind			
		Cumulative Tale			
		Chain Tale			
		Formula Tale			
MOTIFS	–	Religion	TYPE OF		
		Supernatural	FOLKLORE	–	Folk Tales
		Creatures			
		Magic Transforma-			
		tion			

See also   **0062**   **White Rat's Tale, The**

0395 VALENTINE AND ORSON

Reteller, Henry Matthew Brock
Illus. Henry Matthew Brock
London, Warne, n.d. unp.

Twin brothers, Valentine and Orson, are raised by an uncle and a
bear mother respectively. Their mother is captured by a giant. Reunited at manhood, they rescue their mother from the giant.

SUBJECTS	–	Brazen, Oracular	COUNTRY	–	United
		B. Head			Kingdom
		Giant(s)			
		Twins, Separation			
		of T. Through			
		Being Carried Off			
		By a Bear			
		Valentine and Orson			
MOTIFS	–	Legendary Heroes	TYPE OF		
		Tasks and Trials	FOLKLORE	–	Legends
		Supernatural			
		Creatures			

0123 VALIANT CHATTEE-MAKER, THE

Reteller, Christine Price
Illus. Christine Price
New York, Frederick Warner and Co., Inc., 1965. unp.

A timid chattee-maker (pottery maker) experiences a number of hilarious errors—the first when he loses the donkey carrying his wares.

SUBJECTS — Donkey
                   Pottery-Maker
                   Tiger
                   Rajah

COUNTRY — India

MOTIFS — Humor
               Wit Prevails
               Fools and Simpletons

TYPE OF
FOLKLORE — Folk Tales

0013 VALIANT TAILOR, THE

See — 0522 Brave Little Tailor

0352 VASILISA THE BEAUTIFUL

Reteller, Thomas P. Whitney
Illus. Nonny Hogrogian
New York, The MacMillan Company, 1970. unp.

In this version of Cinderella a magic doll replaces the fairy godmother. Baba Yaga is one of the characters in the story. The phenomena of day, night, and the sun are included.

SUBJECTS — Baba Yaga
               Doll (Godmother)
               Skull's Light De-
                 stroys Stepmother
                 and Stepsister

COUNTRY — U.S.S.R.

MOTIFS — Religion
               Supernatural
                 Creatures
               Magic Objects

TYPE OF
FOLKLORE — Folk Tales

See also 0063 Cinderella or The Little Glass Slipper
           0270 Cinderella

0104 VERY SPECIAL BADGERS, THE

Reteller, Claus Stamm
Illus. Kazue Mizumura
New York, Viking Press, 1960. 40p.

Two tribes of badgers in Japan have power to do magical transformations. In a cheat and change contest the winning tribe is given the right to stay and the other tribe has to move away.

SUBJECTS — Badgers
               Contest (Cheat and
                 Change)

COUNTRY — Japan

MOTIFS — Magic Transforma-
                 tion
               Humor
               Wit Prevails
               Trickery
               Talking Animals

TYPE OF
FOLKLORE — Folk Tales

0344 VINLANDERS' SAGA

Reteller, Barbara Schiller
Illus. William Bock
New York, Holt, Rinehart and Winston, 1966. 71p.

>These are the tales of Eric the Red and his sons whose exploits lead to the discovery of North America.

SUBJECTS	–	Eric the Red	COUNTRY	–	North
		Fate			America
		Greenland			
		Leif the Lucky			
		Saga (Icelandic)			
		Vikings			
		Vinland			

MOTIFS	–	Religion	TYPE OF		
		Legendary Heroes	FOLKLORE	–	Epics

0305 WART SNAKE IN A FIG TREE, A

Reteller, George Mendoza
Illus. Etienne Delessert
New York, The Dial Press, Inc., 1968. unp.

>This version of The Twelve Days of Christmas includes a wart snake, two bags of soot, three cobwebs, four raven wings, five useless things, six shadows lurking, seven ghouls a caroling, eight snow wolves wailing, nine nightmares galloping, ten devils grinning, eleven lizards boiling, twelve days of raining. Music is included.

SUBJECTS	–	Christmas	COUNTRY	–	U.S.–Folk-
		Cumulative Tale			songs
		Chain Tale			
		Music			
		Counting			
		Formula Tale			

MOTIFS	–	Humor	TYPE OF		
			FOLKLORE	–	Folk Songs,
					Ballads

See also   **0151**   **Thirteen Days of Yule, The**

0543 WAVE

0026 Burning Rice Fields, The

Reteller, Sara Cone Bryant
Illus. Mamoru Funai
New York, Holt, Rinehart and Winston, Inc., 1963. unp.

>An old man saves the villagers from an oncoming tidal wave by burning his rice fields.

SUBJECTS	–	Farmer	COUNTRY	–	Japan
		Obedience			
		Rice			
		Tidal Wave			

MOTIFS	–	Realistic Events	TYPE OF		
		Nature Calamities	FOLKLORE	–	Folk Tales
		Wit Prevails			

0025 Wave, The

Adapted from Lafcadio Hearn's Gleanings in Buddha-Fields by Margaret Hodges
Illus. Blair Lent
Boston, Houghton Mifflin Company, 1964. 45p.

Similar to title no. 0026 Burning Rice Fields, The.

SUBJECTS	–	Farmer	COUNTRY	–	Japan
		Obedience			
		Rice			
		Tidal Wave			

MOTIFS	–	Realistic Events	TYPE OF		
		Nature Calamities	FOLKLORE	–	Folk Tales
		Wit Prevails			

0025 WAVE, THE

See – 0543 Wave

0046 WAY OF DANGER: THE STORY OF THESEUS, THE

See – 0539 Theseus

0316 WHAT BOBOLINO KNEW

Reteller, Anne Rockwell
Illus. Anne Rockwell
New York, The McCall Publishing Company, 1971. 29p.

Sent to study foreign languages, Bobolino learns the language of the animals, making his father furious. Bobolino runs away and gains a kingship with the help of the animals.

SUBJECTS	–	Royalty	COUNTRY	–	Italy
		Languages, Knowledge			
		of			
		Sicily			

MOTIFS	–	Friendly Animals	TYPE OF		
		Talking Animals	FOLKLORE	–	Folk Tales

0308 WHAT THE GOOD MAN DOES IS ALWAYS RIGHT

By Hans Christian Andersen
Illus. Rick Schreiter
New York, The Dial Press, Inc., 1968. unp.

An old couple decides to trade their horse for something better and after several exchanges ends up with rotten apples. The old man is told his wife will give it to him when he gets home. He says she will kiss him. A wager is placed and he wins.

SUBJECTS	–	Andersen, Hans	COUNTRY	–	Denmark
		Christian			
		Chain Tale			
		Acceptance			
		Farmer			
		Married Bliss			
		Trading of Objects			
		Formula Tale			
		Cumulative Tale			

STORIES BY TITLE

MOTIFS — Humor TYPE OF
Realistic Events FOLKLORE — Folk Tales
See also **0251** **Happy-Go-Lucky**

0345 WHEN THE DRUM SANG

Reteller, Anne Rockwell
Illus. Anne Rockwell
New York, Parents' Magazine Press, 1970. unp.

When the ogre Zimwi hears the little girl singing, he kidnaps her and places her inside his drum. She is rescued by her parents who place a swarm of bees in the drum.

SUBJECTS — Drum Containing COUNTRY — Africa
Singing Girl
Ogre

MOTIFS — Humor TYPE OF
Wit Prevails FOLKLORE — Folk Tales
Trickery
Supernatural
Creatures

0350 WHITE ARCHER, THE

Reteller, James Houston
Illus. James Houston
New York, Harcourt, Brace & World, Inc., 1967. 95p.

After his parents are killed and his sister kidnapped by Indians, Eskimo Kungo seeks revenge. However, he finally achieves a far greater triumph than revenge.

SUBJECTS — Animal Spirits COUNTRY — North
Eskimos America
Night Spirits
Sea Spirits
Survival

MOTIFS — Religion TYPE OF
Realistic Events FOLKLORE — Legends

0062 WHITE RAT'S TALE, THE

Reteller, Barbara Schiller
Illus. Adrienne Adams
New York, Holt, Rinehart and Winston, 1967. unp.

A king and queen ask a fairy queen to transform a white rat into a princess. When it is time for her to marry, she asks for the most powerful husband. The king chooses the sun, cloud, wind and mountain respectively. The final choice is a rat.

SUBJECTS — Chain Tale COUNTRY — France
Rat
Fairy
Sun
Cloud
Wind
Mountain
Formula Tale

MOTIFS — Talking TYPE OF
Animals FOLKLORE — Folk Tales

Supernatural
Creatures
Magic Transforma-
tion
Wit Prevails

See also   0122   Usha the Mouse-Maiden

0175 WHO WAS TRICKED?

Retellers, James Cloyd Bowman & Margery Bianco, Trans. Aili
Kolehmainen
Illus. John Faulkner
Chicago, Albert Whitman & Company, Text c. 1964. Illus. c. 1966. unp.

The farmer's son Pekka outwits two tricksters who try to tell him his
father's cow is a goat and they will pay him accordingly when he
tries to sell it.

SUBJECTS	–	Cow	COUNTRY	–	Finland
		Cap (Pseudo-Magic)			
		Greediness			
		Peasant Outwits			
		Enemies			

MOTIFS	–	Humor	TYPE OF		
		Wit Prevails	FOLKLORE	–	Folk Tales
		Trickery			

0190 WHY THE JACKAL WON'T SPEAK TO THE HEDGEHOG

Reteller, Harold Berson
Illus. Harold Berson
New York, The Seabury Press, 1969. unp.

Jackal picks what grows below the ground one year after he and
Hedgehog plant wheat. The next year he is tricked again when he
picks what grows above ground after they plant onions. Jackal won't
speak to Hedgehog because of this trickery.

SUBJECTS	–	Hedgehog	COUNTRY	–	Tunisia
		Harvesting			
		Jackal			

MOTIFS	–	Talking Animals	TYPE OF		
		Trickery	FOLKLORE	–	Folk Tales
		Pourquoi Stories			

See also   0239   Tops and Bottoms

0353 WHY THE SUN AND THE MOON LIVE IN THE SKY

Reteller, Elphinstone Dayrell
Illus. Blair Lent
Boston, Houghton Mifflin Company, 1968. 27p.

The sun and his wife, the moon, invite the water and all his people
to visit with them. By the time all of water's people arrive, there is
no room for the sun and moon. They have no choice but to float
to the sky and stay there.

| SUBJECTS | – | Moon | COUNTRY | – | Africa |
| | | Friendship | | | |

Sun
Water

MOTIFS	– Pourquoi Stories	TYPE OF FOLKLORE – Folk Tales

0050 WHY THE SUN WAS LATE

Reteller, Benjamin Elkin
Illus. Jerome Snyder
New York, Parents' Magazine Press, 1966. unp.

This chain tale includes one fly, two boys, three squirrels, four snakes, five elephants, and six eggs, respectively. The upset mother bird won't sing to wake the sun, thus causing the world to be in darkness. The great spirit remedies the problem.

SUBJECTS	– Imps	COUNTRY	– Africa
	Formula Tale		
	Bird(s)		
	Egg(s)		
	Sun		
	Spirit		
	Chain Tale		
	Counting		

MOTIFS	– Talking Animals	TYPE OF
	Pourquoi Stories	FOLKLORE – Folk Tales
	Supernatural Creatures	

0253 WIDDECOMBE FAIR

Author Anonymous
Illus. Christine Price
New York, Frederick Warne & Co., Inc., 1968. unp.

This English folksong describes Tom Pearce's mare who dies while carrying all Tom Cobbleigh's friends and whose ghost can still be seen riding across the moor.

SUBJECTS	– Horse	COUNTRY	– United
	Widdicombe Fair		Kingdom

MOTIFS	– Humor	TYPE OF
	Supernatural Creatures	FOLKLORE – Folk Songs, Ballads

0363 WILD DUCKS AND THE GOOSE, THE

Reteller, Carl Withers
Illus. Alan E. Cober
New York, Holt, Rinehart and Winston, 1968. unp.

The Indians are amused to see the old man's futile efforts to shoot the ducks. Storyteller draws while telling the tale.

SUBJECTS	– Duck	COUNTRY	– U.S.–Native
	Drawing Tale		Folk Tales
	Goose		

MOTIFS	– Humor	TYPE OF
		FOLKLORE – Folk Tales

STORIES BY TITLE

0057 WILD SWANS, THE

By Hans Christian Andersen, Trans. M. R. James
Illus. Marcia Brown
New York, Charles Scribner's Sons, 1963. 80p.

Eleven brothers are turned into swans by a wicked stepmother. Their young sister does certain tasks to bring about their transformation.

SUBJECTS	–	Royalty	COUNTRY	–	Denmark
		Witch(es)			
		Swan(s)			
		God			
		Andersen, Hans			
		Christian			
		Courage			
		Love, Selfless			
		Sister Seeks Brothers			

MOTIFS	–	Magic Objects	TYPE OF		
		Magic Transforma-	FOLKLORE	–	Folk Tales
		tion			
		Tasks and Trials			
		Supernatural			
		Creatures			
		Religion			

See also   0203   Seven Ravens, The

0136 WILLIAM TELL AND HIS SON

Reteller, Bettina Hurlimann, Trans. and Adapted by Elizabeth D.
 Crawford
Illus. Paul Nussbaumer
New York, Harcourt, Brace & World, Inc., First American ed., 1967. unp.

Marksman William Tell uses his skill with a bow to do in the Austrian bailiff Gessler who had ordered all Swiss to bow to a hat placed on a pole.

SUBJECTS	–	Apple	COUNTRY	–	Switzerland
		Cross-Bow			
		Tyranny			
		Tell, William			
		Patriotism			

| MOTIFS | – | Realistic Events | TYPE OF | | |
| | | | FOLKLORE | – | Legends |

0097 WILLIAM PLATE, LEGEND OF

See – 0500 Willow Ware

0500 WILLIAM WARE

0097 Willow Plate, Legend of

Retellers, Alvin Tresselt and Nancy Cleaver
Illus. Joseph Low
New York, Parents' Magazine Press, 1968. unp.

Refusing to marry someone she does not love, the cruel mandarin's beautiful daughter runs away to an island with a poet. They live happily until her rejected suitor finds them.

SUBJECTS	– Love Goddess of Mercy (Kwan-Yin) Cruelty Royalty Mandarin	COUNTRY	– China (Mainland)
MOTIFS	– Religion Supernatural Creatures Magic Transforma- tion	TYPE OF FOLKLORE	– Legends

0206 WISE FOOL, THE

By Francois Rabelais, Reteller, Paul Galdone
Illus. Paul Galdone
New York, Pantheon Books, Random House, Inc., 1968. unp.

When the meat seller demands payment for the meat smell that permeates the poor porter's bread, the court jester tells the porter to bounce his coin so all can hear it ring. This sound, he says, is the required payment.

SUBJECTS	– Judge(s) Justice Smell (Selling of)	COUNTRY	– France
MOTIFS	– Humor Wit Prevails Trickery	TYPE OF FOLKLORE	– Folk Tales

See also **0156 Eggs, The**
0082 Judge Not
0322 Mice That Ate Iron, The

0164 WISE ROOSTER, THE

Reteller, Mariana Prieto
Illus. Lee Smith
New York, The John Day Company, 1962. unp.

On the eve Christ is born all the animals in the stable with him are given the gift of speech. The animals use it wisely with the exception of one little vain donkey who says he is even more beautiful than the shining star. At this all the animals lose their power of speech.

SUBJECTS	– Christmas Donkey Rooster Vanity Spain	COUNTRY	– Latin America
MOTIFS	– Religion Talking Animals	TYPE OF FOLKLORE	– Legends

0170 WISEST MAN IN THE WORLD, THE

Reteller, Benjamin Elkin
Illus. Anita Lobel
New York, Parent's Magazine Press, 1968. unp.

Wise King Solomon's only weakness is his pride in his knowledge. When he is tested by the queen of Sheba, it requires the help of a little bee to outsmart her.

SUBJECTS – Bee   COUNTRY – Israel
                Eagle
                Lion(s)
                Queen of Sheba
                Solomon
                Wisdom
                Pride

MOTIFS – Legendary Heroes   TYPE OF
             Religion   FOLKLORE – Legends
             Talking Animals
             Trickery
             Wit Prevails

0035   WOLF AND THE SEVEN LITTLE KIDS, THE

By Grimm, The Brothers
Illus. Felix Hoffmann
New York, Harcourt, Brace and Company, First American ed.,
    1959. unp.

> The wolf swallows six kids alive, but the mother goat rescues them by cutting the wolf's stomach open when he falls asleep. She fills his stomach with stones, and he falls in the well and drowns.

SUBJECTS – Goat(s)   COUNTRY – Germany
                Kids
                Wolf
                Greediness

MOTIFS – Talking Animals   TYPE OF
             Trickery   FOLKLORE – Folk Tales

0408   WONDERFUL EGGS OF FURICCHIA

Reteller, Anne Rockwell
Illus. Anne Rockwell
New York, The World Publishing Company, 1969. unp.

> The wicked Maddelana tries to steal the secret of the magic eggs laid by the good witch Furicchia's hen. A surprising punishment is her lot. She turns into a chicken who lays eggs that turn into mice.

SUBJECTS – Hen Laid Magic Eggs   COUNTRY – Italy
                Italy
                Witch(es)

MOTIFS – Humor   TYPE OF
             Magic Objects   FOLKLORE – Folk Tales
             Magic Transforma-
                tion
             Supernatural
                Creatures

0540   WOODEN HORSE

0289   Trojan Horse, The

Reteller, James Reeves
Illus. Krystyna Turska
New York, Franklin Watts, Inc., First American Edition, 1969. unp.

> Ilias tells his children how the Greeks gained access to his city of Troy with a huge wooden horse filled with Greek soldiers who

opened the city gates for their fellow soldiers, bringing about the downfall of Troy.

SUBJECTS — Helen of Troy   COUNTRY — Greece
             Trojan Horse
             Paris
             Ulysses
             Athena

MOTIFS   — Wit Prevails   TYPE OF
             Trickery   FOLKLORE — Epics
             Legendary Heroes
             Religion

0114 YOU NEVER CAN TELL

Adapted by Janice Holland
Illus. Janice Holland
New York, Charles Scribner's Sons, 1963. unp.

When the horse of a farmer near the Great Wall of China disappears, the villagers see it as an omen of ill-luck but the farmer listens quietly and replies wisely, "You never can tell. You never can tell."

SUBJECTS — Farmer   COUNTRY — China
             China (Great Wall)   (Mainland)
             Fate
             Horse

MOTIFS   — Realistic Events   TYPE OF
                                FOLKLORE — Folk Tales

0399 YURI AND THE MOONEYGOATS

Reteller Charles Robinson
Illus. Charles Robinson
New York, Simon and Schuster, 1969. unp.

Yuri sets out to seek his fortune because there is no food in the house for his 14 brothers and sisters and his mother. Captured by the Mooneygoats, he tricks them into offering him pots of gold.

SUBJECTS — Mooneygoats   COUNTRY — Rumania
             Moon Creatures
             Lucky Successes

MOTIFS   — Humor   TYPE OF
             Wit Prevails   FOLKLORE — Folk Tales
             Trickery
             Tasks and Trials

STORIES BY SUBJECT

ABRAHAM LINCOLN

0261 Ol' Dan Tucker

ACCEPTANCE

0251 Happy-Go-Lucky
0308 What the Good Man Does
Is Always Right

ACORN

0115 Long, Broad and Quickeye

ACORN (HITS CHICKEN'S HEAD)

0278 Henny Penny

ADVICE (COUNSEL–PRECEPT)

0070 No Room, An Old Story
Retold
0189 Three Gold Pieces

AESOP

0010 Donkey Ride, The
0157 Hare and the Tortoise, The
0264 Hee Haw
0205 John J. Plenty and Fiddler
Dan
0315 Maid and Her Pail of
Milk, The
0005 Miller, His Son, and Their
Donkey, The

AFREETS–DEMONS

0131 Sundiata, The Epic of the
Lion King

ALADDIN AND THE LAMP

0402 Aladdin and the Wonderful
Lamp
0404 Aladdin, The Story of

ALGONQUIN NATION

0248 Badger, The Mischief
Maker

ALLAH

0402 Aladdin and the Wonderful Lamp
0404 Aladdin, The Story of
0131 Sundiata, The Epic of
the Lion King

ALLEGORY–MYTH TYPE

0015 Golden Touch, The
0246 Ugly Duckling, The
0061 Ugly Duckling, The

ANANSE BARGAINS WITH SKY GOD

0379 Story, A Story, A

ANDERSEN, HANS CHRISTIAN

0213 Emperor's New Clothes, The
0169 Emperor's New Clothes, The
0360 Fir Tree, The
0059 Little Match Girl, The
0387 Little Mermaid, The
0380 Little Mermaid, The
0058 Little Mermaid, The
0204 Nightingale, The
0060 Nightingale, The
0049 Snow Queen, The
0397 Snow Queen, The
0056 Steadfast Tin Soldier, The
0055 Swineherd, The
0048 Thumbelina
0394 Thumbelina
0247 Tinder Box, The
0246 Ugly Duckling, The
0061 Ugly Duckling, The
0308 What the Good Man Does Is
Always Right
0057 Wild Swans, The

ANDREW JACKSON

0301 Andy Jackson's Water Well

ANGLO-SAXONS

0374 Beowulf
0373 Beowulf The Warrior
0375 Beowulf, Story of
0227 By His Own Might: The
Battles of Beowulf

ANIMAL SPIRITS

0350 White Archer, The

ANIMAL WEDDINGS (COCKROACH AND MOUSE)

0165 Perez and Martina

ANIMAL WEDDINGS (COCK ROBIN AND JENNY WREN)

0235 Cock Robin and Jenny Wren

ANIMAL WEDDINGS (FROG AND MISS MOUSE)

0258 Frog Went A-Courtin'

ANIMALS WITH STRANGE NAMES

0278 Henny Penny
0358 Henny Penny

ANIMALS, FARM

0070 No Room, an Old Story Retold
0003 Turnip, The

ANIMALS, JUNGLE

0191 Beeswax Catches a Thief

ANIMALS, WHO LIVED IN A SHOE

0238 Six Who Were Left in a Shoe

ANIMALS, WILD FOREST

0077 Mitten, The

ANT

0205 John J. Plenty and Fiddler Dan

APPALACHIAN MOUNTAIN SONG

0327 Billy Boy
0258 Frog Went A-Courtin'
0292 Hush Little Baby
0262 Swapping Boy, The

APPLE

0110 Flying Carpet, The
0036 Snow White and the Seven Dwarfs
0136 William Tell and His Son

APPRENTICE

0268 Baker and the Basilisk, The
0135 Sorcerer's Apprentice
0134 Sorcerer's Apprentice, The
0269 Sorcerer's Apprentice, The

ARABIAN NIGHTS

0107 Ali-Baba and the Forty-Thieves
0110 Flying Carpet, The
0109 Joco and the Fishbone (An Arabian Nights Tale)

ARCTIC ANIMALS

0210 Tikta'liktak, an Eskimo Legend

ARROGANCE

0119 Tiger, the Braham, and the Jackal, The

ARROWS MAKE SKY ROPE

0174 Angry Moon, The

ARTHURIAN LEGEND

0366 Challenge of the Green Knight, The
0347 Erec and Enid
0369 Joy of the Court
0153 Kitchen Knight, The
0378 Knight of the Cart, The
0367 Knight of the Lion, The
0154 Sir Gawain and the Green Knight
0372 Taliesin and King Arthur

ASBJORNSEN, P.C. AND MOE, J.E.

0200 Three Billy Goats Gruff, The
0214 Three Billy Goats Gruff, The

ASTROLOGER

0032 Luck Child, The
0132 Thirty Gilt Pennies, The

ATHENA

0289 Trojan Horse, The

BABA YAGA

0076 Baba Yaga
0352 Vasilisa the Beautiful

BABES, THE BLUE OX

0290 Paul Bunyan
0291 Paul Bunyan, The Story of

BABOUSHKA

0312 Baboushka and the Three Kings

BADGERS

0104 Very Special Badgers, The

BAG—CAPTORS B. FILLED WITH STONES WHILE CAPTIVES ESCAPED

0310 Little White Hen

BAG, GIANT'S WIFE TRICKED IN TAKING PRISONER'S PLACE IN B.

0392 Molly Whuppie

STORIES BY SUBJECT

BAGDAD

0109 Joco and the Fishbone (An Arabian Nights Tale)

BAKER

0268 Baker and the Basilisk, The

BALLET

0030 Sleeping Beauty, The

BALLET DANCER

0056 Steadfast Tin Soldier, The

BARGAINING FROM GOOD TO BAD

0181 Hans in Luck

BASILISK (MONSTER)

0268 Baker and the Basilisk, The

BEANS

0226 Jack and the Beanstalk
0144 Jack and the Beanstalk

BEAR(S)

0173 Autun and the Bear
0163 Mourka, the Mighty Cat
0006 Snow White and Rose Red
0008 Snow-White and Rose-Red
0212 Three Bears, The Story of
0137 Three Bears, The Story of
0233 Three Bears, The Story of

BEAST

0020 Beauty and the Bear

BEE

0170 Wisest Man In the World, The

BEESWAX, CAPTURE BY B.

0191 Beeswax Catches a Thief

BEGGAR(S) (SUPERNATURAL CREATURE)

0270 Cinderella
0240 Magic Sack, The

BEOWULF

0374 Beowulf
0373 Beowulf the Warrior
0375 Beowulf, Story of
0227 By His Own Might: The Battles of Beowulf

BILLY BOY

0327 Billy Boy

BIRD(S)

0052 Feather Mountain
0033 Jorinda and Joringel
0113 Peacock and the Crow, The
0050 Why the Sun Was Late

BISHOP TRICKS DEVIL

0386 Bishop and the Devil

BLACK BROTHERS

0201 King of the Golden River, The or the Black Brothers
0152 King of the Golden River, The or the Black Brothers
0284 King of the Golden River, The or the Black Brothers

BLACKS

0207 John Henry and His Hammer
0017 John Henry, an American Legend
0016 Steel Driving Man, the Legend of John Henry

BLIND MEN

0121 Blind Men and the Elephant, The
0120 Blind Men and the Elephant, The

BOAR

0163 Mourka, The Mighty Cat
0013 Valiant Tailor, The

BOASTING

0101 Three Strong Women

BOGGART

0283 Goblin Under the Stairs, The

BOOOIN (WIZARDS)

0248 Badger, The Mischief Maker

BOOTS, MAGIC

0030 Sleeping Beauty, The

BOOTS, SEVEN-LEAGUE

0396 Hop O' My Thumb

BRAHMAN

0119 Tiger, the Brahman, and the Jackal, The

STORIES BY SUBJECT

BRAZEN, ORACULAR B. HEAD

0395 Valentine and Orson

BROOM

0135 Sorcerer's Apprentice
0134 Sorcerer's Apprentice, The
0269 Sorcerer's Apprentice, The

BROTHERS TRICKED BY MOON

0383 Dancing Stars, The

BROTHERS, WHY HEN AND CROCODILE ARE

0194 Crocodile and Hen

BRYNHILD

0286 Sword of Siegfried, The

BUDDHA AS GARDENER

0118 Stolen Necklace, The
0263 Thousand and One Buddas, A

BUDDHA AS MONKEY (BUILT TEMPLE)

0195 Monkey and the Crocodile, The

BUNYAN, PAUL

0290 Paul Bunyan
0291 Paul Bunyan, The Story of

BURNED, CANNOT BE B.

0090 Five Chinese Brothers, The

CAMEL TRICKS MERCHANT

0406 Camel in the Tent

CAMELS

0108 Nine in a Line

CANAL BOATS

0359 Erie Canal, The

CANDLE (MAGIC)

0247 Tinder Box, The

CANTERBURY TALES

0321 Chanticleer and the Fox

CAP (PSEUDO-MAGIC)

0175 Who Was Tricked?

CAPTAIN ICHABOD PADDOCK

0293 Captain Ichabod Paddock, Whaler of Nantucket

CAPTAIN JASON DOW

0299 Cap'n Dow and the Hole in the Doughnut

CARPENTER

0099 Oniroku and the Carpenter

CARPET

0117 Carpet of Solomon
0110 Flying Carpet, The
0112 Three Feathers, The

CASEY JONES

0295 Casey Jones: The Story of a Brave Engineer

CAT

0217 Bremen Town Musicians, The
0237 Dame Wiggins of Lee and Her Seven Wonderful Cats
0357 Dick Whittington
0365 Dick Whittington and His Cat
0244 Fox, the Dog, and the Griffin, The
0009 Great Big Enormous Turnip, The
0255 Little Red Hen, The
0133 Lullaby: Why the Pussy-Cat Washes Himself So Often
0116 Magic Ring, The
0163 Mourka, The Mighty Cat
0229 Peter and the Wolf
0011 Puss in Boots
0007 Puss in Boots
0183 Puss in Boots
0078 Raminagrobis and the Mice
0038 Traveling Musicians, The

CAT EATS POT, ETC.

0329 Fat Cat, The

CAT, REASON DOG FIGHTS C.

0381 Chinese Story Teller, The

CHAIN TALE

0141 All in the Morning Early
0124 Bojabi Tree, The
0192 Bojabi Tree, The
0235 Cock Robin and Jenny Wren
0329 Fat Cat, The
0361 Gingerbread Boy, The
0009 Great Big Enormous Turnip, The
0085 Grindstone of God, The

0181 Hand In Luck
0251 Happy-Go-Lucky
0278 Henny Penny
0358 Henny Penny
0198 House That Jack Built, The
0281 House That Jack Built, The
0150 House That Jack Built, The
or Maison Que Jacques a
Batie, La
0292 Hush Little Baby
0109 Joco and the Fishbone (An
Arabian Nights Tale)
0143 Johnny-Cake
0302 Journey Cake, Ho!
0260 Judge, The
0368 Little Red Hen
0255 Little Red Hen, The
0168 Little Tuppen
0077 Mitten, The
0306 Mommy, Buy Me a China Doll
0318 Monkey's Whiskers, The
0355 Munachar and Manachar
0276 Old Woman and Her Pig, The
0382 One Fine Day
0166 Snow and the Sun, The
0069 Speckled Hen
0054 Such Is the Way of the World
0262 Swapping Boy, The
0243 The Rabbit and the Turnip
0151 Thirteen Days of Yule, The
0003 Turnip, The
0122 Usha the Mouse-Maiden
0305 Wart Snake in a Fig Tree, A
0308 What the Good Man Does Is
Always Right
0062 White Rat's Tale, The
0050 Why the Sun Was Late

CHARACTER FORMING

0042 King Thrushbeard
0095 King Thrushbeard
0182 Rich Man and the
Shoe-Maker, The

CHILDLESS (COUPLE)

0092 Crane Maiden, The
0280 Diverting Adventures of
Tom Thumb, The
0158 Greyling
0091 Issun Boshi. The Inchlins.
0040 Rapunzel
0177 Tale of a Pig

CHILDLESS (MAN)

0093 Golden Crane, The

CHINA

0402 Aladdin and the Wonderful
Lamp

0060 Nightingale, The
0204 Nightingale, The

CHINA (GREAT WALL)

0100 Good-Luck Horse
0114 You Never Can Tell

CHIVALRY

0366 Challenge of the Green
Knight, The
0347 Erec and Enid
0369 Joy of the Court
0153 Kitchen Knight, The
0378 Knight of the Cart, The
0154 Sir Gawain and the Green
Knight
0155 St. George and the Dragon

CHRIST

0346 Every Man Heart Lay Down
0132 Thirty Gilt Pennies, The

CHRISTIANITY

0386 Bishop and the Devil
0366 Challenge of the Green
Knight, The
0347 Erec and Enid
0346 Every Man Heart Lay Down
0401 Golden Cup, The
0377 Havelok the Dane
0369 Joy of the Court
0378 Knight of the Cart, The
0367 Knight of the Lion, The
0058 Little Mermaid, The
0387 Little Mermain, The
0380 Little Mermaid, The
0397 Snow Queen, The
0049 Snow Queen, The
0155 St George and the Dragon

CHRISTMAS

0312 Baboushka and the Three
Kings
0398 Elves and the Shoemaker, The
0346 Every Man Heart Lay Down
0360 Fir Tree, The
0401 Golden Cup, The
0171 Ice Bird, The
0079 Little Juggler, The
0133 Lullaby: Why the Pussy-Cat
Washes Himself So Often
0390 Nutcracker
0165 Perez and Martina
0037 Shoemaker and the Elves, The
0372 Taliesin and King Arthur
0151 Thirteen Days of Yule, The
0132 Thirty Gilt Pennies, The

STORIES BY SUBJECT

COUNTING

0141 All in the Morning Early
0151 Thirteen Days of Yule, The
0305 Wart Snake in a Fig Tree, A
0050 Why the Sun Was Late

COUNTING WRONG BY NOT COUNTING ONESELF

0108 Nine in a Line
0149 Six Foolish Fishermen

COURAGE

0374 Beowulf
0373 Beowulf the Warrior
0375 Beowulf, Story of
0227 By His Own Might: The Battles of Beowulf
0045 Clashing Rocks: The Story of Jason, The
0044 Gorgon's Head: The Story of Perseus, The
0348 Heracles the Strong
0046 Way of Danger: The Story of Theseus, The
0057 Wild Swans, The

COURTSHIP

0042 King Thrushbeard
0095 King Thrushbeard
0362 Laird of Cockpen, The
0165 Perez and Martina
0055 Swineherd, The

COW

0111 Gone Is Gone or The Story of a Man Who Wanted To Do the Housework
0144 Jack and the Beanstalk
0226 Jack and the Beanstalk
0002 Jack and the Three Sillies
0001 Three Sillies, The
0175 Who Was Tricked?

COWBOYS

0019 Pecos Bill and the Mustang

COWHIDE (PSEUDO-MAGIC)

0146 Hudden and Dudden and Donald O'Neary

CRANE

0092 Crane Maiden, The
0236 Crane With One Leg, The
0093 Golden Crane, The
0094 Kap and the Wicked Monkey

CROCODILE

0194 Crocodile and Hen
0195 Monkey and the Crocodile, The

CROSS-BOW

0136 William Tell and His Son

CROW (PAINTS PEACOCK FEATHERS)

0113 Peacock and the Crow, The

CRUELTY

0086 Suho and the White Horse
0097 Willow Plate, Legend of

CRYING

0106 Nine (9) Cry-Baby Dolls

CUMULATIVE TALE

0141 All in the Morning Early
0235 Cock Robin and Jenny Wren
0329 Fat Cat, The
0361 Gingerbread Boy, The
0009 Great Big Enormous Turnip, The
0085 Grindstone of God, The
0181 Hans in Luck
0251 Happy-Go-Lucky
0278 Henny Penny
0358 Henny Penny
0281 House That Jack Built, The
0198 House That Jack Built, The
0150 House That Jack Built, The or Maison Que Jacques a Batie, La
0292 Hush Little Baby
0143 Johnny-Cake
0302 Journey Cake, Ho!
0260 Judge, The
0368 Little Red Hen
0255 Little Red Hen, The
0168 Little Tuppen
0077 Mitten, The
0306 Mommy, Buy Me a China Doll
0318 Monkey's Whiskers, The
0355 Munachar and Manachar
0276 Old Woman and Her Pig, The
0382 One Fine Day
0166 Snow and the Sun, The
0069 Speckled Hen
0054 Such Is the Way of the World
0262 Swapping Boy, The
0243 The Rabbit and the Turnip
0151 Thirteen Days of Yule, The
0003 Turnip, The
0122 Usha the Mouse-Maiden
0305 Wart Snake In a Fig Tree, A
0308 What the Good Man Does Is Always Right

STORIES BY SUBJECT

CURIOSITY

0103 Magic Monkey, The

DAEDALUS FLIES ON ARTIFICIAL WINGS

0319 Fall From the Sky: The Story of Daedalus

DAME WIGGINS

0237 Dame Wiggins of Lee and Her Seven Wonderful Cats

DEATH

0165 Perez and Martina

DECEPTIVE APPEARANCES

0314 Blue Jackal, The

DEMONS

0185 Dumplings and the Demons, The
0091 Issun Boshi. The Inchlins.
0103 Magic Monkey, The

DENMARK

0173 Autun and the Bear
0377 Havelok the Dane

DEVIL

0293 Captain Ichabod Paddock, Whaler of Nantucket
0275 Kellyburn Braes
0351 Painting the Moon

DEVIL (NEARSIGHTED)

0273 Ote

DIAMOND HALF-PENNY

0160 Little Cock, The

DICK WHITTINGTON

0357 Dick Whittington
0365 Dick Whittington and His Cat

DIONYSIS

0356 Dionysos and the Pirates: Homeric Hymn Number Seven

DIONYSOS

0356 Dionysos and the Pirates: Homeric Hymn Number Seven

DISOBEDIENCE

0139 Mr. Miacca

DISPUTE OVER DESCRIPTION OF ELEPHANT

0120 Blind Men and the Elephant, The
0121 Blind Men and the Elephant, The

DJINNS

0131 Sundiata, The Epic of the Lion King

DOG(S)

0217 Bremen Town Musicians, The
0125 Coconut Thieves, The
0244 Fox, the Dog, and the Griffin, The
0009 Great Big Enormous Turnip, The
0255 Little Red Hen, The
0116 Magic Ring, The
0254 Old Mother Hubbard and Her Dog
0247 Tinder Box, The
0038 Traveling Musicians, The

DOLL (GODMOTHER)

0352 Vasilisa the Beautiful

DOLLS

0106 Nine(9) Cry-Baby Dolls

DONKEY

0217 Bremen Town Musicians, The
0010 Donkey Ride, The
0264 Hee Haw
0005 Miller, His Son, and Their Donkey, The
0176 Miller, The Boy, and the Donkey, The
0038 Traveling Musicians, The
0123 Valiant Chattee-Maker, The
0164 Wise Rooster, The

DOUGHNUTS

0299 Cap'n Dow and the Hole in the Doughnut

DRAGON

0039 Four Clever Brothers, The
0023 Ivanko and the Dragon
0155 St. George and the Dragon
0286 Sword of Siegfried, The

DRAGON KILLS BEOWULF

0373 Beowulf the Warrior
0375 Beowulf, Story of

0227 By His Own Might: The
Battles of Beowulf

DRAWING TALE

0363 Wild Ducks and the
Goose, The

DREAM(S)

0208 Gilgamesh: Man's First Story
0033 Jorinda and Joringel
0247 Tinder Box, The
0004 Twelve Dancing Princesses,
The

DREAM, ADVICE TO PEDDLER

0403 Pedlar of Swaffham, The

DREAM, NUTCRACKER, AND SUGAR PLUM FAIRY

0390 Nutcracker
0232 Nutcracker
0231 Nutcracker

DREAMING, DAY

0285 Don't Count Your Chicks
0059 Little Match Girl, The
0315 Maid and Her Pail of Milk, The

DRINKING

0090 Five Chinese Brothers, The

DRONGO BIRD

0126 Rakoto and the Drongo Bird

DROUGHT

0301 Andy Jackson's Water Well
0191 Beeswax Catches a Thief
0410 Palm Tree, The Legend of
the

DRUM CONTAINING SINGING GIRL

0345 When the Drum Sang

DUCK

0031 Good-For-Nothings, The
0255 Little Red Hen, The
0229 Peter and the Wolf
0363 Wild Ducks and the Goose,
The

DUCKLING

0246 Ugly Duckling, The
0061 Ugly Duckling, The

DUMMLING (SIMPLETON)

0343 Grimm's Golden Goose

DUMPLING (COULD TALK AND ROLL)

0185 Dumplings and the Demons, The

DWARF

0284 King of the Golden River, The
or The Black Brothers
0201 King of the Golden River, The
or The Black Brothers
0152 King of the Golden River, The
or The Black Brothers
0378 Knight of the Cart, The
0168 Little Tuppen
0203 Seven Ravens, The
0030 Sleeping Beauty, The
0006 Snow White and Rose Red
0008 Snow-White and Rose-Red
0036 Snow White and the Seven
Dwarfs
0131 Sundiata, The Epic of the
Lion King
0215 Thieving Dwarfs, The

DWARF LONGNOSE

0371 Dwarf Long-Nose

EAGLE

0117 Carpet of Solomon
0349 Eagle Mask: A West Coast
Indian Tale
0170 Wisest Man In the World, The

EARTH

0167 Good Llama, The

EARTHQUAKE

0189 Three Gold Pieces

EGG(S)

0156 Eggs, The
0069 Speckled Hen
0050 Why the Sun Was Late

EGYPT

0155 St. George and the Dragon

ELEPHANT

0121 Blind Men and the Elephant,
The
0120 Blind Men and the Elephant,
The
0186 Emperor's Big Gift, The

STORIES BY SUBJECT

0375 Beowulf, Story of
0227 By His Own Might: The Battles of Beowulf
0045 Clashing Rocks: The Story of Jason, The
0356 Dionysos and the Pirates: Homeric Hymn Number Seven
0354 Fisherman and the Goblet, The
0044 Gorgon's Head: The Story of Perseus, The
0348 Heracles the Strong
0272 Ramayana, The
0286 Sword of Siegfried, The
0344 Vinlanders' Saga
0046 Way of Danger: The Story of Theseus, The
0114 You Never Can Tell

FEATHERS

0052 Feather Mountain

FIGS AND CHERRIES (MAGIC)

0311 Too Much Nose

FIREBIRD

0073 Humpy
0065 Prince Ivan, the Firebird, and the Gray Wolf, The Story of

FISH

0116 Magic Ring, The

FISH (FLOUNDER)

0179 Fisherman and His Wife, The
0084 Fisherman and His Wife, The

FISH EYE

0174 Angry Moon, The

FISHBONE

0109 Joco and the Fishbone (An Arabian Nights Tale)

FISHERMAN (MEN)

0179 Fisherman and His Wife, The
0084 Fisherman and His Wife, The
0093 Golden Crane, The
0149 Six Foolish Fishermen

FISHERMAN PLAYS FLUTE FOR PRINCESS

0354 Fisherman and the Goblet, The

FLAX

0053 Golden Seed, The

FLEA

0328 Steel Flea, The

FLOOD

0208 Gilgamesh: Man's First Story
0167 Good Llama, The

FLOWER KING

0048 Thumbelina
0394 Thumbelina

FLOWER, BLACK SUNFLOWER

0076 Baba Yaga
0033 Jorinda and Joringel

FLOWERS

0113 Peacock and the Crow, The

FLOWERS (SNOWDROP)

0341 Month Brothers, The

FLUTE

0129 Princess of the Full Moon

FLUTE AND SILVER BELLS (MAGIC)

0271 Magic Flute, The

FLY (FLIES)

0087 Sixty At a Blow
0013 Valiant Tailor, The

FOLKSONG

0327 Billy Boy
0359 Erie Canal, The
0320 Fox Went Out On a Chilly Night, The

FOOD

0127 Never-Empty

FOREST SPRITES

0047 Heart of Stone. A Fairy Tale

FOREST SPIRITS

0105 Black Heart of Indri, The

FORGETTING (FORGETFULNESS)

0124 Bojabi Tree, The
0192 Bojabi Tree, The
0082 Judge Not

STORIES BY SUBJECT

0083 Just Say Hic!
0273 Ote

FORMULA TALE

0141 All in the Morning Early
0192 Bojabi Tree, The
0124 Bojabi Tree, The
0235 Cock Robin and Jenny Wren
0329 Fat Cat, The
0361 Gingerbread Boy, The
0009 Great Big Enormous Turnip, The
0085 Grindstone of God, The
0181 Hans In Luck
0251 Happy-Go-Lucky
0278 Henny Penny
0358 Henny Penny
0198 House That Jack Built, The
0281 House That Jack Built, The
0150 House That Jack Built, The
     or Maison Que Jacques a
     Batie, La
0292 Hush Little Baby
0109 Joco and the Fishbone (An
     Arabian Nights Tale)
0143 Johnny-Cake
0302 Journey Cake, Ho!
0260 Judge, The
0368 Little Red Hen
0255 Little Red Hen, The
0168 Little Tuppen
0077 Mitten, The
0306 Mommy, Buy Me a China Doll
0318 Monkey's Whiskers, The
0355 Munachar and Manachar
0276 Old Woman and Her Pig, The
0382 One Fine Day
0166 Snow and the Sun, The
0069 Speckled Hen
0054 Such Is the Way of the World
0262 Swapping Boy, The
0243 The Rabbit and the Turnip
0151 Thirteen Days of Yule, The
0003 Turnip, The
0122 Usha the Mouse-Maiden
0305 Wart Snake In a Fig Tree, A
0308 What the Good Man Does Is
     Always Right
0062 White Rat's Tale, The
0050 Why the Sun Was Late

FOX REGAINS HIS TAIL

0382 One Fine Day

FOX(ES)

0187 Fox Wedding, The
0320 Fox Went Out On a Chilly
     Night, The
0225 Fox, and the Hare, The

0244 Fox, the Dog, and the Griffin,
     The
0085 Grindstone of God, The
0041 Horse, the Fox, and the Lion,
     The
0143 Johnny-Cake
0310 Little White Hen
0163 Mourka, The Mighty Cat
0071 Neighbors, The
0325 Rooster, Mouse, and Little Red
     Hen, The
0324 Rooster, the Mouse, and the Little
     Red Hen, The

FRIENDSHIP

0173 Autun and the Bear
0125 Coconut Thieves, The
0012 Elephants and the Mice, The
     (Panchatantra Tale)
0208 Gilgamesh: Man's First Story
0171 Ice Bird, The
0307 Lion and the Rat, The
0027 Nail Soup
0028 Stone Soup, an Old Tale
0215 Thieving Dwarfs, The
0353 Why the Sun and the Moon
     Live In the Sky

FROG

0029 Sleeping Beauty, The
0112 Three Feathers, The

FROG AND MOUSE

0258 Frog Went A-Courtin'

FRONTIER AND PIONEER LIFE

0393 Monkey See, Monkey Do
0389 Story of Johnny Appleseed
0250 Big Fraid Little Fraid

GEESE

0034 Goose Girl, The
0023 Ivanko and the Dragon

GENI AND THE LAMP

0402 Aladdin and the Wonderful
     Lamp
0404 Aladdin, The Story of

GERDA AND KAY ESCAPE THE SNOW QUEEN

0397 Snow Queen, The
0049 Snow Queen, The

GHOSTS

0250 Big Fraid Little Fraid

STORIES BY SUBJECT

GIANT(S)

0227 By His Own Might: The
     Battles of Beowulf
0045 Clashing Rocks: The Story of
     Jason, The
0218 Count Carrot
0369 Joy of the Court
0011 Puss In Boots
0068 Salt
0087 Sixty At a Blow
0230 Tom Thumb
0395 Valentine and Orson
0013 Valiant Tailor, The

GINGERBREAD BOY

0361 Gingerbread Boy, The

GINGERBREAD HOUSE

0267 Hansel and Gretel
0216 Nibble, Nibble Mousekin

GLASS MOUNTAIN

0203 Seven Ravens, The

GLASSMAN

0047 Heart of Stone. A Fairy
     Tale

**GLOOSCAP (GOD OF THE
WABANAKI INDIANS)**

0248 Badger, The Mischief Maker

GOAT(S)

0192 Bojabı Tree, The
0124 Bojabi Tree, The
0214 Three Billy Goats Gruff, The
0200 Three Billy Goats Gruff, The
0161 Three Poor Tailors, The
0035 Wolf and the Seven Little
     Kids, The

GOBLET (UNANSWERED LOVE)

0354 Fisherman and the Goblet,
     The

GOBLIN

0239 Tops and Bottoms

GOD

0374 Beowulf
0373 Beowulf the Warrior
0375 Beowulf, Story of
0227 By His Own Might: The
     Battles of Beowulf
0117 Carpet of Solomon
0084 Fisherman and His Wife, The

0179 Fisherman and His Wife, The
0085 Grindstone of God, The
0073 Humpy
0079 Little Juggler, The
0351 Painting the Moon
0057 Wild Swans, The

GODDESS OF MERCY (KWAN-YIN)

0097 Willow Plate, Legend of

GODDESS OF THE FOREST

0096 Two Stonecutters, The

GODS

0045 Clashing Rocks: The Story of
     Jason, The
0356 Dionysos and the Pirates:
     Homeric Hymn Number Seven
0044 Gorgon's Head: The Story of
     Perseus, The
0348 Heracles the Strong
0286 Sword of Siegfried, The
0046 Way of Danger: The Story of
     Theseus, The

GODS OF GILGAMESH

0208 Gilgamesh: Man's First Story

GOLD

0053 Golden Seed, The
0015 Golden Touch, The
0182 Rich Man and the Shoe-Maker,
     The

GOLD PIECES

0189 Three Gold Pieces

GOLDEN GOOSE

0222 Golden Goose, The

GOLDILOCKS

0137 Three Bears, The Story of
0233 Three Bears, The Story of

GOOSE

0363 Wild Ducks and the Goose, The

GOOSE SWALLOWS NECKLACE

0188 Juan Bobo and the Queen's
     Necklace

GOVERNOR

0086 Suho and the White Horse

GRAIN HARVESTING

0172 Seven Silly Wise Men

STORIES BY SUBJECT

GRASSHOPPER

0205 John J. Plenty and Fiddler Dan

GRASSHOPPER WAR

0297 Hippity Hopper, The or Why There Are No Indians In Pennsylvania

GRATEFUL ANIMALS

0220 Monkey, the Lion, and the Snake, The

GREEDINESS

0107 Ali-Baba and the Forty-Thieves Thieves
0105 Black Heart of Indri, The
0179 Fisherman and His Wife, The
0084 Fisherman and His Wife, The
0093 Golden Crane, The
0015 Golden Touch, The
0146 Hudden and Dudden and Donald O'Neary
0355 Munachar and Manachar
0127 Never-Empty
0089 Stargazer to the Sultan
0175 Who Was Tricked?

GREEN CHILDREN

0364 Green Children, The

GREEN KNIGHT

0366 Challenge of the Green Knight, The
0154 Sir Gawain and the Green Knight

GREENLAND

0344 Vinlanders' Saga

GRIFFIN

0244 Fox, the Dog, and the Griffin, The

GRIMM, THE BROTHERS

0217 Bremen Town Musicians, The
0313 Elves and the Shoemaker, The
0398 Elves and the Shoemaker, The
0179 Fisherman and His Wife, The
0084 Fisherman and His Wife, The
0039 Four Clever Brothers, The
0222 Golden Goose, The
0031 Good-For-Nothings, The
0034 Goose Girl, The
0343 Grimm's Golden Goose
0181 Hans In Luck

0267 Hansel and Gretel
0219 Hedgehog and the Hare, The
0041 Horse, the Fox, and the Lion, The
0033 Jorinda and Joringel
0095 King Thrushbeard
0042 King Thrushbeard
0180 Little Red Riding Hood
0211 Little Red Riding Hood
0032 Luck Child, The
0216 Nibble, Nibble Mousekin
0040 Rapunzel
0287 Rumpelstiltskin
0203 Seven Ravens, The
0037 Shoemaker and the Elves, The
0029 Sleeping Beauty, The
0006 Snow White and Rose Red
0008 Snow-White and Rose-Red
0036 Snow white and the Seven Dwarfs
0038 Traveling Musicians, The
0178 Twelve Dancing Princesses
0013 Valiant Tailor, The
0035 Wolf and the Seven Little Kids, The

GRINDSTONE

0085 Grindstone of God, The

GUN

0039 Four Clever Brothers, The
0066 Seven Simeons

HAIRSTRING (MAGIC)

0248 Badger, The Mischief Maker

HARE TRICKS ANIMALS

0128 Extraordinary Tug-of-War

HARE(S)

0225 Fox, and the Hare, The
0157 Hare and the Tortoise, The
0081 Hare and the Tortoise, The
0219 Hedgehog and the Hare, The
0127 Never-Empty

HARP (GOLDEN)

0226 Jack and the Beanstalk
0144 Jack and the Beanstalk

HARVESTING

0239 Tops and Bottoms
0190 Why the Jackal Won't Speak to the Hedgehog

HAT, HORN, COIN PURSE

0311 Too Much Nose

STORIES BY SUBJECT

HAVELOK

0377 Havelok the Dane

HAWAII

0304 Punia and the King of the
Sharks

HEDGEHOG

0076 Baba Yaga
0219 Hedgehog and the Hare, The
0190 Why the Jackal Won't Speak
to the Hedgehog

HELEN OF TROY

0289 Trojan Horse, The

HELPFULNESS

0279 Buried Moon, The
0313 Elves and the Shoemaker,
The
0398 Elves and the Shoemaker,
The
0168 Little Tuppen
0037 Shoemaker and the Elves, The
The

HEN

0194 Crocodile and Hen
0031 Good-For-Nothings, The
0310 Little White Hen

HEN LAID MAGIC EGGS

0408 Wonderful Eggs of
Furicchia

HEN LAYS GOLDEN EGGS

0144 Jack and the Beanstalk
0226 Jack and the Beanstalk

HERB ENCHANTMENT

0371 Dwarf Long-Nose
0372 Taliesin and King Arthur

HERCULES

0348 Heracles the Strong

HERMIT TRANSF. MOUSE

0323 Once a Mouse

HERONS

0051 Look, There Is a Turtle Flying

HINDU TRINITY (BRAHMA, VISHNU, AND SHIVA)

0272 Ramayana, The

HIPPOPOTAMUS

0128 Extraordinary Tug-of-War

HITOPADESA

0323 Once a Mouse

HOLLANDER MIKE, LUMBERJACK

0047 Heart of Stone: A Fairy Tale

HOLY MAN

0122 Usha the Mouse-Maiden

HOLY WATER

0152 King of the Golden River, The
or the Black Brothers
0201 King of the Golden River, The
or the Black Brothers
0284 King of the Golden River, The
or the Black Brothers

HOP O' MY THUMB

0396 Hop O' My Thumb

HORN WAKENS KNIGHTS FROM ENCHANTED SLEEP

0369 Joy of the Court

HORSE

0100 Good-Luck Horse
0034 Goose Girl, The
0085 Grindstone of God, The
0041 Horse, the Fox, and the Lion,
The
0073 Humpy
0021 Kappa's Tug-of-War With Big
Brown Horse. The Story of
a Japanese Water Imp
0065 Prince Ivan, The Firebird, and
the Gray Wolf, The Story of
0086 Suho and the White Horse
0064 Tsar's Riddle or the Wise
Little Girl
0253 Widdecombe Fair
0114 You Never Can Tell

HORSE-HEAD FIDDLE

0086 Suho and the White Horse

HOUSES MADE OF WOOD AND ICE

0225 Fox, and the Hare, The

HOUSEWORK

0111 Gone Is Gone or The Story of
a Man Who Wanted to Do the
Housework

STORIES BY SUBJECT

0138 Pixy and the Lazy Housewife, The

HUMBABA (MONSTER)

0208 Gilgamesh: Man's First Story

HUMILITY

0117 Carpet of Solomon

ICARUS' WINGS MELT

0319 Fall From the Sky: The Story of Daedalus

IMMORTALITY

0208 Gilgamesh: Man's First Story

IMPS

0050 Why the Sun Was Late

INCAS

0167 Good Llama, The

INDIA

0186 Emperor's Big Gift, The
0110 Flying Carpet, The

INDIANS, NORTHWESTERN AMERICA

0349 Eagle Mask: A West Coast Indian Tale

INDIVIDUALITY, EXPRESSING

0010 Donkey Ride, The
0264 Hee Haw
0005 Miller, His Son, and Their Donkey, The
0176 Miller, the Boy, and the Donkey, The

INDUSTRIOUS

0368 Little Red Hen
0255 Little Red Hen, The

INDUSTRIOUS ANT VERSUS LAZY GRASSHOPPER

0205 John J. Plenty and Fiddler Dan

INDUSTRY

0296 Joe Magarac and His USA Citizen Papers

INITIATION RITUALS

0349 Eagle Mask: A West Coast Indian Tale

INSTRUCTIONS OF MOTHER FOLLOWED FOLLOWED LITERALLY BY SON

0294 Epaminondas and His Auntie
0256 Lazy Jack
0145 Lazy Jack
0199 Silly Simon

INVENTION

0319 Fall From the Sky: The Story of Daedalus

INVISIBILITY

0117 Carpet of Solomon
0044 Gorgon's Head: The Story of Perseus, The
0103 Magic Monkey, The
0129 Princess of the Full Moon
0379 Story, a Story, A
0215 Thieving Dwarfs, The
0311 Too Much Nose
0178 Twelve Dancing Princesses
0004 Twelve Dancing Princesses, The

IRON-EATING MICE

0322 Mice That Ate Iron, The

IRON-NECK

0090 Five Chinese Brothers, The

ITALY

0220 Monkey, the Lion, and the Snake, The
0408 Wonderful Eggs of Furicchia

JACK AND THE BEANSTALK

0144 Jack and the Beanstalk
0226 Jack and the Beanstalk

JACK SPRAT

0259 Jack Sprat, His Wife and His Cat, The Life of

JACK TALES

0002 Jack and the Three Sillies

JACK, THE HOUSE THAT J. BUILT

0281 House That Jack Built, The
0198 House That Jack Built, The
0150 House That Jack Built, The or Maison Que Jacques a Batie, La

STORIES BY SUBJECT

JACKAL

JACOBS, JOSEPH

JATAKA

JEALOUSY

JEWEL (PRECIOUS STONE)

JIZO, GOD OF THE CHILDREN

JOE MAGARAC, STEEL MAN

JOHN HENRY

JOHN TABOR

JOHNNY APPLESEED

JUDAS

JUDGE PERSUADED BY HIGH-FLOWN SPEECH

JUDGE(S)

JUGGLER

JUSTICE

KAPPA – WATER SPIRIT

KEY (GOLD)

KIDS

STORIES BY SUBJECT

KINDNESS

0020 Beauty and the Beast
0270 Cinderella
0063 Cinderella or the Little
      Glass Slipper
0092 Crane Maiden, The
0398 Elves and the Shoemaker, The
0313 Elves and the Shoemaker, The
0093 Golden Crane, The
0041 Horse, the Fox, and the Lion,
      The
0023 Ivanko and the Dragon
0094 Kap and the Wicked Monkey
0284 King of the Golden River, The
      or the Black Brothers
0152 King of the Golden River, The
      or the Black Brothers
0201 King of the Golden River, The
      or the Black Brothers
0307 Lion and the Rat, The
0116 Magic Ring, The
0204 Nightingale, The
0060 Nightingale, The
0242 Otwe
0037 Shoemaker and the Elves,
      The
0006 Snow White and Rose Red
0008 Snow-White and Rose-Red
0243 The Rabbit and the Turnip
0400 Three Brothers, The
0096 Two Stonecutters, The

KING ARTHUR

0280 Diverting Adventures of Tom
      Thumb, The
0230 Tom Thumb

KITE

0098 Emperor and the Kite, The

KNIFE

0087 Sixty At a Blow

KNIGHTHOOD

0366 Challenge of the Green
      Knight, The
0153 Kitchen Knight, The
0154 Sir Gawain and the Green
      Knight
0155 St. George and the
      Dragon

**KNOTHOLE, ELVES CAN BE VIEWED
THROUGH IT**

0283 Goblin Under the Stairs, The

LA FONTAINE

0081 Hare and the Tortoise, The
0307 Lion and the Rat, The
0176 Miller, the Boy, and the
      Donkey, The
0080 North Wind and the Sun
0182 Rich Man and the Shoe-Maker,
      The

**LADDER TO HEAVEN MADE OF
SPIDER WEB**

0379 Story, a Story, A

LAIRD

0362 Laird of Cockpen, The

LAMP, MAGIC

0402 Aladdin and the Wonderful
      Lamp
0404 Aladdin, The Story of

LANCELOT

0378 Knight of the Cart, The

LANGUAGES, KNOWLEDGE OF

0316 What Bobolino Knew

LAZY JACK

0145 Lazy Jack
0256 Lazy Jack
0199 Silly Simon

LAZY WOMAN

0138 Pixy and the Lazy Housewife,
      The

LEAR, EDWARD

0391 Owl and the Pussy-Cat, The

LEIF THE LUCKY

0344 Vinlanders' Saga

LENNI LENAPE INDIANS

0297 Hippity Hopper, The or Why
      There Are No Indians In
      Pennsylvania

LEPRECHAUN

0355 Munachar and Manachar

**LEPRECHAUN HELPS PRINCESS
CLIMB MT.**

0388 Blue Mountain, The

STORIES BY SUBJECT

LIFE, ETERNAL

0103 Magic Monkey, The

LION HELPS MAN IN GRATITUDE

0367 Knight of the Lion, The

LION(S)

0041 Horse, the Fox, and the
      Lion, The
0307 Lion and the Rat, The
0220 Monkey, the Lion, and
      the Snake, The
0170 Wisest Man In the World, The

LITTLE PEOPLE

0280 Diverting Adventures of
      Tom Thumb, The
0091 Issun Boshi. The Inchlins.
0048 Thumbelina
0394 Thumbelina
0184 Timimoto's Great Adventures
0230 Tom Thumb

LITTLE RED HEN (ASKS ANIMALS TO HELP HER)

0368 Little Red Hen
0255 Little Red Hen, The

LITTLE TOM TUCKER

0257 Little Tom Tucker, The
      History of

LIZARDS

0063 Cinderella or the Little
      Glass Slipper

LLAMA

0167 Good Llama, The

LOBSTERS

0304 Punia and the King of
      the Sharks

LONDON BRIDGE

0197 London Bridge Is Falling
      Down
0282 London Bridge Is Falling
      Down

LONELINESS

0238 Six Who Were Left in a
      Shoe

LOVE

0254 Fisherman and the Goblet, The
0309 King Carlo of Capri
0072 My Mother Is the Most Beautiful
      Woman In the World
0097 Willow Plate, Legend of

LOVE, SELFLESS

0105 Black Heart of Indri, The
0092 Crane Maiden, The
0098 Emperor and the Kite, The
0380 Little Mermaid, The
0387 Little Mermaid, The
0058 Little Mermaid, The
0384 Orange Princess, The Legend
      of the
0129 Princess of the Full Moon
0203 Seven Ravens, The
0057 Wild Swans, The

LOYALTY

0107 Ali-Baba and the Forty-Thieves
0244 Fox, the Dog, and the Griffin,
      The
0251 Happy-Go-Lucky
0377 Havelok the Dane
0065 Prince Ivan, the Firebird, and
      the Gray Wolf, The Story of
0007 Puss In Boots
0011 Puss In Boots
0183 Puss In Boots
0397 Snow Queen, The
0049 Snow Queen, The

LUCKY SUCCESSES

0399 Yuri and the Mooneygoats

LULLABY

0292 Hush Little Baby
0306 Mommy, Buy Me a China Doll
0133 Lullaby: Why the Pussy Cat
      Washes Himself So Often

MAGIC BASKET, COCK AND BROOMSTICK

0221 Cobbler's Dilemma, The

MAGIC FIDDLE, STICK, SACK

0240 Magic Sack, The

MAGIC WAND

0103 Magic Monkey, The

MAGICIAN

0402 Aladdin and the Wonderful
      Lamp

0404 Aladdin, The Story of
0074 Golden Cockerel, The
0100 Good-Luck Horse
0103 Magic Monkey, The

MAHARAJAH

0116 Magic Ring, The

MAINE

0299 Cap'n Dow and the Hole
In the Doughnut

MAKING PRINCESS, GIRL LAUGH

0222 Golden Goose, The
0343 Grimm's Golden Goose
0145 Lazy Jack
0199 Silly Simon

MALLET (MAGIC)

0091 Issun Boshi. The Inchlins.

MANDARIN

0105 Black Heart of Indri, The
0354 Fisherman and the Goblet,
The
0097 Willow Plate, Legend of

MANKIND, STORY OF

0208 Gilgamesh: Man's First
Story

MARRIED BLISS

0251 Happy-Go-Lucky
0308 What the Good Man Does
Is Always Right

MASSACHUSETTS

0293 Captain Ichabod Paddock,
Whaler of Nantucket

MATCHES

0059 Little Match Girl, The

MAZEL AND SHIMAZEL

0266 Mazel and Shimazel or
the Milk of a Lioness

MERLIN, MAGICIAN

0280 Diverting Adventures of
Tom Thumb, The
0230 Tom Thumb

MERMAID

0293 Captain Ichabod Paddock,
Whaler of Nantucket

MERMAID RESCUES HERO FROM SHIPWRECK

0058 Little Mermaid, The
0387 Little Mermaid, The
0380 Little Mermaid, The

MIDDLE EAST

0132 Thirty Gilt Pennies, The

MILKY WAY

0103 Magic Monkey, The

MILLER

0187 Fox Wedding, The
0005 Miller, His Son, and Their
Donkey, The

MIRROR

0020 Beauty and the Beast
0245 Mai-Ling and the Mirror
0036 Snow White and the Seven
Dwarfs

MISFORTUNE (MONSTER)

0241 I Am Your Misfortune

MITTEN(S)

0077 Mitten, The

MOLLY WHUPPIE

0392 Molly Whuppie

MONK

0098 Emperor and the Kite, The

MONKEY

0250 Big Fraid Little Fraid
0094 Kap and the Wicked Monkey
0021 Kappa's Tug-of-War With Big
Brown Horse. The Story of a
Japanese Water Imp
0103 Magic Monkey, The
0195 Monkey and the Crocodile, The
0220 Monkey, the Lion, and the
Snake, The
0318 Monkey's Whiskers, The
0118 Stolen Necklace, The
0054 Such Is the Way of the World

MONKEY MAKES FRONTIER LIFE EXCITING

0393 Monkey See, Monkey Do

MONSTER

0241 I Am Your Misfortune

STORIES BY SUBJECT

STORIES BY SUBJECT

STORIES BY SUBJECT

162

STORIES BY SUBJECT

164

STORIES BY SUBJECT

SERBIA

0400 Three Brothers, The

SERGEANT O'KEEFE

0252 Sergeant O'Keefe and His Mule, Balaam

SERPENT'S TEETH

0045 Clashing Rocks: The Story of Jason, The

SHARING

0236 Crane With One Leg, The
0222 Golden Goose, The
0053 Golden Seed, The
0343 Grimm's Golden Goose
0079 Little Juggler, The
0133 Lullaby: Why the Pussy-Cat Washes Himself So Often
0240 Magic Sack, The
0070 No Room, An Old Story Retold
0006 Snow White and Rose Red
0008 Snow-White and Rose-Red

SHARING OF HOUSE WITH TRAVELERS

0370 Always Room for One More

SHARKS

0304 Punia and the King of the Sharks

SHAVING BRUSH TAILS

0209 Old Satan

SHAWNEE INDIANS

0297 Hippity Hopper, The or Why There Are No Indians in Pennsylvania

SHEPHERD(S)

0086 Suho and the White Horse

SHIELD, MAGIC

0044 Gorgon's Head: The Story of Perseus, The

SHIP (MAGIC)

0075 Fool of the World and the Flying Ship, The
0066 Seven Simeons

SHIRT

0002 Jack and the Three Sillies

SHOEMAKER

0398 Elves and the Shoemaker, The
0313 Elves and the Shoemaker, The
0182 Rich Man and the Shoemaker, The
0037 Shoemaker and the Elves, The

SICILY

0316 What Bobolino Knew

SIEGFRIED

0286 Sword of Siegfried, The

SIMPLE SIMON

0277 Simon's Song

SIMPLETON

0222 Golden Goose, The
0256 Lazy Jack

SINGING GAMES

0282 London Bridge is Falling Down
0261 Ol' Dan Tucker

SISTER SEEKS BROTHERS

0203 Seven Ravens, The
0057 Wild Swans, The

SKULL'S LIGHT DESTROYS STEPMOTHER AND STEPSISTER

0352 Vasilisa the Beautiful

SKY COUNTRY

0194 Angry Moon, The

SKY GOD

0379 Story, A Story, A

SLAPPY HOOPER, SIGN PAINTER

0303 Slappy Hooper the Wonderful Sign Painter

SLAVERY

0126 Rakoto and the Drongo Bird

SLEEP EXTENDED OVER MANY YEARS

0218 Count Carrot
0376 Rip Van Winkle

SMELL (SELLING OF)

0206 Wise Fool, The

SNAKE

0125 Coconut Thieves, The
0116 Magic Ring, The

STORIES BY SUBJECT

0220　Monkey, the Lion, and
　　　　the Snake, The
0242　Otwe

SNOBBERY

0055　Swineherd, The

SNOBBISHNESS

0042　King Thrushbeard
0095　King Thrushbeard
0129　Princess of the Full
　　　　Moon

SNOW

0166　Snow and the Sun,
　　　　The

SNOW QUEEN

0397　Snow Queen, The
0049　Snow Queen, The

SOAP, SOFT

0209　Old Satan

SOLDIER(S)

0162　Brave Soldier Janosh
0056　Steadfast Tin Soldier,
　　　　The
0028　Stone Soup, An Old
　　　　Tale
0247　Tinder Box, The
0178　Twelve Dancing
　　　　Princesses

SOLOMON

0117　Carpet of Solomon
0170　Wisest Man in the
　　　　World, The

SOONER, HOUND DOG

0298　Fast Sooner Hound,
　　　　The

SOOTHSAYER

0131　Sundiata, The Epic
　　　　of the Lion King

SORCERER(S)

0135　Sorcerer's Apprentice, The
0269　Sorcerer's Apprentice, The
0134　Sorcerer's Apprentice, The
0131　Sundiata, The Epic of the
　　　　Lion King
0067　Tale of Stolen Time, A

SORCERESS

0155　St. George and the Dragon

SOUP

0027　Nail Soup
0028　Stone Soup, An Old Tale

SOUTH-WEST WIND

0152　King of the Golden River, The
　　　　or The Black Brothers
0201　King of the Golden River, The
　　　　or The Black Brothers
0284　King of the Golden River, The
　　　　or The Black Brothers

SPAIN

0322　Mice That Ate Iron, The
0165　Perez and Martina
0164　Wise Rooster, The

SPINDLE

0029　Sleeping Beauty, The

SPINNING

0287　Rumpelstiltskin
0142　Tom Tit Tot

SPIRIT

0052　Feather Mountain
0050　Why the Sun Was Late

ST. NICHOLAS RESCUES BASILIO

0401　Golden Cup, The

STEALING

0118　Stolen Necklace, The

STEAM DRIVEN DRILL

0207　John Henry and His Hammer
0017　John Henry, An American
　　　　Legend
0016　Steel Driving Man, The Legend
　　　　of John Henry

STEEL

0296　Joe Magarac and His USA
　　　　Citizen Papers

STONE TRANSF. INTO
MOUNTAIN

0174　Angry Moon, The

STONECUTTERS

0096　Two Stonecutters, The

STORIES BY SUBJECT

TAR

0088 Hilili and Dilili

TELESCOPE (MAGIC)

0110 Flying Carpet, The
0039 Four Clever Brothers,
The

TELL, WILLIAM

0136 William Tell and His
Son

TENNESSEE

0301 Andy Jackson's Water
Well

THEFT

0191 Beeswax Catches A
Thief
0125 Coconut Thieves, The
0188 Juan Bobo and the
Queen's Necklace
0089 Stargazer to the
Sultan
0215 Theiving Dwarfs, The

**THIRTY PIECES OF SILVER
(GOLD)**

0132 Thirty Gilt Pennies,
The

THUMBELINA

0048 Thumbelina
0394 Thumbelina

TIDAL WAVE

0026 Burning Rice Fields,
The
0025 Wave, The

TIGER

0119 Tiger, The Brahman,
and the Jackal, The
0123 Valiant Chattee-Maker

TIME

0067 Tale of Stolen Time,
A

TIMIDITY

0314 Blue Jackal, The

TINDER BOX (MAGIC)

0247 Tinder Box, The

TLINGIT INDIANS (ALASKAN)

0174 Angry Moon, The

TOAD

0105 Black Heart of Indri, The

TOM THUMB

0280 Diverting Adventures of Tom
Thumb, The
0230 Tom Thumb

TOM, TOM THE PIPER'S SON

0317 Tom, Tom the Piper's Son

TORTOISE

0124 Bojabi Tree, The
0192 Bojabi Tree, The
0157 Hare and the Tortoise, The
0081 Hare and the Tortoise, The

TORTOISE TRICKS ANIMALS

0385 Tortoise's Tug of War, The

TOWER

0040 Rapunzel
0066 Seven Simeons

TRADING (SWAPPING SONG)

0262 Swapping Boy, The

TRADING OF OBJECTS

0308 What the Good Man Does Is
Always Right

TRAMP

0027 Nail Soup

**TREE, FIR WISHES FOR
UNOBTAINABLE**

0360 Fir Tree, The

TREES

0052 Feather Mountain

TROJAN HORSE

0289 Trojan Horse, The

TROLL
0200 Three Billy Goats Gruff, The
0214 Three Billy Goats Gruff, The

TROUSERS

0001 Three Sillies, The

STORIES BY SUBJECT

TRUTH

0109 Joco and the Fishbone
(An Arabian Nights Tale)

TSAR

0064 Tsar's Riddle or The Wise
Little Girl

TUG-OF-WAR

0128 Extraordinary Tug-Of-War
0385 Tortoise's Tug of War, The

TUPPEN

0168 Little Tuppen

TURKISH SULTAN

0160 Little Cock, The

TURNIP(S)

0076 Baba Yaga
0009 Great Big Enormous
Turnip, The
0243 The Rabbit and the
Turnip
0003 Turnip, The

TURTLE

0193 Clever Turtle, The
0125 Coconut Thieves, The
0051 Look, There Is A
Turtle Flying

**TWINS, SEPARATION OF T.
THROUGH BEING CARRIED
OFF BY A BEAR**

0395 Valentine and Orson

TYRANNY

0136 William Tell and His
Son

ULYSSES

0289 Trojan Horse, The

UMBRELLA

0288 One-Legged Ghost, The

UNICORN

0013 Valiant Tailor, The

UNSELFISHNESS

0004 Twelve Dancing
Princesses, The

VAGABOND

0342 Derby Ram, The

VALENTINE AND ORSON

0395 Valentine and Orson

VANITY

0381 Chinese Story Teller, The
0169 Emperor's New Clothes, The
0213 Emperor's New Clothes, The
0081 Hare and the Tortoise, The
0051 Look, There Is A Turtle Flying
0129 Princess of the Full Moon
0118 Stolen Necklace, The
0164 Wise Rooster, The

VIENNA

0268 Baker and the Basilisk, The

VIKINGS

0173 Autun and the Bear
0286 Sword of Siegfried, The
0344 Vinlanders' Saga

VINLAND

0344 Vinlanders' Saga

VISION

0117 Carpet of Solomon

WAR

0100 Good-Luck Horse
0263 Thousand and One Buddhas, A

WATER

0353 Why the Sun and the Moon
Live In the Sky

WATER SPIRIT (SPRITE)

0105 Black Heart of Indri, The
0021 Kappa's Tug-of-War With Big
Brown Horse. The Story of a
Japanese Water Imp

WEALTH

0096 Two Stonecutters, The

WEALTH, CURSE OF

0015 Golden Touch, The

WEAVER

0082 Judge Not

STORIES BY SUBJECT

WOMAN AND HEN

    0285 Don't Count Your Chicks

WOMAN AND PAIL OF MILK

    0315 Maid and Her Pail of Milk, The

WOMAN, OLD W. WITH MAGIC POWERS

    0400 Three Brothers, The

WOODCUTTER

    0089 Stargazer to the Sultan
    0177 Tale of A Pig
    0148 Three Wishes, The

YWAIN

    0367 Knight of the Lion, The

ENCHANTED PEOPLE

0218 Count Carrot
0110 Flying Carpet, The
0074 Golden Cockerel, The
0091 Issun Boshi. The Inchlins.
0369 Joy of the Court
0115 Long, Broad and Quickeye
0106 Nine(9) Cry-Baby Dolls
0376 Rip Van Winkle
0030 Sleeping Beauty, The
0029 Sleeping Beauty, The
0036 Snow White and the Seven
      Dwarfs
0286 Sword of Siegfried, The
0178 Twelve Dancing Princesses
0004 Twelve Dancing Princesses,
      The
0046 Way of Danger: The Story
      of Theseus, The

FOOLS AND SIMPLETONS

0406 Camel in the Tent
0010 Donkey Ride, The
0213 Emperor's New Clothes,
      The
0169 Emperor's New Clothes,
      The
0294 Epaminondas and His
      Auntie
0111 Gone is Gone or the Story
      of a Man Who Wanted
      To Do the Housework
0181 Hans In Luck
0264 Hee Haw
0088 Hilili and Dilili
0146 Hudden and Dudden and
      Donald O'Neary
0002 Jack and the Three Sillies
0109 Joco and the Fishbone
      (An Arabian Nights Tale)
0083 Just Say Hic!
0256 Lazy Jack
0145 Lazy Jack
0005 Miller, His Son, and Their
      Donkey, The
0176 Miller, The Boy, and The
      Donkey, The
0108 Nine in a Line
0140 Old Woman and the Pedlar,
      The
0287 Rumpelstiltskin
0172 Seven Silly Wise Men
0199 Silly Simon
0149 Six Foolish Fishermen

0087 Sixty at a Blow
0069 Speckled Hen
0054 Such Is the Way of the World
0161 Three Poor Tailors, The
0001 Three Sillies, The
0148 Three Wishes, The
0142 Tom Tit Tot
0064 Tsar's Riddle or The Wise
      Little Girl
0123 Valiant Chattee-Maker, The

FRIENDLY ANIMALS

0141 All In the Morning Early
0124 Bojabi Tree, The
0192 Bojabi Tree, The
0125 Coconut Thieves, The
0187 Fox Wedding, The
0225 Fox, and the Hare, The
0258 Frog Went A-Courtin'
0093 Golden Crane, The
0100 Good-Luck Horse
0171 Ice Bird, The
0094 Kap and the Wicked Monkey
0021 Kappa's Tug-of-War With Big
      Brown Horse. The Story of a
      Japanese Water Imp
0367 Knight of the Lion, The
0307 Lion and the Rat, The
0168 Little Tuppen
0133 Lullaby: Why the Pussy-Cat
      Washes Himself So Often
0116 Magic Ring, The
0341 Month Brothers, The
0391 Owl and the Pussy-Cat, The
0019 Pecos Bill and the Mustang
0165 Perez and Martina
0126 Rakoto and the Drongo Bird
0238 Six Who Were Left In a Shoe
0397 Snow Queen, The
0389 Story of Johnny Appleseed
0177 Tale of a Pig
0243 The Rabbit and the Turnip
0112 Three Feathers, The
0316 What Bobolino Knew

HUMOR

0141 All In the Morning Early
0370 Always Room For One More
0301 Andy Jackson's Water Well
0248 Badger, The Mischief Maker
0268 Baker and the Basilisk, The
0191 Beeswax Catches a Thief
0250 Big Fraid Little Fraid
0300 Big Mose

STORIES BY MOTIF

0393 Monkey See, Monkey Do
0318 Monkey's Whiskers, The
0163 Mourka, The Mighty Cat
0139 Mr. Miacca
0355 Munachar and Manachar
0027 Nail Soup
0108 Nine in a Line
0106 Nine (9) Cry-Baby Dolls
0070 No Room, An Old Story Retold
0080 North Wind and the Sun
0261 Ol' Dan Tucker
0254 Old Mother Hubbard and Her Dog
0209 Old Satan
0276 Old Woman and Her Pig, The
0140 Old Woman and the Pedlar, The
0382 One Fine Day
0202 One Good Deed Deserves Another
0288 One-legged Ghost, The
0273 Ote
0242 Otwe
0391 Owl and the Pussy-cat, The
0351 Painting the Moon
0290 Paul Bunyan
0291 Paul Bunyan, The Story of
0019 Pecos Bill and the Mustang
0403 Pedlar of Swaffham, The
0165 Perez and Martina
0265 Pigs and Pirates
0138 Pixy and the Lazy Housewife, The
0304 Punia and the King of the Sharks
0182 Rich Man and the Shoe-Maker, The
0376 Rip Van Winkle
0287 Rumpelstiltskin
0252 Sergeant O'Keefe and His Mule, Balaam
0172 Seven Silly Wise Men
0199 Silly Simon
0277 Simon's Song
0149 Six Foolish Fishermen
0238 Six Who Were Left In a Shoe
0087 Sixty at a Blow
0303 Slappy Hooper the Wonderful Sign Painter
0166 Snow and the Sun, The
0135 Sorcerer's Apprentice
0269 Sorcerer's Apprentice, The
0134 Sorcerer's Apprentice, The
0069 Speckled Hen
0089 Stargazer to the Sultan
0328 Steel Flea, The
0118 Stolen Necklace, The
0028 Stone Soup, An Old Tale
0379 Story, a Story, A

0054 Such Is the Way of the World
0262 Swapping Boy, The
0177 Tale of a Pig
0215 Thieving Dwarfs, The
0151 Thirteen Days of Yule, The
0214 Three Billy Goats Gruff, The
0200 Three Billy Goats Gruff, The
0161 Three Poor Tailors, The
0001 Three Sillies, The
0101 Three Stong Women
0148 Three Wishes, The
0119 Tiger, the Brahman, and The Jackal, The
0102 Tikki Tikki Tembo
0230 Tom Thumb
0142 Tom Tit Tot
0317 Tom, Tom the Piper's Son
0311 Too Much Nose
0239 Tops and Bottoms
0385 Tortoise's Tug of War, The
0038 Traveling Musicians, The
0064 Tsar's Riddle or The Wise Little Girl
0003 Turnip, The
0123 Valiant Chattee-Maker, The
0104 Very Special Badgers, The
0305 Wart Snake In a Fig Tree, A
0308 What the Good Man Does Is Always Right
0345 When the Drum Sang
0175 Who Was Tricked?
0353 Why the Sun and the Moon Live in the Sky
0253 Widdecombe Fair
0363 Wild Ducks and the Goose, The
0206 Wise Fool, The
0408 Wonderful Eggs of Furicchia
0399 Yuri and the Mooneygoats

LEGENDARY HEROES

0173 Autun and the Bear
0374 Beowulf
0373 Beowulf the Warrior
0375 Beowulf, Story of
0227 By His Own Might: The Battles of Beowulf
0117 Carpet of Solomon
0366 Challenge of the Green Knight, The
0347 Erec and Enid
0346 Every Man Heart Lay Down
0319 Fall From the Sky: The Story of Daedalus
0208 Gilgamesh: Man's First Story
0377 Havelok the Dane
0348 Heracles the Strong
0369 Joy of the Court
0284 King of the Golden River, The or the Black Brothers

STORIES BY MOTIF

0153 Kitchen Knight, The
0378 Knight of the Cart, The
0367 Knight of the Lion, The
0272 Ramayana, The
0154 Sir Gawain and the Green Knight
0155 St. George and the Dragon
0286 Sword of Siegfried, The
0372 Taliesin and King Arthur
0210 Tikta'liktak, An Eskimo Legend
0289 Trojan Horse, The
0395 Valentine and Orson
0344 Vinlanders' Saga
0170 Wisest Man in the World, The

LOCAL LEGENDARY HEROES

0301 Andy Jackson's Water Well
0248 Badger, The Mishief Maker
0300 Big Mose
0299 Cap'n Dow and the Hole In the Doughnut
0293 Captain Ichabod Paddock, Whaler of Nantucket
0295 Casey Jones: The Story of a Brave Engineer.
0298 Fast Sooner Hound, The
0047 Heart of Stone: A Fairy Tale
0326 How Old Stormalong Captured Mocha Dick
0296 Joe Magarac and His USA Citizen Papers
0207 John Henry and His Hammer
0017 John Henry, An American Legend
0340 John Tabor's Ride
0249 Magnificent House of Man Alone, The
0290 Paul Bunyan
0291 Paul Bunyan, The Story of
0019 Pecos Bill and the Mustang
0376 Rip Van Winkle
0252 Sergeant O'Keefe and His Mule, Balaam
0303 Slappy Hooper the Wonderful Sign Painter
0016 Steel Driving Man, The Legend of John Henry
0389 Story of Johnny Appleseed
0101 Three Strong Women

MAGIC OBJECTS

0402 Aladdin and the Wonderful Lamp
0404 Aladdin, The Story of
0107 Ali-Baba and the Forty-Thieves
0174 Angry Moon, The
0076 Baba Yaga

0020 Beauty and the Beast
0117 Carpet of Solomon
0381 Chinese Story Teller, The
0270 Cinderella
0063 Cinderella or the Little Glass Slipper
0045 Clashing Rocks: The Story of Jason, The
0221 Cobbler's Dilemma, The
0092 Crane Maiden, The
0371 Dwarf Long-nose
0398 Elves and the Shoemaker, The
0354 Fisherman and the Goblet, The
0110 Flying Carpet, The
0075 Fool of the World and the Flying Ship, The
0039 Four Clever Brothers, The
0361 Gingerbread Boy, The
0222 Golden Goose, The
0100 Good-Luck Horse
0034 Goose Girl, The
0044 Gorgon's Head: The Story of Perseus, The
0343 Grimm's Golden Goose
0396 Hop O' My Thumb
0073 Humpy
0091 Issun Boshi. The Inchlins.
0144 Jack and the Beanstalk
0226 Jack and the Beanstalk
0143 Johnny-Cake
0033 Jorinda and Joringel
0302 Journey Cake, Ho!
0369 Joy of the Court
0201 King of the Golden River, The or the Black Brothers
0152 King of the Golden River, The or the Black Brothers
0284 King of the Golden River, The or the Black Brothers
0380 Little Mermaid, The
0387 Little Mermaid, The
0058 Little Mermaid, The
0115 Long, Broad and Quickeye
0271 Magic Flute, The
0103 Magic Monkey, The
0116 Magic Ring, The
0240 Magic Sack, The
0341 Month Brothers, The
0127 Never-Empty
0106 Nine (9) Cry-Baby Dolls
0390 Nutcracker
0384 Orange Princess, The Legend of the
0065 Prince Ivan, the Firebird, and the Gray Wolf, The Story of
0129 Princess of the Full Moon
0272 Ramayana, The
0155 St. George and the Dragon
0203 Seven Ravens, The
0066 Seven Simeons

0030 Sleeping Beauty, The
0029 Sleeping Beauty, The
0049 Snow Queen, The
0036 Snow White and the Seven Dwarfs
0135 Sorcerer's Apprentice
0134 Sorcerer's Apprentice, The
0269 Sorcerer's Apprentice, The
0056 Steadfast Tin Soldier, The
0131 Sundiata, The Epic of the Lion King
0055 Swineherd, The
0286 Sword of Siegfried, The
0067 Tale of Stolen Time, A
0372 Taliesin and King Arthur
0215 Thieving Dwarfs, The
0247 Tinder Box, The
0311 Too Much Nose
0178 Twelve Dancing Princesses
0004 Twelve Dancing Princesses, The
0352 Vasilisa the Beautiful
0057 Wild Swans, The
0408 Wonderful Eggs of Furicchia

MAGIC TRANSFORMATION

0402 Aladdin and the Wonderful Lamp
0404 Aladdin, The Story of
0174 Angry Moon, The
0076 Baba Yaga
0020 Beauty and the Beast
0105 Black Heart of Indri, The
0270 Cinderella
0063 Cinderella or the Little Glass Slipper
0218 Count Carrot
0092 Crane Maiden, The
0356 Dionysos and the Pirates: Homeric Hymn Number Seven
0280 Diverting Adventures of Tom Thumb, The
0371 Dwarf Long-Nose
0244 Fox, the Dog, and the Griffin, The
0074 Golden Cockerel, The
0158 Greyling
0047 Heart of Stone: A Fairy Tale
0348 Heracles the Strong
0023 Ivanko and the Dragon
0144 Jack and the Beanstalk
0033 Jorinda and Joringel
0284 King of the Golden River, The or the Black Brothers
0152 King of the Golden River, The or the Black Brothers
0201 King of the Golden River, The or the Black Brothers

0058 Little Mermaid, The
0380 Little Mermaid, The
0387 Little Mermaid, The
0115 Long, Broad and Quickeye
0271 Magic Flute, The
0103 Magic Monkey, The
0341 Month Brothers, The
0390 Nutcracker
0232 Nutcracker, The
0231 Nutcracker, The
0323 Once a Mouse
0384 Orange Princess, The Legend of the
0410 Palm Tree, The Legend of the
0129 Princess of the Full Moon
0183 Puss in Boots
0007 Puss in Boots
0272 Ramayana, The
0203 Seven Ravens, The
0066 Seven Simeons
0154 Sir Gawain and the Green Knight
0006 Snow White and Rose Red
0008 Snow-White and Rose-Red
0131 Sundiata, The Epic of the Lion King
0177 Tale of a Pig
0067 Tale of Stolen Time, A
0372 Taliesin and King Arthur
0400 Three Brothers, The
0112 Three Feathers, The
0394 Thumbelina
0048 Thumbelina
0230 Tom Thumb
0311 Too Much Nose
0096 Two Stonecutters, The
0122 Usha the Mouse-Maiden
0104 Very Special Badgers, The
0062 White Rat's Tale, The
0057 Wild Swans, The
0097 Willow Plate, Legend of
0408 Wonderful Eggs of Furicchia

NATURE CALAMITIES

0301 Andy Jackson's Water Well
0026 Burning Rice Fields, The
0208 Gilgamesh: Man's First Story
0167 Good Llama, The
0410 Palm Tree, The Legend of the
0189 Three Gold Pieces
0025 Wave, The

POURQUOI STORIES

0299 Cap'n Dow and the Hole in the Doughnut
0381 Chinese Story Teller, The
0194 Crocodile and Hen
0383 Dancing Stars, The

STORIES BY MOTIF

REALISTIC EVENTS

RELIGION

STORIES BY MOTIF

0152 King of the Golden River,
     The or The Black Brothers
0284 King of the Golden River,
     The or The Black Brothers
0201 King of the Golden River,
     The or The Black Brothers
0367 Knight of the Lion, The
0160 Little Cock, The
0079 Little Juggler, The
0058 Little Mermaid, The
0387 Little Mermaid, The
0380 Little Mermaid, The
0168 Little Tuppen
0271 Magic Flute, The
0103 Magic Monkey, The
0240 Magic Sack, The
0266 Mazel and Shimazel or The
     Milk of a Lioness
0392 Molly Whuppie
0341 Month Brothers, The
0139 Mr. Miacca
0355 Munachar and Manachar
0216 Nibble, Nibble Mousekin
0080 North Wind and the Sun
0390 Nutcracker
0231 Nutcracker, The
0232 Nutcracker, The
0099 Oniroku and the Carpenter
0273 Ote
0242 Otwe
0351 Painting the Moon
0138 Pixy and the Lazy Housewife,
     The
0065 Prince Ivan, the Firebird, and
     the Gray Wolf, The Story
     of
0129 Princess of the Full Moon
0007 Puss In Boots
0183 Puss In Boots
0011 Puss In Boots
0126 Rakoto and the Drongo
     Bird
0272 Ramayana, The
0040 Rapunzel
0287 Rumpelstiltskin
0155 St. George and the Dragon
0068 Salt
0203 Seven Ravens, The
0037 Shoemaker and the Elves,
     The
0154 Sir Gawain and the Green
     Knight
0087 Sixty At a Blow
0030 Sleeping Beauty, The
0029 Sleeping Beauty, The
0397 Snow Queen, The
0049 Snow Queen, The
0006 Snow White and Rose Red
0008 Snow-White and Rose-Red
0036 Snow White and the Seven

     Dwarfs
0135 Sorcerer's Apprentice
0134 Sorcerer's Apprentice, The
0269 Sorcerer's Apprentice, The
0131 Sundiata, The Epic of the Lion
     King
0286 Sword of Siegfried, The
0177 Tale of a Pig
0067 Tale of Stolen Time, A
0215 Thieving Dwarfs, The
0263 Thousand and One Buddhas, A
0200 Three Billy Goats Gruff, The
0214 Three Billy Goats Gruff, The
0400 Three Brothers, The
0112 Three Feathers, The
0184 Timimoto's Great Adventures
0247 Tinder Box, The
0230 Tom Thumb
0142 Tom Tit Tot
0239 Tops and Bottoms
0178 Twelve Dancing Princesses
0004 Twelve Dancing Princesses, The
0096 Two Stonecutters, The
0122 Usha the Mouse-Maiden
0395 Valentine and Orson
0013 Valiant Tailor, The
0352 Vasilisa the Beautiful
0046 Way of Danger: The Story of
     Theseus, The
0345 When the Drum Sang
0062 White Rat's Tale, The
0050 Why the Sun Was Late
0253 Widdecombe Fair
0057 Wild Swans, The
0097 Willow Plate, Legend of
0408 Wonderful Eggs of Furicchia

TALKING ANIMALS

0141 All in the Morning Early
0191 Beeswax Catches a Thief
0105 Black Heart of Indri, The
0192 Bojabi Tree, The
0124 Bojabi Tree, The
0217 Bremen Town Musicians, The
0406 Camel in the Tent
0117 Carpet of Solomon
0321 Chanticleer and the Fox
0381 Chinese Story Teller, The
0193 Clever Turtle, The
0235 Cock Robin and Jenny Wren
0125 Coconut Thieves, The
0194 Crocodile and Hen
0371 Dwarf Long-Nose
0012 Elephants and the Mice, The
     (Panchatantra Tale)
0128 Extraordinary Tug-of-War
0329 Fat Cat, The
0052 Feather Mountain
0360 Fir Tree, The

STORIES BY MOTIF

STORIES BY MOTIF

TASKS AND TRIALS

0045 Clashing Rocks: The Story of Jason, The
0349 Eagle Mask: A West Coast Indian Tale
0090 Five Chinese Brothers, The
0110 Flying Carpet, The
0075 Fool of the World and the Flying Ship, The
0208 Gilgamesh: Man's First Story
0044 Gorgon's Head: The Story of Perseus, The
0343 Grimm's Golden Goose
0348 Heracles the Strong
0073 Humpy
0095 King Thrushbeard
0042 King Thrushbeard
0153 Kitchen Knight, The
0378 Knight of the Cart, The
0115 Long, Broad and Quickeye
0116 Magic Ring, The
0266 Mazel and Shimazel or The Milk of a Lioness
0392 Molly Whuppie
0065 Prince Ivan, the Firebird, and the Gray Wolf, The Story of
0155 Saint George and the Dragon
0203 Seven Ravens, The
0066 Seven Simeons
0154 Sir Gawain and the Green Knight
0087 Sixty At a Blow
0379 Story, a Story, A
0067 Tale of Stolen Time, A
0395 Valentine and Orson
0013 Valiant Tailor, The
0046 Way of Danger: The Story of Theseus, The
0057 Wild Swans, The
0399 Yuri and the Mooneygoats

TRICKERY

0402 Aladdin and the Wonderful Lamp
0404 Aladdin, The Story of
0107 Ali-Baba and the Forty-Thieves
0174 Angry Moon, The
0248 Badger, the Mischief Maker
0191 Beeswax Catches a Thief
0105 Black Heart of Indri, The
0321 Chanticleer and the Fox
0381 Chinese Story Teller, The
0193 Clever Turtle, The
0221 Cobbler's Dilemma, The
0125 Coconut Thieves, The
0218 Count Carrot
0156 Eggs, The

0169 Emperor's New Clothes, The
0213 Emperor's New Clothes, The
0128 Extraordinary Tug-of-War
0319 Fall From the Sky: The Story of Daedalus
0225 Fox, and the Hare, The
0244 Fox, the Dog, and the Griffin, The
0074 Golden Cockerel, The
0031 Good-For-Nothings, The
0034 Goose Girl, The
0405 Green Noses
0267 Hansel and Gretel
0047 Heart of Stone: A Fairy Tale
0219 Hedgehog and the Hare, The
0041 Horse, the Fox, and the Lion, The
0146 Hudden and Dudden and Donald O'Neary
0241 I Am Your Misfortune
0143 Johnny-Cake
0188 Juan Bobo and the Queen's Necklace
0082 Judge Not
0094 Kap and the Wicked Monkey
0021 Kappa's Tug-of-War With Big Brown Horse. The Story of a Japanese Water Imp
0095 King Thrushbeard
0042 King Thrushbeard
0211 Little Red Riding Hood
0180 Little Red Riding Hood
0043 Little Red Riding Hood, The Renowned History of
0310 Little White Hen
0032 Luck Child, The
0116 Magic Ring, The
0266 Mazel and Shimazel or The Milk of a Lioness
0322 Mice That Ate Iron, The
0392 Molly Whuppie
0195 Monkey and the Crocodile, The
0220 Monkey, the Lion, and the Snake, The
0318 Monkey's Whiskers, The
0127 Never-Empty
0216 Nibble, Nibble Mousekin
0140 Old Woman and the Pedlar, The
0202 One Good Deed Deserves Another
0273 Ote
0113 Peacock and the Crow, The
0229 Peter and the Wolf
0265 Pigs and Pirates
0138 Pixy and the Lazy Housewife, The

STORIES BY MOTIF

STORIES BY COUNTRY

0260 Judge, The
0309 King Carlo of Capri
0307 Lion and the Rat, The
0079 Little Juggler, The
0043 Little Red Riding Hood, The Renowned History of
0176 Miller, the Boy, and the Donkey, The
0080 North Wind and the Sun
0007 Puss In Boots
0183 Puss In Boots
0011 Puss In Boots
0078 Raminagrobis and the Mice
0182 Rich Man and the Shoe-Maker, The
0030 Sleeping Beauty, The
0028 Stone Soup, An Old Tale
0004 Twelve Dancing Princesses, The
0062 White Rat's Tale, The
0206 Wise Fool, The

GERMANY

0217 Bremen Town Musicians, The
0218 Count Carrot
0371 Dwarf Long-Nose
0398 Elves and the Shoemaker, The
0313 Elves and the Shoemaker, The
0084 Fisherman and His Wife, The
0179 Fisherman and His Wife, The
0039 Four Clever Brothers, The
0222 Golden Goose, The
0031 Good-For-Nothings, The
0034 Goose Girl, The
0343 Grimm's Golden Goose
0181 Hans In Luck
0267 Hansel and Gretel
0047 Heart of Stone: A Fairy Tale
0219 Hedgehog and the Hare, The
0041 Horse, the Fox, and the Lion, The
0033 Jorinda and Joringel
0095 King Thrushbeard
0042 King Thrushbeard
0180 Little Red Riding Hood
0211 Little Red Riding Hood
0032 Luck Child, The
0216 Nibble, Nibble Mousekin
0390 Nutcracker
0231 Nutcracker, The
0232 Nutcracker, The
0040 Rapunzel
0287 Rumpelstiltskin
0203 Seven Ravens, The
0037 Shoemaker and the Elves, The
0029 Sleeping Beauty, The
0006 Snow White and Rose Red
0036 Snow White and the Seven Dwarfs

0008 Snow-White and Rose-Red
0135 Sorcerer's Apprentice
0269 Sorcerer's Apprentice, The
0134 Sorcerer's Apprentice, The
0286 Sword of Siegfried, The
0215 Thieving Dwarfs, The
0132 Thirty Gilt Pennies, The
0112 Three Feathers, The
0038 Traveling Musicians, The
0178 Twelve Dancing Princesses
0013 Valiant Tailor, The
0035 Wolf and the Seven Little Kids, The

GREECE

0407 Bundle of Sticks, A
0406 Camel In the Tent
0045 Clashing Rocks: The Story of Jason, The
0356 Dionysos and the Pirates: Homeric Hymn Number Seven
0010 Donkey Ride, The
0156 Eggs, The
0319 Fall From the Sky: The Story of Daedalus
0015 Golden Touch, The
0044 Gorgon's Head: The Story of Perseus, The
0157 Hare and the Tortoise, The
0264 Hee Haw
0348 Heracles the Strong
0205 John J. Plenty and Fiddler Dan
0051 Look, There Is a Turtle Flying
0315 Maid and Her Pail of Milk, The
0005 Miller, His Son, and Their Donkey, The
0265 Pigs and Pirates
0189 Three Gold Pieces
0289 Trojan Horse, The
0046 Way of Danger: The Story of Theseus, The

HUNGARY

0162 Brave Soldier Janosh
0160 Little Cock, The
0161 Three Poor Tailors, The

ICELAND

0173 Autun and the Bear

ITALY

0270 Cinderella
0221 Cobbler's Dilemma, The
0236 Crane With One Leg, The
0311 Too Much Nose
0316 What Bobolino Knew
0408 Wonderful Eggs of Furicchia

STORIES BY COUNTRY

LITHUANIA

0241 I Am Your Misfortune
0240 Magic Sack, The

NORWAY

0171 Ice Bird, The
0214 Three Billy Goats Gruff, The
0200 Three Billy Goats Gruff, The

POLAND

0053 Golden Seed, The
0251 Happy-Go-Lucky
0133 Lullaby: Why the Pussy-Cat
Washes Himself So Often
0106 Nine (9) Cry-Baby Dolls

PORTUGAL–ANGOLA

0193 Clever Turtle, The

RUMANIA

0399 Yuri and the Mooneygoats

SWEDEN

0027 Nail Soup

SCANDINAVIA

0285 Don't Count Your Chicks
0168 Little Tuppen

SWITZERLAND

0136 William Tell and His Son

U.S.S.R.

0076 Baba Yaga
0312 Baboushka and the Three
Kings
0075 Fool of the World and the
Flying Ship, The
0225 Fox, and the Hare, The
0074 Golden Cockerel, The
0009 Great Big Enormous Turnip,
The
0085 Grindstone of God, The
0073 Humpy
0341 Month Brothers, The
0163 Mourka, the Mighty Cat
0071 Neighbors, The
0070 No Room, An Old Story Retold
0229 Peter and the Wolf
0065 Prince Ivan, the Firebird, and
the Gray Wolf, The Story of
0068 Salt
0066 Seven Simeons
0069 Speckled Hen
0328 Steel Flea, The

0177 Tale of a Pig
0067 Tale of Stolen Time, A
0064 Tsar's Riddle or The Wise Little
Girl
0352 Vasilisa the Beautiful

U.S.S.R.–UKRAINE

0023 Ivanko and the Dragon
0077 Mitten, The
0072 My Mother Is the Most
Beautiful Woman In the World

UNITED KINGDOM

0141 All In the Morning Early
0370 Always Room For One More
0374 Beowulf
0373 Beowulf the Warrior
0375 Beowulf, Story of
0386 Bishop and the Devil
0388 Blue Mountain, The
0279 Buried Moon, The
0227 By His Own Might: The Battles
of Beowulf
0159 Callow Pit Coffer, The
0366 Challenge of the Green Knight,
The
0321 Chanticleer and the Fox
0235 Cock Robin and Jenny Wren
0237 Dame Wiggins of Lee and Her
Seven Wonderful Cats
0342 Derby Ram, The
0357 Dick Whittington
0365 Dick Whittington and His Cat
0280 Diverting Adventures of Tom
Thumb, The
0347 Erec and Enid
0361 Gingerbread Boy, The
0283 Goblin Under the Stairs, The
0364 Green Children, The
0158 Greyling
0377 Havelok the Dane
0358 Henny Penny
0278 Henny Penny
0396 Hop O' My Thumb
0281 House That Jack Built, The
0198 House That Jack Built, The
0150 House That Jack Built, The or
Maison Que Jacques a Batie,
La
0146 Hudden and Dudden and Donald
O'Neary
0144 Jack and the Beanstalk
0226 Jack and the Beanstalk
0259 Jack Sprat, His Wife and His Cat,
The Life of
0143 Johnny-Cake
0369 Joy of the Court
0275 Kellyburn Braes

STORIES BY COUNTRY

0284 King of the Golden River, The
    or The Black Brothers
0152 King of the Golden River, The
    or The Black Brothers
0201 King of the Golden River, The
    or The Black Brothers
0153 Kitchen Knight, The
0378 Knight of the Cart, The
0367 Knight of the Lion, The
0362 Laird of Cockpen, The
0145 Lazy Jack
0256 Lazy Jack
0368 Little Red Hen
0255 Little Red Hen, The
0257 Little Tom Tucker, The
    History of
0282 London Bridge Is Falling
    Down
0197 London Bridge Is Falling
    Down
0392 Molly Whuppie
0139 Mr. Miacca
0355 Munachar and Manachar
0254 Old Mother Hubbard and Her
    Dog
0276 Old Woman and Her Pig, The
0140 Old Woman and the Pedlar,
    The
0391 Owl and the Pussy-Cat, The
0403 Pedlar of Swaffham, The
0138 Pixy and the Lazy Housewife,
    The
0325 Rooster, Mouse, and Little
    Red Hen, The
0324 Rooster, the Mouse, and the
    Little Red Hen, The
0199 Silly Simon
0277 Simon's Song
0154 Sir Gawain and the Green
    Knight
0149 Six Foolish Fishermen
0238 Six Who Were Left In a Shoe
0155 St. George and the Dragon
0372 Taliesin and King Arthur
0151 Thirteen Days of Yule, The
0212 Three Bears, The Story of
0233 Three Bears, The Story of
0137 Three Bears, The Story of
0223 Three Little Pigs, The
0224 Three Little Pigs, The
0147 Three Little Pigs, The Story
    of the
0234 Three Little Pigs, The Story
    of the
0001 Three Sillies, The
0148 Three Wishes, The
0230 Tom Thumb
0142 Tom Tit Tot
0317 Tom, Tom the Piper's Son
0239 Tops and Bottoms

0395 Valentine and Orson
0253 Widdecombe Fair

YUGOSLAVIA

0116 Magic Ring, The
0400 Three Brothers, The
0003 Turnip, The

FAR EAST

CHINA (MAINLAND)

0105 Black Heart of Indri, The
0381 Chinese Story Teller, The
0098 Emperor and the Kite, The
0186 Emperor's Big Gift, The
0090 Five Chinese Brothers, The
0100 Good-Luck Horse
0103 Magic Monkey, The
0245 Mai-Ling and the Mirror
0113 Peacock and the Crow, The
0243 The Rabbit and the Turnip
0102 Tikki Tikki Tembo
0097 Willow Plate, Legend of
0114 You Never Can Tell

JAPAN

0026 Burning Rice Fields, The
0092 Crane Maiden, The
0185 Dumplings and the Demons, The
0187 Fox Wedding, The
0093 Golden Crane, The
0091 Issun Boshi. The Inchlins.
0094 Kap and the Wicked Monkey
0021 Kappa's Tug-of-War With Big
    Brown Horse. The Story of a
    Japanese Water Imp
0310 Little White Hen
0288 One-Legged Ghost, The
0099 Oniroku and the Carpenter
0263 Thousand and One Buddhas, A
0101 Three Strong Women
0184 Timimoto's Great Adventures
0096 Two Stonecutters, The
0104 Very Special Badgers, The
0025 Wave, The

MONGOLIAN PEOPLE'S REPUBLIC

0086 Suho and the White Horse

MIDDLE EAST

MIDDLE EAST

0082 Judge Not

IRAN

0402 Aladdin and the Wonderful Lamp
0404 Aladdin, The Story of

0107 Ali-Baba and the Forty-Thieves
0110 Flying Carpet, The
0109 Joco and the Fishbone (An Arabian Nights Tale)

IRAQ

0208 Gilgamesh: Man's First Story

ISRAEL

0117 Carpet of Solomon
0266 Mazel and Shimazel or The Milk of a Lioness
0170 Wisest Man In the World, The

SAUDI ARABIA

0401 Golden Cup, The
0220 Monkey, the Lion, and the Snake, The
0108 Nine In a Line

TURKEY

0088 Hilili and Dilili
0083 Just Say Hic!
0382 One Fine Day
0087 Sixty At a Blow
0089 Stargazer To the Sultan

NORTH AMERICA

NORTH AMERICA

0210 Tikta'liktak, An Eskimo Legend
0344 Vinlanders' Saga
0350 White Archer, The

NORTH AMERICA–INDIANS OF NORTH AMERICA

0349 Eagle Mask: A West Coast Indian Tale

CANADA

0248 Badger, the Mischief Maker

MEXICO

0202 One Good Deed Deserves Another

U.S.–VARIANTS OF THE EUROPEAN STORIES

0294 Epaminondas and His Auntie
0002 Jack and the Three Sillies
0302 Journey Cake, Ho!
0376 Rip Van Winkle

U.S.–TALES FROM THE NORTH AMERICAN INDIANS

0174 Angry Moon, The
0383 Dancing Stars, The
0052 Feather Mountain
0297 Hippity Hopper, The or Why There Are No Indians In Pennsylvania
0249 Magnificent House of Man Alone, The

U.S.–NATIVE TALL TALES OF THE PAUL BUNYAN VARIETY

0301 Andy Jackson's Water Well
0300 Big Mose
0299 Cap'n Dow and the Hole In the Doughnut
0293 Captain Ichabod Paddock, Whaler of Nantucket
0295 Casey Jones: The Story of a Brave Engineer
0298 Fast Sooner Hound, The
0326 How Old Stormalong Captured Mocha Dick
0296 Joe Magarac and His USA Citizen Papers
0207 John Henry and His Hammer
0017 John Henry, An American Legend
0340 John Tabor's Ride
0209 Old Satan
0290 Paul Bunyan
0291 Paul Bunyan, The Story of
0019 Pecos Bill and the Mustang
0252 Sergeant O'Keefe and His Mule, Balaam
0303 Slappy Hooper the Wonderful Sign Painter
0016 Steel Driving Man, The Legend of John Henry
0389 Story of Johnny Appleseed

U.S.–PUERTO RICO

0188 Juan Bobo and the Queen's Necklace
0273 Ote
0165 Perez and Martina

U.S.–NATIVE FOLK TALES

0250 Big Fraid Little Fraid
0393 Monkey See, Monkey Do
0363 Wild Ducks and the Goose, The

U.S.–FOLKSONGS

0327 Billy Boy
0359 Erie Canal, The

0320 Fox Went Out On a Chilly Night, The
0258 Frog Went A-Courtin'
0292 Hush Little Baby
0306 Mommy, Buy Me a China Doll
0261 Ol' Dan Tucker
0262 Swapping Boy, The
0305 Wart Snake In a Fig Tree, A

U.S.–VARIANTS OF THE AFRICAN TALES

0304 Punia and the King of the Sharks

OCEANIA

SOUTH AMERICA

SOUTH AMERICA

0166 Snow and the Sun, The
0385 Tortoise's Tug of War, The

BRAZIL

0318 Monkey's Whiskers, The
0410 Palm Tree, The Legend of the

PERU

0167 Good Llama, The

SOUTH ASIA

INDIA

0120 Blind Men and the Elephant, The
0121 Blind Men and the Elephant, The
0314 Blue Jackal, The
0012 Elephants and the Mice, The (Panchatantra Tale)
0322 Mice That Ate Iron, The
0195 Monkey and the Crocodile, The
0323 Once a Mouse
0384 Orange Princess, The Legend of the
0272 Ramayana, The
0118 Stolen Necklace, The
0119 Tiger, the Brahman, and the Jackal, The
0122 Usha the Mouse-Maiden
0123 Valiant Chattee-Maker, The

VIETNAM

0354 Fisherman and the Goblet, The

STORIES BY TYPE OF FOLKLORE

EPICS

0374 Beowulf
0373 Beowulf, The Warrior
0375 Beowulf, Story of
0227 By His Own Might: The Battles of Beowulf
0366 Challenge of the Green Knight, The
0347 Erec and Enid
0208 Gilgamesh: Man's First Story
0377 Havelok the Dane
0369 Joy of the Court
0153 Kitchen Knight, The
0378 Knight of the Cart, The
0367 Knight of the Lion, The
0272 Ramayana, The
0154 Sir Gawain and the Green Knight
0131 Sundiata, the Epic of the Lion King
0286 Sword of Siegfried, The
0372 Taliesin and King Arthur
0289 Trojan Horse, The
0344 Vinlanders' Saga

FABLES

0120 Blind Men and the Elephant, The
0121 Blind Men and the Elephant, The
0314 Blue Jackal, The
0407 Bundle of Sticks, A
0406 Camel In the Tent
0321 Chanticleer and the Fox
0010 Donkey Ride, The
0012 Elephants and the Mice, The (Panchatantra Tale)
0130 Emir's Son, The
0244 Fox, the Dog and the Griffin, The
0085 Grindstone of God, The
0157 Hare and the Tortoise, The
0081 Hare and the Tortoise, The
0264 Hee Haw
0205 John J. Plenty and Fiddler Dan
0307 Lion and the Rat, The
0103 Magic Monkey, The
0315 Maid and Her Pail of Milk, The
0322 Mice That Ate Iron, The

0005 Miller, His Son, and Their Donkey, The
0176 Miller, the Boy, and the Donkey, The
0195 Monkey and the Crocodile, The
0220 Monkey, the Lion, and the Snake, The
0080 North Wind and the Sun
0323 Once a Mouse
0202 One Good Deed Deserves Another
0243 Rabbit and the Turnip, The
0182 Rich Man and the Shoe-Maker, The
0119 Tiger, Brahman, and the Jackal
0114 You Never Can Tell

FOLK SONGS, BALLADS

0370 Always Room For One More
0327 Billy Boy
0295 Casey Jones: The Story of a Brave Engineer
0359 Erie Canal, The
0320 Fox Went Out On a Chilly Night, The
0258 Frog Went A-Courtin'
0292 Hush Little Baby
0275 Kellyburn Braes
0362 Laird of Cockpen, The
0306 Mommy, Buy Me a China Doll
0261 Ol' Dan Tucker
0262 Swapping Boy, The
0151 Thirteen Days of Yule, The
0305 Wart Snake In a Fig Tree, A
0253 Widdecombe Fair

FOLK TALES

0402 Aladdin and the Wonderful Lamp
0404 Aladdin, The Story of
0107 Ali-Baba and the Forty-Thieves
0141 All In the Morning Early
0301 Andy Jackson's Water Well
0174 Angry Moon, The
0076 Baba Yaga
0312 Baboushka and the Three Kings
0268 Baker and the Basilisk, The
0220 Beauty and the Beast
0191 Beeswax Catches a Thief
0250 Big Fraid Little Fraid
0300 Big Mose

190

STORIES BY TYPE OF FOLKLORE

0105 Black Heart of Indri, The
0388 Blue Mountain, The
0192 Bojabi Tree, The
0124 Bojabi Tree, The
0162 Brave Soldier Janosh
0217 Bremen Town Musicians, The
0279 Buried Moon, The
0026 Burning Rice Fields, The
0159 Callow Pit Coffer, The
0299 Cap'n Dow and the Hole In
     the Doughnut
0293 Captain Ichabod Paddock,
     Whaler of Nantucket
0381 Chinese Story Teller, The
0270 Cinderella
0063 Cinderella or The Little Glass
     Slipper
0193 Clever Turtle, The
0221 Cobbler's Dilemma, The
0125 Coconut Thieves, The
0218 Count Carrot
0092 Crane Maiden, The
0236 Crane With One Leg, The
0194 Crocodile and Hen
0383 Dancing Stars, The
0357 Dick Whittington
0365 Dick Whittington and His Cat
0280 Diverting Adventures of Tom
     Thumb, The
0285 Don't Count Your Chicks
0185 Dumplings and the Demons,
     The
0371 Dwarf Long-Nose
0156 Eggs, The
0398 Elves and the Shoemaker, The
0313 Elves and the Shoemaker, The
0098 Emperor and the Kite, The
0186 Emperor's Big Gift, The
0169 Emperor's New Clothes, The
0213 Emperor's New Clothes, The
0294 Epaminondas and His Auntie
0128 Extraordinary Tug-of-War
0298 Fast Sooner Hound, The
0329 Fat Cat, The
0052 Feather Mountain
0360 Fir Tree, The
0179 Fisherman and His Wife, The
0084 Fisherman and His Wife, The
0354 Fisherman and the Goblet,
     The
0090 Five Chinese Brothers, The
0110 Flying Carpet, The
0075 Fool of the World and the
     Flying Ship, The
0039 Four Clever Brothers, The
0187 Fox Wedding, The
0225 Fox, and the Hare, The
0361 Gingerbread Boy, The
0283 Goblin Under the Stairs, The

0074 Golden Cockerel, The
0093 Golden Crane, The
0222 Golden Goose, The
0053 Golden Seed, The
0111 Gone Is Gone or The Story of
     a Man Who Wanted To Do the
     Housework
0167 Good Llama, The
0031 Good-For-Nothings, The
0034 Goose Girl, The
0009 Great Big Enormous Turnip,
     The
0364 Green Children, The
0405 Green Noses
0158 Greyling
0343 Grimm's Golden Goose
0181 Hans In Luck
0267 Hansel and Gretel
0251 Happy-Go-Lucky
0047 Heart of Stone. A Fairy Tale
0219 Hedgehog and the Hare, The
0358 Henny Penny
0278 Henny Penny
0088 Hilili and Dilili
0297 Hippity Hopper, The or Why
     There Are No Indians In
     Pennsylvania
0396 Hop O' My Thumb
0041 Horse, the Fox, and the Lion,
     The
0281 House That Jack Built, The
0326 How Old Stormalong Captured
     Mocha Dick
0146 Hudden and Dudden and
     Donald O'Neary
0073 Humpy
0241 I Am Your Misfortune
0091 Issun Boshi. The Inchlins.
0023 Ivanko and the Dragon
0144 Jack and the Beanstalk
0226 Jack and the Beanstalk
0002 Jack and the Three Sillies
0109 Joco and the Fishbone (An
     Arabian Nights Tale)
0296 Joe Magarac and His USA
     Citizen Papers
0207 John Henry and His Hammer
0017 John Henry, An American
     Legend
0340 John Tabor's Ride
0143 Johnny-Cake
0033 Jorinda and Joringel
0302 Journey Cake, Ho!
0188 Juan Bobo and the Queen's
     Necklace
0082 Judge Not
0083 Just Say Hic!
0094 Kap and the Wicked
     Monkey

STORIES BY TYPE OF FOLKLORE

0135 Sorcerer's Apprentice
0134 Sorcerer's Apprentice, The
0269 Sorcerer's Apprentice, The
0089 Stargazer To the Sultan
0056 Steadfast Tin Soldier, The
0016 Steel Driving Man, The
     Legend of John Henry
0328 Steel Flea, The
0118 Stolen Necklace, The
0028 Stone Soup, An Old Tale
0379 Story, a Story, A
0054 Such Is the Way of the World
0086 Suho and the White Horse
0055 Swineherd, The
0177 Tale of a Pig
0067 Tale of Stolen Time, A
0215 Thieving Dwarfs, The
0212 Three Bears, The Story of
0233 Three Bears, The Story of
0137 Three Bears, The Story of
0214 Three Billy Goats Gruff, The
0200 Three Billy Goats Gruff, The
0400 Three Brothers, The
0112 Three Feathers, The
0189 Three Gold Pieces
0223 Three Little Pigs, The
0224 Three Little Pigs, The
0234 Three Little Pigs, The Story
     of the
0147 Three Little Pigs, The Story
     of the
0161 Three Poor Tailors, The
0001 Three Sillies, The
0101 Three Strong Women
0148 Three Wishes, The
0048 Thumbelina
0394 Thumbelina
0102 Tikki Tikki Tembo
0184 Timimoto's Great Adventures
0247 Tinder Box, The
0230 Tom Thumb
0142 Tom Tit Tot
0311 Too Much Nose
0239 Tops and Bottoms
0385 Tortoise's Tug of War, The
0038 Traveling Musicians, The
0064 Tsar's Riddle or The Wise
     Little Girl
0003 Turnip, The
0178 Twelve Dancing Princesses
0004 Twelve Dancing Princesses, The
0096 Two Stonecutters, The
0061 Ugly Duckling, The
0246 Ugly Duckling, The
0122 Usha the Mouse-Maiden
0123 Valiant Chattee-Maker, The
0013 Valiant Tailor, The
0352 Vasilisa the Beautiful
0104 Very Special Badgers, The
0025 Wave, The

0316 What Bobolino Knew
0308 What the Good Man Does Is
     Always Right
0345 When the Drum Sang
0062 White Rat's Tale, The
0175 Who Was Tricked?
0190 Why the Jackal Won't Speak
     To the Hedgehog
0353 Why the Sun and the Moon
     Live In the Sky
0050 Why the Sun Was Late
0363 Wild Ducks and the Goose, The
0057 Wild Swans, The
0206 Wise Fool, The
0035 Wolf and the Seven Little Kids,
     The
0408 Wonderful Eggs of Furicchia
0399 Yuri and the Mooneygoats

LEGENDS

0173 Autun and the Bear
0248 Badger, the Mischief Maker
0386 Bishop and the Devil
0117 Carpet of Solomon
0349 Eagle Mask: A West Coast
     Indian Tale
0346 Every Man Heart Lay Down
0401 Golden Cup, The
0100 Good-Luck Horse
0171 Ice Bird, The
0079 Little Juggler, The
0410 Palm Tree, The Legend of the
0376 Rip Van Winkle
0155 St. George and the Dragon
0389 Story of Johnny Appleseed
0132 Thirty Gilt Pennies, The
0263 Thousand and One Buddhas, A
0210 Tikta'liktak, An Eskimo Legend
0395 Valentine and Orson
0350 White Archer, The
0136 William Tell and His Son
0097 Willow Plate, Legend of
0164 Wise Rooster, The
0170 Wisest Man In the World, The

MYTHS

0045 Clashing Rocks: The Story of
     Jason, The
0356 Dionysos and the Pirates:
     Homeric Hymn Number
     Seven
0319 Fall From the Sky: The Story
     of Daedalus
0015 Golden Touch, The
0044 Gorgon's Head: The Story of
     Perseus, The
0348 Heracles the Strong
0046 Way of Danger: The Story of
     Theseus, The

STORIES BY TYPE OF FOLKLORE

NURSERY RHYMES

0235 Cock Robin and Jenny Wren
0237 Dame Wiggins of Lee and Her
   Seven Wonderful Cats
0342 Derby Ram, The
0198 House That Jack Built, The
0150 House That Jack Built, The
   or Maison Que Jacques a
   Batie, La
0259 Jack Sprat, His Wife and His
   Cat, The Life of
0260 Judge, The

0257 Little Tom Tucker, The History
   of
0168 Little Tuppen
0282 London Bridge Is Falling Down
0197 London Bridge Is Falling Down
0254 Old Mother Hubbard and Her
   Dog
0391 Owl and the Pussy-Cat, The
0277 Simon's Song
0166 Snow and the Sun, The
0069 Speckled Hen
0317 Tom, Tom the Piper's Son

STORIES BY ILLUSTRATOR

ADAMS, ADRIENNE
0388 Blue Mountain, The
0033 Jorinda and Joringel
0362 Laird of Cockpen, The
0351 Painting the Moon
0037 Shoemaker and the Eleves, The
0006 Snow White and Rose Red
0048 Thumbelina
0004 Twelve Dancing Princesses, The
0061 Ugly Duckling, The
0062 White Rat's Tale, The

AKABA, SUEKICHI
0099 Oniroku and the Carpenter
0086 Suho and the White Horse

AKINO, FUKO
0091 Issun Boshi. The Inchlins.
0288 One Legged Ghost, The

ALIKI
0156 Eggs, The
0292 Hush Little Baby
0389 Story of Johnny Appleseed
0189 Three Gold Pieces

AMBRUS, VICTOR G.
0162 Brave Soldier Janosh
0366 Challenge of the Green Knight, The
0161 Three Poor Tailors, The

ANGLUND, JOAN WALSH
0216 Nibble, Nibble Mousekin

ARDIZZONE, EDWARD
0357 Dick Whittington

ARTZYBASHEFF, BORIS
0066 Seven Simeons

AYER, JACQUELINE
0073 Humpy
0287 Rumpelstiltskin

BARRER-RUSSELL, GERTRUDE
0173 Autun and the Bear

BARSS, BILL
0088 Hilili and Dilili

BAYNES, PAULINE
0369 Joy of the Court

BERKOYA, DAGMAR
0232 Nutcracker, The

BERNADETTE
0211 Little Red Riding Hood

BERSON, HAROLD
0204 Nightingale, The
0390 Nutcracker
0265 Pigs and Pirates
0078 Raminagrobis and the Mice
0190 Why the Jackal Won't Speak To the Hedgehog

BIANCO, PAMELA
0387 Little Mermaid, The

BLEGVAD, ERIK
0213 Emperor's New Clothes, The
0055 Swineherd, The

BOGDANOVIC, TOMA
0397 Snow Queen, The

BOLOGNESE, DON
0083 Just Say Hic!
0304 Punia and the King of the Sharks

BOOTH, GRAHAM
0140 Old Woman and the Pedlar, The

BOTKIN, GLEB
0124 Bojabi Tree, The

BRANDT, KATRIN
0398 Elves and the Shoemaker, The

STORIES BY ILLUSTRATOR

BRAUNE, ANNA

0192 Bojabi Tree, The

BROCK, EMMA

0143 Johnny-Cake

BROCK, HENRY MATTHEW

0396 Hop O' My Thumb
0395 Valentine and Orson

BROOKE, LESLIE

0233 Three Bears, The Story of
0234 Three Little Pigs, The Story of the
0230 Tom Thumb

BROOMFIELD, ROBERT

0237 Dame Wiggins of Lee and Her Seven Wonderful Cats

BROWN, MARCIA

0063 Cinderella or The Little Glass Slipper
0365 Dick Whittington and His Cat
0110 Flying Carpet, The
0071 Neighbors, The
0323 Once a Mouse
0007 Puss In Boots
0056 Steadfast Tin Soldier, The
0028 Stone Soup, An Old Tale
0200 Three Billy Goats Gruff, The
0057 Wild Swans, The

BROWNING, COLLEEN

0346 Every Man Heart Lay Down

BRYSON, BERNARDA

0208 Gilgamesh: Man's First Story
0085 Grindstone of God, The

BUCK, WILLIAM

0344 Vinlanders' Saga

BURKERT, NANCY EKHOLM

0360 Fir Tree, The
0060 Nightingale, The

BURN, DORIS

0146 Hudden and Dudden and Donald O'Neary

BURNINGHAM, JOHN

0128 Extraordinary Tug-of-War

BURTON, VIRGINIA LEE

0169 Emperor's New Clothes, The
0298 Fast Sooner Hound, The

CHAN, PLATO

0100 Good-Luck Horse
0103 Magic Monkey, The

CHAPMAN, GAYNOR

0032 Luck Child, The

CHAPPELL, WARREN

0231 Nutcracker, The
0229 Peter and the Wolf
0030 Sleeping Beauty, The

COBER, ALAN E.

0363 Wild Ducks and the Goose, The

COOKE, DONALD E.

0135 Sorcerer's Apprentice

COONEY, BARBARA

0321 Chanticleer and the Fox
0235 Cock Robin and Jenny Wren
0356 Dionysos and the Pirates: Homeric Hymn Number Seven
0079 Little Juggler, The
0008 Snow-White and Rose-Red

CORWIN, JUNE ATKIN

0049 Snow Queen, The

CREDLE, ELLIS

0250 Big Fraid Little Fraid
0393 Monkey See, Monkey Do

D'AULAIRE, INGRI & EDGAR PARIN

0285 Don't Count Your Chicks

DAUGHERTY, JAMES

0296 Joe Magarac and His USA Citizen Papers

DE ANGELI, MARGUERITE

0034 Goose Girl, The

DELESSERT, ETIENNE

0305 Wart Snake In a Fig Tree, A

DENNIS, WESLEY

0171 Ice Bird, The

STORIES BY ILLUSTRATOR

DOANE, PELAGIE

0392 Molly Whuppie

DOMANSKA, JANINA

0105 Black Heart of Indri, The
0125 Coconut Thieves, The
0053 Golden Seed, The
0051 Look, There Is a Turtle
  Flying
0328 Steel Flea, The
0003 Turnip, The

DOMJAN, JOSEPH

0160 Little Cock, The

DU BOIS, WILLIAM PENE

0391 Owl and the Pussy-Cat, The
0224 Three Little Pigs, The

DUCORNET, ERICA

0020 Beauty and the Beast

DUVOISIN, ROGER

0005 Miller, His Son, and Their
  Donkey, The

ECCLES

0199 Silly Simon

EICHENBERG, FRITZ

0070 No Room, An Old Story
  Retold

EMBERLEY, ED

0282 London Bridge Is Falling
  Down
0291 Paul Bunyan, The Story of
0277 Simon's Song

EVANS, KATHERINE

0407 Bundle of Sticks, A
0406 Camel In the Tent
0315 Maid and Her Pail of Milk,
  The
0322 Mice That Ate Iron, The
0202 One Good Deed Deserves
  Another
0149 Six Foolish Fishermen

FABRES, OSCAR

0394 Thumbelina

FAULKNER, JOHN

0082 Judge Not

0172 Seven Silly Wise Men
0175 Who Was Tricked?

FAX, ELTON

0242 Otwe

FISCHER, HANS

0031 Good-For-Nothings, The
0011 Puss In Boots
0038 Traveling Musicians, The

FISHER, LEONARD EVERETT

0290 Paul Bunyan
0376 Rip Van Winkle
0252 Sergeant O'Keefe and His Mule,
  Balaam

FLOETHE, RICHARD

0263 Thousand and One Buddhas, A

FLOYD, GARETH

0130 Emir's Son, The

FORBERG, ATI

0347 Erec and Enid

FRANCIS, FRANK

0184 Timimoto's Great Adventures

FRASCINO, EDWARD

0380 Little Mermaid, The

FRASCONI, ANTONIO

0150 House That Jack Built, The or
  Maison Que Jacques a Batie,
  La
0166 Snow and the Sun, The

FUNAI, MAMORU

0026 Burning Rice Fields, The
0119 Tiger, the Brahman, and the
  Jackal, The

GAG, WANDA

0111 Gone Is Gone or The Story of
  a Man Who Wanted To Do
  the Housework
0036 Snow White and the Seven
  Dwarfs

GALDONE, PAUL

0120 Blind Men and the Elephant,
  The
0217 Bremen Town Musicians, The

0015 Golden Touch, The
0157 Hare and the Tortoise, The
0278 Henny Penny
0041 Horse, the Fox, and the Lion, The
0198 House That Jack Built, The
0259 Jack Sprat, His Wife and His Cat, The Life of
0257 Little Tom Tucker, The History of
0168 Little Tuppen
0195 Monkey and the Crocodile, The
0254 Old Mother Hubbard and Her Dog
0276 Old Woman and Her Pig, The
0273 Ote
0223 Three Little Pigs, The
0148 Three Wishes, The
0317 Tom, Tom the Piper's Son
0064 Tsar's Riddle or The Wise Little Girl
0206 Wise Fool, The

GANNETT, RUTH

0072 My Mother Is the Most Beautiful Woman In the World

GEKIERE, MADELEINE

0084 Fisherman and His Wife, The
0205 John J. Plenty and Fiddler Dan

GOBBATO, IMERO

0241 I Am Your Misfortune
0239 Tops and Bottoms

GOBHAI, MEHILLI

0314 Blue Jackal, The
0384 Orange Princess, The Legend of the
0122 Usha the Mouse-Maiden

GORDON, MARGARET

0159 Callow Pit Coffer, The
0364 Green Children, The
0403 Pedlar of Swaffham, The

GORSLINE, DOUGLAS

0286 Sword of Siegfried, The

GRAHAM, MARGARET BLOY

0300 Big Mose

GRETZER, JOHN

0378 Knight of the Cart, The

GRUTTNER, ROSWITHA

0243 The Rabbit and the Turnip

GUIRMA, GREDERIC

0129 Princess of the Full Moon

HALEY, GAIL E.

0379 Story, a Story, A

HAMBERGER, JOHN

0248 Badger, the Mischief Maker

HANE, SETSUKO

0310 Little White Hen

HEWITT, JOYCE

0313 Elves and the Shoemaker, The

HIRSH, MARILYN

0012 Elephants and the Mice, The (Panchatantra Tale)

HOFFMANN, FELIX

0039 Four Clever Brothers, The
0095 King Thrushbeard
0040 Rapunzel
0203 Seven Ravens, The
0029 Sleeping Beauty, The
0035 Wolf and the Seven Little Kids, The

HOGAN, INEZ

0294 Epaminondas and His Auntie

HOGENBYL, JAN

0186 Emperor's Big Gift, The

HOGROGIAN, NONNY

0370 Always Room For One More
0153 Kitchen Knight, The
0043 Little Red Riding Hood, The Renowned History of
0382 One Fine Day
0065 Prince Ivan, the Firebird, and the Gray Wolf, The Story of
0067 Tale of Stolen Time, A
0151 Thirteen Days of Yule, The
0352 Vasilisa the Beautiful
0046 Way of Danger: The Story of Theseus, The

STORIES BY ILLUSTRATOR

STORIES BY ILLUSTRATOR

LOW, JOSEPH

0226 Jack and the Beanstalk
0367 Knight of the Lion, The
0089 Stargazer to the Sultan
0097 Willow Plate, Legend of

MAESTRO, GIULIO

0385 Tortoise's Tug of War, The

MALOY, LOIS

0155 St. George and the Dragon

MATULAY, LASZLO

0227 By His Own Might: The Battles of Beowulf

MC CAFFERY, JANET

0283 Goblin Under the Stairs, The
0138 Pixy and the Lazy Housewife, The
0215 Thieving Dwarfs, The

MC CLOSKEY, ROBERT

0302 Journey Cake, Ho!

MC KAY, DONALD

0326 How Old Stormalong Captured Mocha Dick

MC KEE, DAVID

0181 Hans In Luck

MIKOLAYCAK, CHARLES

0343 Grimm's Golden Goose
0163 Mourka, The Mighty Cat

MITSUHASHI, YOKO

0054 Such Is the Way of the World
0096 Two Stonecutters, The

MITSUI, ELLCHI

0094 Kap and the Wicked Monkey

MIZUMURA, KAZUE

0185 Dumplings and the Demons, The
0101 Three Strong Women
0104 Very Special Badgers, The

MONTRESOR, BENI

0270 Cinderella

0271 The Magic Flute

MURE, ELEANOR

0212 Three Bears, The Story of

NARDINI, SANDRO

0201 King of the Golden River, The or The Black Brothers

NEGRI, ROCCO

0348 Heracles the Strong

NESS, EVALINE

0141 All In the Morning Early
0275 Kellyburn Braes
0115 Long, Broad and Quickeye
0139 Mr. Miacca
0142 Tom Tit Tot

NOLDEN, VICTOR

0225 Fox, and the Hare, The

NUSSBAUMER, PAUL

0136 William Tell and His Son

OAKLEY, GRAHAM

0112 Three Feathers, The

OLDS, ELIZABETH

0052 Feather Mountain

OXENBURY, HELEN

0009 Great Big Enormous Turnip, The

PALAZZO, TONY

0255 Little Red Hen, The

PINCUS, HARRIET

0180 Little Red Riding Hood

PINTO, RALPH

0240 Magic Sack, The

PITZ, HENRY H.

0375 Beowulf, Story of

POGANY, WILLY

0074 Golden Cockerel, The

PRESTOPINO, GREGORIO

0131 Sundiata, The Epic of the Lion King

STORIES BY ILLUSTRATOR

PRICE, CHRISTINE
- 0188 Juan Bobo and the Queen's Necklace
- 0087 Sixty At A Blow
- 0123 Valiant Chattee-Maker, The
- 0253 Widdecombe Fair

QUACKENBUSH, ROBERT
- 0268 Baker and the Basilisk, The
- 0126 Rakoto and the Drongo Bird

RAMUS, MICHAEL
- 0301 Andy Jackson's Water Well

RAPHAEL, ELAINE
- 0377 Havelok the Dane

REIFSNYDER, MARYLOU
- 0401 Golden Cup, The

ROBBINS, RUTH
- 0372 Taliesin and King Arthur

ROBINSON, CHARLES
- 0399 Yuri and the Mooneygoats

ROCHE, A. K.
- 0193 Clever Turtle, The

ROCKWELL, ANNE
- 0383 Dancing Stars, The
- 0167 Good Llama, The
- 0318 Monkey's Whiskers, The
- 0355 Munachar and Manachar
- 0118 Stolen Necklace, The
- 0316 What Bobolino Knew
- 0345 When the Drum Sang
- 0408 Wonderful Eggs of Furicchia

ROGERS, JOE
- 0281 House That Jack Built, The

ROJANKOVSKY, FEODOR
- 0258 Frog Went A-Courtin'

ROUNDS, GLEN
- 0327 Billy Boy
- 0295 Casey Jones: The Story of a Brave Engineer

RUTHERFORD, BONNIE & BILL & EUALIE
- 0361 Gringerbread Boy, The
- 0325 Rooster, Mouse, and Little Red Hen, The

SAKAI, SANRYO
- 0021 Kappa's Tug-of-War With Big Brown Horse. The Story of A Japanese Water Imp

SANCHEZ., CARLOS M.
- 0165 Perez and Martina

SANDIN, JOAN
- 0194 Crocodile and Hen

SARG, TONY
- 0324 Rooster, the Mouse, and the Little Red Hen, The

SATORSKY, CYRIL
- 0247 Tinder Box, The

SCHINDELMAN, JOSEPH
- 0238 Six Who Were Left In A Shoe

SCHREITER, RICK
- 0342 Derby Ram, The
- 0308 What the Good Man Does Is Always Right

SEGAWA, YASUO
- 0187 Fox Wedding, The

SELIG, SYLVIE
- 0127 Never-Empty

SENDAK, MAURICE
- 0371 Dwarf Long-Nose

SEVERIN
- 0373 Beowulf the Warrior

SHEKERJIAN, REGINA
- 0381 Chinese Story Teller, The

SHORTALL, LEONARD
- 0019 Pecos Bill and the Mustang

SHULEVITZ, URI
- 0117 Carpet of Solomon

STORIES BY ILLUSTRATOR

STORIES BY ILLUSTRATOR

0307 Lion and the Rat, The
0176 Miller, the Boy, and the
     Donkey, The
0080 North Wind and the Sun
0182 Rich Man and the Shoe-
     Maker, The

WILKINSON, BARRY

0404 Aladdin, The Story of
0280 Diverting Adventures of
     Tom Thumb, The
0256 Lazy Jack
0183 Puss In Boots

WILKON, JOZEF

0236 Crane With One Leg, The

WISKUR, DARRELL

0016 Steel Driving Man, The
     Legend of John Henry

YAMAGUCHI, MARIANNE

0093 Golden Crane, The

YAROSLAVA

0023 Ivanko and the Dragon
0077 Mitten, The

YASHIMA, TARO

0354 Fisherman and the Goblet, The

YOUNG, ED

0098 Emperor and the Kite, The

ZEMACH, MARGOT

0179 Fisherman and His Wife, The
0260 Judge, The
0266 Mazel and Shimazel or The
     Milk of A Lioness
0306 Mommy, Buy Me A
     China Doll
0027 Nail Soup
0068 Salt
0069 Speckled Hen
0001 Three Sillies, The
0311 Too Much Nose